"No stranger to controvers   y
British government." *Irish* \

"MacDonogh has often appeared to be engaged in one man's war against censorship and 'the authorities'. He has brought out a list of controversial books, and tested the legal bounds of what may and may not be published." *Sunday Business Post*

"MacDonogh has a formidable talent for discovering and promoting new writers... one of the few Irish publishers who is well-known in Europe and beyond. One of his greatest strengths is without doubt his internationalism." *European Bookseller*

"Steve MacDonogh, the editorial director of Brandon, deserves to be saluted for his repeated attempts to undermine official censorship ... [His relationship with Gerry Adams has been] a literary collaboration that must surely have contributed more to the 'peace process' than all the gagging orders signed, sealed and delivered by London and Dublin officialdom. There will be no peace prizes for MacDonogh, for he has rocked too many establishment boats, and never even contemplated licking the appropriate number of boots, often necessary as a pre-condition for official recognition and congratulation." *Derry Journal*

"An intelligent, articulate and quiet-spoken man who could so easily be seated at the opposite side of the negotiating table from Adams et al., a high-ranking civil servant with a gong and an index-linked pension to look forward to." *Publishing News*

"Everyone in the business knows that publishing is a gambler's game, but not many publishers in this country or elsewhere can match Steve MacDonogh when it comes to taking risks... Forward-thinking and ambitious... a facility with the international marketplace has become one of MacDonogh's trademarks." *Books Ireland*

OPEN BOOK

STEVE MACDONOGH, son of a Church of Ireland clergyman, was born in Dublin and educated in England. He is the editor of *The Brandon Book of Irish Short Stories* and *The Rushdie Letters*; he is a former chairperson of the Irish Writers' Co-operative and former president of CLÉ, the Irish Book Publishers' Association. In 1982 he founded Brandon Book Publishers, in 1997 Mount Eagle Publications. He is the author of a history of the Dingle Peninsula, a book on folk custom, and three collections of poetry.

Also by Steve MacDonogh

Local History
A Visitor's Guide to the Dingle Peninsula
The Dingle Peninsula: History, Folklore, Archaeology

Folklore
Green and Gold: The Wrenboys of Dingle

Poetry
York Poems
My Tribe
By Dingle Bay and Blasket Sound

Collections edited
The Rushdie Letters: Freedom to Speak, Freedom to Write
The Brandon Book of Irish Short Stories

Steve MacDonogh

OPEN BOOK

ONE PUBLISHER'S WAR

A Brandon Original Paperback

Published in 1999 by
Brandon
an imprint of Mount Eagle Publications Ltd.
Dingle, Co. Kerry, Ireland

10 9 8 7 6 5 4 3 2 1

Copyright © Steve MacDonogh 1999

The author has asserted his moral rights

ISBN 0 86322 263 3
(original paperback)

Cover design by id communications, Tralee
Typeset by Red Barn Publishing, Skibbereen
Printed by The Guernsey Press Ltd, Channel Islands

Contents

INTRODUCTION

G OOD WRITING INCREASES the sum of human understanding and extends the range of human expression. If we see publishing simply as a business in which one seeks to move more units than last year, this social and cultural, this human aspect is irrelevant. But if one is talking about the art of publishing then it is of the essence. Independent, innovative publishing provides a platform for diverse voices, and I believe that it is the suppression of voices which is a major source of social violence. If we can understand people, understand their motivations, their hopes, fears and aspirations, we may not find that we agree with them, but we may find that we can accept their reality as human beings like ourselves. And we may find that this acceptance guides our actions.

Capitalism seeks to atomise us, to isolate us as individuals whose function is to consume. It seeks, as Margaret Thatcher sought, to abolish the idea of society. But it also seeks to promote feelings of competitiveness which can fuel consumption. I believe that if we wish to achieve reconciliation, be it between Muslims and Christians, between settled and nomadic peoples, between nationalists and unionists, then we must find vigorous and creative antidotes to the competitive, exploitative values of capitalism. And we must recognise that the apparent freedom and diversity of capitalism are largely bogus, that the free market is not a free market for ideas.

For one reason and another I emerged from my background into the adult world with a certain disregard for political, religious

9

and social institutions. It is not my intention in this book to convince you to think as I do. And anyway my views are a shifting phenomenon; I subscribe to no set political programme, and I would certainly not claim to be a provider of answers. More an asker of questions.

What I do intend is to tell a story: a story of my own experience, in which I have found that the role of the state is to control and to limit; that the role of multinational capitalism is also to control and limit, but in a different and more insidiously effective way.

All over the world there are more significant independent voices than mine, and many have been subjected to real repression, rather than the mere inconveniences that have been visited on me. It is to those independent voices that I dedicate this book.

Chapter One

ORIGINS

I T BEGAN ON a Greyhound bus between Chicago and Milwaukee in June 1968. The man in the next seat was a talker, and we had three hundred miles to travel. A TV executive, he was taking the bus for the first time in his life because the airline had screwed up his reservation and he was damned sure he was going to prove a point, no matter how much discomfort it cost him.

I experienced my own discomfort when I became aware that he couldn't seem to keep his eyes off the floor down around my feet. I looked but could see nothing to explain his staring, no hole in the floor with the tarmac zipping by below. Then he turned his eager, well-scrubbed face and spoke to me and his intense interest gained a more definite focus.

"Where'd you get those shoes?" he asked. "London?"

"Ah, ahm, yes; yes, London," I replied.

"They're unlined buffalo hide!" he exclaimed in some excitement.

I rifled the ill-assorted files of my brain for references to foot-fetishism and its particular perils when encountered in a mobile situation.

After half an hour which contained every one of thirty minutes he finally exhausted the topic of buffalo-hide shoes, their geographical distribution and their rarity, and he moved on then to some rather more revealing insights into the world of Democratic Party politics and the preparations for their convention in Chicago later in the year, which he would be covering for his network.

Eventually he asked what I was doing. I was somewhat stuck for what might seem an acceptable answer to this paragon of energy and enthusiasm. I was eighteen years old. I had been appointed as an assistant lecturer in creative writing at the New School for Social Research in New York, but my promised work permit had failed to materialise. In New York City I had given readings of my poetry, had met writers – Anne Waldman, Lewis Warsh, Gilbert Sorrentino – and had spent a day in Grove Press. This visit – to the publisher of *Evergreen Review* – now presented me with a hook, I realised, to hang something resembling the kind of career aspiration that this media man might want to hear about.

"Oh, yes," I said. "I shall be living in England once my American summer is over, and I shall be setting up and publishing an international literary magazine. Right now I'm travelling across the States meeting writers who will feature in my magazine."

He seemed duly impressed. As for myself, I realised that I had articulated, almost by accident, exactly what I wanted to do. As I travelled on that Greyhound bus on my days and nights journey across America, I began to know that I was making my first move along the road to becoming a publisher.

*   *   *   *   *

I had the privilege of a relatively comfortable middle-class family background, and I grew up in a context which was a mixture of Irish and British elements and identifications. Perhaps I was stranded in the middle of the Irish Sea.

Born in the Rotunda Hospital in Dublin on 3 September 1949, the last of three children, I was named after Saint Stephen's Church in Mount Street in Dublin, popularly known as the Peppercanister. It was there that my father, also born in Dublin, had his first posting as a Church of Ireland curate.

The MacDonogh family line stretches back to Kanturk in County Cork, where Donogh Mac Carthy founded a sub-sept of the Mac Carthy More. In the early seventeenth century, as the lord of Duhallow barony, my ancestor embarked on the construction of a magnificent castle at Kanturk. It still stands today, almost as complete as when it was first built in about 1609, but in fact it was never finished. The English Privy Council ordered that building work be stopped, on the grounds that it was much too large for a native Irish chieftain. The man who acted for the English and conveyed the news was named Taylor; centuries later one of his descendants would play an important role in my life.

Innovative glass tiles had been manufactured for the roof, but these were now thrown away, giving the name of "Bluepool" to an area to the south of Kanturk. A field beside the river near the castle is known as the Glassford, which also seems to derive from this instance. But historic parochial conflicts such as this are rarely attended by only one story, and another one has it that Mac Donogh's servants were bringing the glass from Cork but dumped it in the river at Assolas when they heard that further building had been stopped; this, it is said, gave Assolas its longer name in Irish of *Atha soluis na gloinne*, the ford of the light of the glass.

In more recent times the MacDonogh tradition has expressed itself in the peaceful groves of scholarship and religion. My father's father, who died before I was born, founded Avoca, a Protestant school in Blackrock, County Dublin, in 1891. His mother, whose maiden name was Fisher, presided in an entirely Victorian drawing room in Belgrave Square in Monkstown, County Dublin, constantly cared for by my long-suffering and wonderful Aunt Ida, who also taught at Avoca, for some thirty years. My father himself – Jack Albert Midleton MacDonogh – was ordained a clergyman and became a teacher. Both he and his older brother Paddy combined scholarship and sport while studying at Trinity College Dublin. Both played hockey for Ireland and cricket for Trinity, Paddy also representing Ireland at long jump in the Olympics. Their representative sporting careers were cut short by the rise of fascism and the Second World War, initially when they were unable to compete in the 1938 Olympics due to the Irish government's decision to withdraw. Nevertheless, my father became a celebrated centre forward in the Irish hockey team.

As a student of divinity, Hebrew, Irish and modern languages, my father was a member of Gaelic societies which brought him into contact with Irish scholars such as David Greene, with whom he shared rooms at Trinity, and Tomás de Bhaldraithe. While still studying divinity he became a teacher at St Columba's College, a Protestant school in Rathfarnham, County Dublin, and in his enthusiasm for the Irish language he brought students to Dún Chaoin and the Blasket Islands, off the coast of the Dingle Peninsula, where he came to know storyteller Peig Sayers and author Robin Flower. He also preached in Irish in the Protestant church in Ventry and was remembered by Dún Chaoin teacher and folklore collector Dr Seosamh Ó Dálaigh as having had excellent spoken as well as fine academic Irish.

My mother, Barbara Kathleen Sullivan, was the daughter of a Church of Ireland clergyman who became archdeacon of Dublin. The Sullivans were from Bandon in County Cork, which they had left in 1919, their unionist politics and close association with the British armed forces rendering them objects of nationalist hostility. Her father, whose own father was a barrister, had worked in a bank in Cork city before taking holy orders. Although I was only about five years old when he died, I still remember his kindly face, wisps of white hair, his top hat, frock coat and gaiters. Her mother was related to families from the Parkinson-Cummins in the north-east to the Godfreys in the south-west, and she had an abiding interest in archaeology and all things antiquarian, which she pursued energetically through the medium of the Royal Dublin Society.

By the time of my parents' marriage in Saint Anne's Church in Dawson Street, Dublin, in 1943, my father had already been appointed chaplain, hockey coach and teacher at Rugby School in England, but they returned to Ireland for long summer holidays.

My brother Terry was born a year or so later, followed two years afterwards by my sister Deirdre.

I was brought up in England, and my parents assimilated into English society, but contact was maintained with Ireland through the long summer holidays in Dublin and Portnoo in Donegal where my mother's family had a holiday cottage. Rugby was an undistinguished town, noted principally for having given its name to a sport. But it was also a junction of the railway system, and Dickens had bestowed upon it the fictional name of Mugby junction.

Close to my eighth birthday I was dispatched to boarding "preparatory" school, and at twelve I graduated to Marlborough College in Wiltshire. At both schools teachers spoke of the community of pupils and teachers constituting a microcosm of the community at large, yet they were all-male establishments populated by children of approximately the same age and rarefied social class. We were deprived of any kind of normal social relationships and unable to build lasting friendships at home, being away so much of the time.

Many of us at both boarding schools experienced great loneliness, some suffered visibly from the brutality of the regimes, but we survived for the most part – children being, to outward appearances at least, resilient – and made the best of our situations. We were imbued with a sense of correct behaviour and discouraged from displaying emotion. I never cried as I parted from my parents to resume another term, though some boys did. Whether we cried or not, almost all experienced a wrenching sense of separation.

In my early years at prep school I lay awake every night long after lights out, finally alone with emotions I dared not show, and as time went on I composed verses in my head to fill a desperate void. I also employed my imagination to counter punishments, reciting verses in my head as the headmaster's cane thrashed down; making up stories to hold at bay the pitch darkness of the musty, spider-filled cupboard under the stairs into which I was locked for misbehaving. Only when I was about ten did I start to write any of my compositions down, but even before that age I used to recall the verses of the previous night in the course of lessons, which inevitably gained me a record as being an inattentive dreamer, more interested in fruitless imaginings than practical application. Almost always the responsibility for this characteristic was ascribed to my Irishness; the Irish, it seemed, were, amongst other things, incorrigible dreamers. I acquired nicknames based on a quite different alleged national characteristic: "the wild Irishman" and "wild Irish wart-hog", and one teacher frequently livened up classes by placing a chair over my head and screaming at me that I was an Irish savage as he pelted me with fusillades of chalk, followed by the wooden board-rubber.

The atmosphere at both boarding schools was rancid with racism, religious sectarianism and class hatred. Attitudes to women combined aggressive contempt with sentimental condescension. England was the centre of the world, and the parts that had been touched by the benefits of its civilisation were coloured celebratory red on the maps.

Discipline was strict and often arbitrary, and beatings were common. There was nothing to be gained by complaining at punishment, whether it was cold showers at 6.00am, five-mile runs or repeated beatings with the cane. Indeed, any complaint invited only further punishment. But one of the most effective means of discipline was the general ethos, a kind of team spirit complete with sporting metaphors such as "playing a straight bat" and buttressed by the intimidatory power of religion and its own particular language of authority. We quickly learned that if we went against authority to the slightest degree we were going against God, religion and the established order.

Much of the discipline at school was exercised through peer pressure: any boy stepping out of line would usually be dealt with by other, more senior boys. Any child showing too much sensitivity would be mercilessly "baited". One boy at prep school was constantly ridiculed for talking lovingly of his parents, yet he continued to do it. His breaking point came with the Cuban missile crisis of 1962. Tormented by his classmates with the image of his parents being painfully fried in the coming nuclear holocaust, he cracked; whatever happened to him, he was not seen in the school again.

I became quite good at playing the game and, indeed, at playing the games that were so important to the schools' ethos – hockey, cricket and rugby. Marlborough was characterised by traditional warfare between "aesthetes" and "athletes" but – perhaps following the family trait exemplified by my father and Uncle Paddy – I managed to get on quite well in both camps. There was an Anglican religious tradition and an armed forces tradition: two pillars of the establishment which always complemented each other with great ease. Sports and daily religion were compulsory, as was basic military training; the aesthetes were, by and large, sceptical about these fundamental elements of the school. The aesthetes cohered around the Literary Society, of which Siegfried Sassoon, who lived nearby, was president, and occasional magazines and stage revues.

As an almost immutable rule it was the so-called "thicks" who went into the army. The form for a boy applying for Sandhurst military academy listed a number of qualities with boxes to be ticked which indicated "excellent", "above average", "average", "below average" or "poor", and then had a space beneath for comments. One housemaster, celebrated for his absent-mindedness and wry wit, ticked "below average" for all the qualities and beneath added the comment: "This man is admirably suited to be an army officer." I recall only one of my friends, Mark Phillips, going to Sandhurst. We were in the same school house and were made prefects at the same time; an amiable fellow, he was certainly not ranked amongst the aesthetes and he exemplified more than any other pupil the old-fashioned values expressed in the words of the school song: "Staunch do we stand and stalwart-hearted".

The notion that one's schooldays were the happiest days of one's life gained some kind of confirmation in the large numbers of Old Boys who returned to visit the school. My own feeling was that there was some truth in the notion if one substituted the words "most intense" for "happiest". That the intensity could be very unhappy was illustrated by one rather strange character who used to arrive at the nearby village of Preshute on a particular day each year in a London taxi dressed in the archetypal garb of the city gent. The taxi would stop at the graveyard, where this sober figure of a middle-aged man would walk to a particular grave and proceed to jump up and down on it. He would then walk back to the taxi and return the 120 miles to London. The grave was that of his former housemaster.

A frequent Old Boy visitor was Rab Butler, who cut a pathetic figure in my eyes as he sat eating school lunch at a table with the boys in the dining room. I was quite sure that the last thing I would want to do when I left school would be to return; yet here was this elderly prominent politician, who had been regarded as a likely leader of the Tory Party, who wanted nothing more, it seemed, than to regress to the unedifying ambience of his schooldays.

On Field Days the school would be turned over to military parades which were inspected by one of the top brass of the armed forces, who usually turned out to be an Old Marlburian. I went on at least one exercise to the army training establishment at Warminster and I soon became handy with a .303, but I was beginning to develop pacifist thoughts and I was amongst those "aesthetes" who pressed successfully for alternative options to military activities. So, instead of drilling and shooting on Corps Day each week, I found myself visiting old people, in particular a First World War veteran who constantly recounted the story of how he had lost a leg at Gallipoli. He spoke more in sadness than in anger of the incompetence of the military authorities and officers, of the casual sacrifice of the ordinary working men. Perhaps his restraint was in response to the fact that I possessed the accent and manner of the officer class, but I felt that his sad gentleness and dignity carried as intense an experience and significance as an angry rant could have. I tended his garden and listened to him, felt guilty when I missed visits. His story and character took on for me a kind of emblematic significance. When I read Robert Tressell's *The Ragged-Trousered Philanthropists* and Patrick MacGill's *Children of the Dead End* at around this time, I associated them in part with him.

The aesthetes' incipient pacifism broke out one Poppy Day when, in protest at the Vietnam War, a group of us made and handed out white poppies. This caused some small annoyance in the school itself, but we came in for heavier criticism when we handed out the same white poppies in the town of Marlborough. The experience sharpened my ardour against the Vietnam War and combined with influences coming through such diverse writings as those of the American "beat generation", Sartre, Oscar Wilde, Jonathan Swift, Wilfred Owen, George Orwell, Aldous Huxley, Ezra Pound and Bob Dylan.

Brought up not just to respect but to revere authority without questioning, I was also encouraged by some of my teachers to begin to think for myself and to question authority. My English teacher at Marlborough especially insisted that no assertion should pass unquestioned and insisted also on the importance of clarity in the use of language, relating the dangers of rhetoric to political consequences such as the triumph of Nazism in pre-war Germany. Orwell's essays provided an eloquent development of his basic concern, and I found that I took to Orwell with an energetic enthusiasm.

Mock elections at school failed to generate any breach in the prevailing notion that the Conservative Party was the sole inheritor of any right to govern England, and any debate that was engendered reflected debate within conservatism. Yet I was rapidly coming to the conclusion that none of the major parties possessed ideas appropriate to the age in the world I was about to enter. I took quiet pleasure in the fact that my Irishness gave me a sense of separation from the English malaise of the time, but I was also strongly influenced by an interest in North American writing and music.

Books had become an increasing passion from the age of twelve; I was writing and by the age of sixteen my poetry and prose fiction were relatively adventurous, if often gauche and mannered, and my criticism was relatively original, if also at times over-written. My first bookshop was the White Horse in Marlborough, and there I loved to browse and view covetously the volumes I could not afford, volumes venerable with age, exotic in materials, exciting in contents. I wanted them all, and most of all I wanted an early collected edition of Byron. To my amazement my housemaster bought the collection for me, and I can still remember the smell not only of the books themselves but of the paper and string in which they were wrapped. The books boasted green paper-covered board and the pages of cream paper had uncut edges; a light dust rose into the air when I blew on the upper edges of the volumes. The brown wrapping paper had a slightly waxy, creased feel to it and a kind of ribbed design, while the string possessed an aromatic dryness; this was string that would burn the skin if wrongly handled, string of a kind that was no stranger to wax. The gift had the effect of confirming my fascination with books, and particularly with editions that had the power to bring me closer to their authors. I began to pay close attention to paper, binding, impression and other details of a book's history and character.

I developed an interest in translating German poetry, particularly that of Heine and Rilke, and was encouraged by winning a competition for translation. At sixteen I passed exams for an award to Cambridge but was asked to try again the next year as I was considered too young. I took the exams again but became exasperated by my interviewer in Cambridge and ended up opting for York University, though I was by no means sure that I wanted to attend any university. I came to know writers and broadcasters through the Literary Society at school, through the Cheltenham Literary Festival, where I plunged passionately into love with a young woman novelist, and through frequent visits to London where I attended poetry readings, plays and literary launchings. Meanwhile, some of my poetry and criticism were being published in magazines, and I had written a critical study comparing Bob Dylan's lyrics with Robert Browning's use of the dramatic monologue, which was scheduled for publication in the US as a monograph. On the strength of this I was appointed in mid-1967 as an assistant lecturer in creative writing for television, films and radio at the New School for Social Research in New York. The paradox of an eighteen-year-old lecturing to mature students in New York simply didn't strike me, but as it turned out this was one paradox I didn't have to face.

I applied to the US embassy in London for visa and work permit, providing appropriate documents from my prospective employers, and was assured that all was in order. As the time approached for me to travel to New York in January 1968 I had still not received my visa and work permit; despite promises that I would be given it before the date of my departure, it never arrived, and the embassy refused to give any explanation. Friends suggested that my participation in demonstrations outside the embassy protesting against the US war on Vietnam might have had some bearing. I learned that embassy personnel had been assiduous in photographing demonstrators, but I preferred the cock-up theory to the conspiracy theory.

In late 1967 I had taken up my first job on leaving school as the assistant warden at a hostel for deprived boys in Putney in London. From here I was able to attend new plays, usually taking the cheapest seats in the "gods" at previews, and to go to poetry readings, which were flourishing throughout the city.

I was an idealist, though I was by no means sure at the time what my ideals were, and with the arrogance of youth I felt that in some inchoate way I had been put on the earth to make it a better place and to be of some kind of service to my fellow human beings. Maybe it wasn't just arrogance: the better part of it probably came from my father, who was a model of the wish to serve – in his case particularly God, the Church and Rugby School.

The world appeared to me to be changing, and I wanted to be part of that change. My idealism was becoming more defined and was cohering in a way that was fundamentally opposed to the notion of service to the state. The old structures, the establishment norms were antediluvian: I didn't so much feel that I wished to overthrow them as that they were on the way out anyway and there was other, more relevant business to be getting on with.

I became disillusioned with my work at the hostel for boys in the care of the local authorities and sought to become involved with drug-related social work. However, the only drug addiction programme in London, it seemed, was based on the precept that the only means to defeat addiction was Christian conversion, a concept with which I was not at all in sympathy.

All the time, my literary interests flourished. I continued to write translations of German poetry, but I also wrote more and more poetry of my own, while reading voraciously. I had met writers while still at school, some of whom I had encountered on their visits to speak at the Literary Society; others I had engaged in conversation at the Cheltenham Literary Festival. Alan Brownjohn, Shena Mackay, Anthony Thwaite and Kenneth Alsop were a few of those I had come to know in 1965 and 1966. But if ever a year was experienced as a year of change, 1967 was a year of change for me. I attended countless poetry readings, avant-garde films and experimental theatre, and was a regular visitor to the Arts Lab in Drury Lane. I spent a day with members of the Los Angeles chapter of the Hell's Angels listening to tapes of Lenny Bruce, who had been banned from entering Great Britain. I met Michael X in Notting Hill, a clutch of poets in Kensington, actors in Putney. Wherever I went I met more and more writers, engaging with great enthusiasm in conversation with one and all.

Looking now for a new job, I became part-time personal secretary to Harold Norse, an American poet living in St Mark's Crescent in Camden Town. He was recovering from a near-fatal dose of hepatitis, and I shopped for his salt-free vegetarian diet and assisted him in preparing his contribution to the *Penguin Modern Poets* series edited by Nikos Stangos. Surviving on the barest subsistence support from Norse, I toyed with the idea of taking up an offer to teach English in Japan, relishing the prospect of travelling there by the Trans-Siberian Express. But I was broke and reality required small steps. For a time I earned extra money by selling fire extinguishers door-to-door. I explored every inch of Camden, borough of commodious contrasts, succeeding for some reasons in selling mostly to West Indian women. But my thoughts were concentrated almost exclusively on writing, literature, theatre, film and art. Although I had almost no money, I managed to get cheap tickets and free passes to a wide range of events, and went especially to events in the burgeoning "alternative" arts world. Unable to afford transport, I came to know and love London by foot, often walking home late at night from Covent Garden to Camden. Meanwhile, life amongst the people I knew was suffused with the political culture of opposition to the continuing war in Vietnam and identification with the new outbreaks of rebellion in Paris and Prague.

Friends of Norse called: Gerard Belaart, a Dutch artist who had turned to poetry and who insisted on scribbling rapid notes in biro on any book he took into his hands; American poet Charles Plymmell, who arrived from the States en route for Paris in May 1968; writers Carl Weissner and Jan Herman on their way to New York; film maker Donald Cammell who was making *Performance*; William Burroughs, who phoned to talk about writing sometimes but more often seeking to persuade Harold Norse to become involved in Scientology. Our landlord, who lived upstairs, was freelance documentary maker Roger Graef, and parties both upstairs and in the neighbourhood seemed at times like animated versions of "Life and Times in NW1", the *New Statesman* cartoon strip.

Harold was of the generation of American writers that included Allen Ginsberg, Gregory Corso, Lawrence Ferlinghetti, William Burroughs and Philip Lamantia. He had been with many of those, and others, in Tangiers and at the "beat hotel" in Paris; he had lived in six or seven European countries since leaving the United States in 1953 and had arrived in London from Greece. There, in July 1967, his fourth book of poems, *Karma*

Circuit, was published by Anthony Barnett's Nothing Doing in London imprint. He in particular, but also his friends, associates, books and magazines, introduced me to a wealth of writing and ideas that I had only sampled in my enthusiastic reading of the beat generation while at school. I was especially interested to encounter the "cut-up conspiracy", for I had already begun writing in my own kind of cut-up mode, influenced more by my continuing insomnia of inherited aloneness and its strange rhythms than by what I was reading, though that, too, played its role.

Suddenly London lost its attraction when my novelist did the sensible thing and ended our relationship. I wanted to get away, and I found that the US embassy were prepared to give me a visitor's visa now. I arrived in New York in early June.

Martin Luther King had been shot dead in Memphis in April; Andy Warhol had been shot and almost killed by Valerie Solanas on 3 June in New York, and Bobby Kennedy had been shot and killed in Los Angeles on 5 June. In my first week on the Lower East Side in New York, I came upon the scenes of three killings, one of them in the apartment beneath the one in which I was staying. The gun lobby demanded that the constitutional right to bear arms be interpreted in terms of all citizens having free access to all kinds of weapons at all times. People that I met in middle America insisted that they needed guns. "For what?" I asked. "For when *they* come," I was told. And *they* turned out to be either communists – Russian or otherwise – or anyone with the slightest inclination towards liberal opinions.

I had arrived several months late for the spring semester at the New School for Social Research; nevertheless I was offered employment for the few weeks remaining of the semester. With the ingratitude of a precocious brat, I shrugged aside any residual responsibility towards the institution that had invited me to the New World. I remained in New York for a few weeks before setting off on my travels into the heart of the United States.

Staying initially with Jan Herman and Carl Weissner on the Lower East Side, I saw tenement tempers flare in the heat and in the stench caused by a garbage strike. One day as Carl entered the apartment block, a Puerto Rican boy of about fourteen thrust a gun up at his temple and demanded money; Carl brushed him aside. The city seemed to conform to the media clichés about muggings and murders. Yet I fell in with musicians who had begun to adopt a conscious African style; saw *Black Hamlet* performed in a nearby square by Joe Papp's New York Public Theatre and met Joe Papp himself. I dropped into the Ikon Gallery where I learned about writer Margaret Randall and the magazine *El Corno Emplumado*; I attended and gave poetry readings there and elsewhere and and visited Ed Sanders' Peace Eye bookstore.

I encountered the hospitality of New Yorkers: the mere possession of someone's phone number seemed sufficient to get an invitation to call over for a party, to join a group going out to Max's Kansas City Restaurant, to a play, or just to call in for a drink and a chat. I went to genteel literary tea parties uptown, but mostly I hung around the East Village in my white denim suit and a broad-brimmed hat decorated with a silver butterfly, being greeted with catcalls of "Cowboy".

I called a few times to see Al Aronowitz, a journalist friend of Bob Dylan's. I had been considering expanding my critical study, *Robert Browning and Bob Dylan: Uses of the Dramatic Monologue*, and wondered if I might be able to meet Dylan. Al Aronowitz gave a copy of it to Dylan and later communicated his response to me.

"So," Dylan had said, "this is what the academe will make of me in twenty years!" I was invited to join him for a game of chess, but it was an invitation I never took up because, as I had to admit, I didn't play chess. In fact, I was already somewhat embarrassed at the academicism of my study and resolved that I should learn to appreciate and understand his music rather better before, if ever, I would meet him.

From writer Gilbert Sorrentino I got an invitation, which I did take up, to visit him where he worked at the Grove Press, which published both an interesting range of books – with authors including Samuel Beckett, Charles Olson, Alain Robbe-Grillet –

and the splendid *Evergreen Review*. There I spent a day in what was for me fascinating conversation with Gilbert and others and was set to work briefly on writing blurbs for titles in their Victorian porn series, a chore they were keen to off-load. Whether my blurbs were ever used or not I do not know, but I was presented with a very welcome collection of Grove Press books.

Full of yearnings to explore, I left New York on a Greyhound bus trip across America to California, stopping off en route at Cambridge, Massachusetts, Buffalo Springs and Niagara Falls, Chicago, Milwaukee and Yellowstone National Park. In the course of my journey I met the television executive with an interest in shoes and began to plan my my first steps in publishing.

In San Francisco I gave poetry readings at the Coffee Gallery in North Beach and other venues and as part of a weekly series called "Poets on Fire", where we read our poems beside a bonfire in the open-air auditorium in MacArthur Park in Oakland. Using the venue after us every week were the Black Panthers; I spoke to some of them and as a consequence went to the courthouse where Huey Newton was on trial and had further meetings with black militants. At the Wheeler auditorium in Berkeley, Ginsberg read, and I met many writers associated with City Lights around both Berkeley and San Francisco. In Provo Park, Janis Joplin sang for free on Sundays, and while we swigged wine from bottles in brown paper bags she drank from a bottle of bourbon on stage. At the Avalon Ballroom, Country Joe and the Fish, the Grateful Dead and Janis performed. When I asked Janis at a party why she had changed her band from Big Brother and the Holding Company, she half-sang, half-growled: "Not heavy enough, man, not heavy enough!"

Meanwhile I was writing a few lyrics for a San Francisco rock band which was going nowhere and received an invitation to be guest poet at the Esalen Institute in Big Sur, which Ginsberg had just returned from. I was asked to write lyrics for a children's film by Herb Meadow, creator of *Have Gun Will Travel*, but recommended Donovan, for whom I felt the script would have been perfect. While at Big Sur, where Michael Murphy introduced me to the delights of kneading dough, I luxuriated in the sulphur baths, to which I repaired at dusk to watch the ineffable Pacific sunset.

At the Coffee Gallery I met Jack Micheline, Jimmy Silver, Carol Lee Sanchez and other writers, and I wound up staying for a while at Carol's with both her and Jack. When I found myself a month or two later later alone and ill on my birthday in New York, Jack, who had just moved back to his base in Little Italy, remembered to ring and then came over on the subway to arrive at my apartment door clutching a bottle of whiskey. I was meeting more and more writers in San Francisco whose work I felt I would like to publish, and I decided I wanted to scout out some writers in Los Angeles.

I spent a couple of weeks down around the LA area, arriving first at Jimmy Silver's in Marina del Rey, having hitched a ride from the corner of Shattuck and Telegraph in a Stingray. Jimmy was a musician and a poet, and as soon as I sat down at his kitchen table we were off on a couple of hours' talk back and forth about this writer and that musician. As the light began to fade to thin yellow on the sea's horizon, I mentioned to Jimmy that there was a writer in LA I'd like to meet, Charles Bukowski. I had read and admired his poetry while helping Harold Norse, with whom he shared *Penguin Modern Poets 15*, and I had read in magazines a number of stunning prose pieces by him, most of which had first been published in the *Los Angeles Free Press*. Harold had spoken of him, as had Carl Weissner and Jan Herman and others, and I really hoped I might meet him.

At that moment I heard a low sound from the far side of the sitting room leading off the kitchen in open-plan style. I looked across and saw a sofa, from behind which a hand emerged, clutching an empty wine bottle. There followed a more startling revelation as hand and arm were slowly followed by a face of battered meat. It was Charles Bukowski.

Recovering from one hangover and game to induce another, Bukowski was as soft, kind and indulgent towards me and my young pretensions as I could have wished. When he promised to give me poems for my magazine, I believed he would, even though other, more outwardly organised writers might not fulfil their promises.

I had called to see Jimmy partly because he knew Dylan and played music with him occasionally. I was tending towards the feeling that I should simply drop the book about Dylan. Okay, I might make a name for myself, or make some money, but I wasn't at all sure that the time was right for the kind of approach I was taking, and Dylan himself had discouraged me by his mention of twenty years as much as by his mention of academia. Maybe more time was needed to consider the lyrics as writing. But above all I felt that my approach lacked integrity because it failed to get inside the songs as music. I talked with Jimmy and listened to him talk about Dylan. He felt that Al Aronowitz had offered me an opening, and I should take it up.

From Jimmy's in Marina del Rey I moved to Severn Darden's in Hollywood. Severn welcomed me with a fresh and generous openness, even though I only had his phone number from a friend, and even though he already had people staying with him, as well as a Great Dane stud flown in from his home town of Chicago to service his bitch. One night, after a birthday party for Tiny Tim at Zsa Zsa Gabor's, Denis Hopper, Michael McClure, his wife and I stayed over at Severn's, all trying to get to sleep while the ageing Great Dane stud, who was getting on a bit, tried to do his stuff. I knocked around with Dennis Hopper for a few days; he was trying to get backing for *Easy Rider*, but everyone in Hollywood thought of him only as Jimmy Dean's sidekick. He gunned his jeep up and down streets in Beverley Hills, declaring that grass improved the speed of your reflexes. Delightful as Severn and others were, the scene at Barney's Beanery soon palled and I decided to head back to San Francisco, but not before I had prevailed upon Michael McClure to send me poems for my magazine.

On my return I met Ginsberg in a supermarket – which was not unusual and singularly apposite – with his father, which *was* unusual. Somewhat gruffly he demanded to know where the fuck

I'd been when the party was held in my honour at Lee Gallaher's in Waverly Place. I had heard about the party but had had no idea it was in my honour. There was a lot of mixed-up confusion.

My visa was about to expire. I had a place at York University, which I was less than enthusiastic about taking up, but I could remain no longer in the land of the free, and I was clutching in my meagre possessions an interesting miscellany of new poetry manuscripts. I left the US in September and enrolled as a student at York University in England. I immediately set about publishing a literary magazine, which I called *Cosmos*. The first issue came out before the end of the year. In informal meetings and at poetry readings in New York and California, I had acquired contributions from American poets which reflected my own literary taste. Amongst those who graced the first issue were Michael McClure, Charles Bukowski, Edward Kissam, Harold Norse and Jack Micheline; and with the second issue, published in the following year, I brought in more British writers, including George Dowden, Jeff Nuttall, Michael Horovitz and Geoffrey Holloway, while retaining the American presence.

In that first issue I extolled, in what I called an "editorial review", the work of the French writer and dramatist Alfred Jarry. I linked Jarry to 1968 by reference not only to the production of two of his Ubu plays in Czechoslovakia in the momentous previous year but also to a continuity of personnel from Roger Vitrac and Antonin Artaud, through Gemier, Roger Blin, Dadaism, Surrealism and the Theatre of the Absurd, to Samuel Beckett and the developing interest in the Japanese Noh theatre.

I was now nineteen years old. I was publishing, but I didn't think of myself as a publisher, still less as any kind of proprietor, though I owned my magazine. I saw the world as a place in which the authorities of all sorts had forfeited all moral standing. I believed I was one tiny element in an alternative moral, spiritual and political order. Yet so transforming were the circumstances as I experienced them that each of these words was suspect and inappropriate: moral, spiritual, political and order were all words which represented a reality which would be, which was being, superseded. I was happy to be engaged in what I was doing, and I sincerely believed that literature could possess and express a liberating humanity.

Argument and conflict with the old order inevitably occurred – especially where old affections still exerted their pull, such as in the family. Yet argument and conflict were peripheral to the experience. We were moving on out past the old ways. We had no need to confront them, to destroy them, to overcome them. We believed that they were crumbling, bereft of power and true authority.

I spent the summer of 1969 in Paddington in London: it was a time of dropping out and an inchoate movement to build "the alternative society"; the arts seemed to assume a new position centre stage as Arts Labs flourished. It was the time of the big squat; the Arts Lab in Drury Lane; Indica Gallery and *International Times*; the Stones in Hyde Park; man on the moon; Bernadette Devlin in the Commons. I met John Lennon and agreed to distribute films from the Yippies and Yoko Ono in the north of England.

One night half the Arts Lab crowd met half of NW1 at a party in the flat I was sharing in Paddington. Starting early, the night was still bright when Donald Gardner thrust into my hand a manuscript and extracted from me the promise that I would read it. Donald was a poet and actor who had recently joined the Living Theatre; we shared an interest in Antonin Artaud, street theatre and poetry. I read his manuscript the very next day, sitting cross-legged in the grass in Hyde Park and registering all the time the London chant voiced by the constant hum of thousands upon thousands of cars and trucks and lorries and vans. I read and I read it again; I sat, circled by the city's traffic, and entered the circle created by the manuscript he had left with me.

What he had given me was his translation of a long poem by Octavio Paz called *Piedra de Sol* ("The Sun Stone"). This poem created a circular world, a world of recurrence; it told a story, but a story without beginning, without end. It caught me in the compelling grip of its language.

a willow of crystal, a poplar of water,
a tall waterjet that the wind arches,
a tree deep-rooted though it dances,
the path of a river which curves, goes forward,
bends back on itself, turns circle
and is always arriving:

These were the lines with which the poem, in Donald's translation, both began and ended. It was a triumph, a masterpiece, and I knew immediately that I would publish it.

I had never published a book before, but I had published two issues of *Cosmos*. Octavio Paz's poetry had not been published before in book form in England, but the North American poets whose work had provided the central element and impetus of *Cosmos* had also not been well known in Britain – poets such as Michael McClure, Harold Norse, Jack Micheline. The rights in his work were held by Jonathan Cape, to whom I wrote. I received a reply from Grahame C. Greene, saying that, while he had no objection in principle to my plans to publish, he would prefer if I would hold off until after they had published their own edition. I enquired as to when that might be, and it was clear that it was not scheduled.

On 2 October 1968 Octavio Paz had resigned his post of Mexican ambassador to India as a protest against his government's violent suppression of student demonstrators in Mexico City. I resolved to publish *Piedra de Sol* in a bilingual edition on the first anniversary of his resignation. This required breakneck speed of production, but the cultural attaché to the Mexican embassy proved instantly sympathetic and helpful in clearing permission for me to reproduce a photograph of the Aztec calendar stone on the front cover.

I was too ignorant to know that it could not be done. By 2 October 1969 *Piedra de Sol* was, indeed, published and on sale in the leading bookstores in London. I printed 750 copies, selling at 5 shillings or, anticipating decimalisation, 25p. Within two months this first printing had sold out, but the first printing proved to be the last. I had learned one hard and important lesson of publishing: it is one thing to sell books, it is another thing to collect the money owed to you for their sale. The following year Cape Goliard Press published Donald's translation of Octavio Paz's essay, *Marcel Duchamp or The Castle of Purity*. In the same year in the US, October House published Eliot Weinberger's translations of Paz's prose poetry, which were later revised and published as *Eagle or Sun?* by New Directions in 1976.

Piedra de Sol is a poetic tour de force which has stood the test of time. It is a poem to which I return again and again, as to a well of inexhaustible metaphor. It is a poem, too, which provided me with my introduction to the exacting, exciting and exasperating addiction of book publishing.

Chapter Two

THE IRISH WRITERS' CO-OPERATIVE

*C*OSMOS LOST MONEY, of which I had none beyond my student grant, but somehow it staggered on while I also joined the management committee of York Arts Centre, organised poetry readings around Yorkshire, and became involved in agitation for a greater proportion of Arts Council funds to go to living artists. I took part in the National Artists' Assembly in St Pancras Town Hall in London, and wound up involved in its committee sessions.

At the university I was critical of the conventional forms of study and assessment, and I persuaded the Department of English to accept my radio production of a play in translation, together with production notes, as part of my final exams. The play was *Pour en finir avec le jugement de Dieu* by Antonin Artaud, a work which he had been commissioned to write in 1947 by French radio, which then banned it shortly before broadcast. In addition to my radio production, which was broadcast on the student radio service, I also mounted a stage production in York Arts Centre, using sculpted models which I constructed principally from wire and a pig's head.

When I was supposed to be preparing for my final exams, I was instead performing with the John Bull Puncture Repair Kit – a theatre group that was something of an offshoot of the People Show – at the New Arts Lab in London. Amongst our motley crew were Jeff Nuttall, Roland Miller and Al Beach, and on at least one of the nights Cornelius Cardew played music as part of our performance. After our last show I took the overnight mail train to York, just in time to stagger in to my first exam at 9.00 in the morning.

I graduated in 1971 and took a job as the sole employee in the antiquarian department at Godfrey's bookshop in York, where I was initiated into the mysteries of *Book Auction Records* by the colourful bookshop manager, Jan Janiurek. Since 1969 I had been living with Pat Farrell, who had already proved an excellent book-seller in the university branch of Godfrey's, and no doubt Jan hoped that I would be her equal in the shop in town. I enjoyed that job, despite its very low wages, as it gave me an opportunity to roam through a mazy collection of ancient rooms housing a large variety of books, where one of the desks I worked at had been Anthony Trollope's, and to compile a catalogue of the most interesting items. However, much of my energies I devoted to local political activism, poetry and other writing, editing *Cosmos*, and involvement in the Arts Centre and in the poetry readings organised at a riverside pub and at the York Festival.

Pat and I visited Ireland, calling one summer to my sister in Coleraine en route to Donegal, another year spending a magnifi-cent two weeks of May in the Dingle Peninsula. With increasing determination we planned to move to Dublin, and in early 1972 I went job-hunting there. I received a provisional promise of a job in Irish University Press. However, by the time I made my move – kitchen sink, manuscripts, cat and all – to Dublin, the company was getting into difficulties and the job prospect had evaporated. I enquired at the nearest bookshop and was taken on by Hanna's in Nassau Street. Despite my degree in English and my experience in antiquarian books, I was put selling technical and scientific books, for which I had no feeling.

I applied for hundreds of jobs but was unsuccessful, often because of my lack of Irish language qualifications, which in par-ticular ruled me out of any teaching job. My attention was drawn to Alan Figgis's small publishing company, with its interesting Riverrun fiction series; it was in terminal decline but I thought it could be reinvigorated, and I proposed to Alan Figgis that I should administer it for him. He knew both my mother's and my father's families, and remembered my father well; ignoring my proposal about the publishing company, he offered to help get me fixed up with a job at St Columba's College in Rathfarnham, where my father had been a teacher forty years before. This was not, however well intentioned, at all what I wanted or why I had approached him. Sadly his publishing died for lack of attention.

I worked on a mink farm in Swords, County Dublin, for a winter, where many of my fellow-workers had arrived at the end of one tether or another. In the winter dusk, one of our number was inclined to wander the long sheds singing, "'Twill not be long, love, till next market day", while another repeatedly remarked, quite appositely, "We are the night shift shite shifters."

I looked up some contacts in England, and asked around about jobs in publishing. I concluded that the kind of job I was looking for, an editorial job, was very hard to find, and anyway I didn't want to leave Ireland, where there was, unfortunately, almost no publishing industry. So I decided to set myself up as a publishers' agent, in the hope that my experience in the field might lead in a couple of years to my getting an editorial position. My first agency, McBride & Broadley, delighted me with its links to my time in the United States, because it meant that I was forging a path into Irish bookshops with the very poetry I most admired, promoting many authors with whom I felt a great affinity. The publishers were City Lights, New Directions, Black Sparrow, Something Else Press and a scattering of other adventurous literary lists. The authors included Denise Levertov, Allen Ginsberg, Charles Bukowski, Michael McClure, Lawrence Ferlinghetti.

Much as I loved such writers and publishers, they were not going to make me a living, and so I set about acquiring other lists. Wildwood House had been set up by two ex-Penguin editors, Dieter Pevsner and Oliver Caldecott, together with sales manager

David Harrison. Their list included a large proportion of "alternative" American material, for which there was a substantial market in London and some of the British university towns. Projections for Ireland were modest, and I knew that most of my booksellers would find the list "weird", but I reckoned that with enough energy and commitment I could generate about 5 per cent of their combined British and Irish turnover, which would go some way towards lifting me towards a minimum wage.

Gradually I added more publishers to my stable: Pluto Press, Pathfinder Press, Journeyman Press, Merlin Press, New Left Books, Lawrence & Wishart. And Wildwood took on new lists themselves, which then became part of my portfolio. Then, in 1976, along came Virago, one of the most remarkable publishers of my generation – remarkable not only for the new feminist perspective they brought but also for publishing style, irrespective of gender agendas. To represent their list was a challenge in a country where many of my customers were deeply prejudiced against the whole idea of a women's press, let alone one that screamed out its name as Virago did. I enjoyed every inch of ground I gained for their books, respected Carmen Callil and the whole team, and welcomed the fact that they appreciated what I was able to achieve. It was inspiring to see them learning, developing and growing; as they learnt and moved on they left a few bruised male egos in their wake, and there were cases, too, when women felt they had cause for complaint, and they may have. They built a new road through British publishing, and in changing the landscape they naturally caused some upsets, but their great achievement was in terms of the outlet they provided for women authors, old and new; they brought about re-evaluations and published their authors with conviction, energy and professionalism.

In 1975 I had moved with my companion Pat to Spiddal, eleven miles west of Galway city, where she had been appointed manager of the Galway university bookshop. From our rough-and-ready two-storey house in the village, rented from Mairtín Thornton, the well-known former heavyweight boxer, now cattle-dealer and much else besides, I set out on my 1963 Triumph 500 to visit bookshops the length and breadth of Ireland, the only publishers' rep covering the territory by motorbike. Despite the delights of musical sessions in Hughes's pub, which often carried on across the road in our house, I resolved when my relationship with Pat broke down to return to Dublin, but not before I had been visited by two young writers, Neil Jordan and Desmond Hogan, who were thinking about setting up a press to publish new Irish writing. They had no experience in publishing or the book trade, and I was able to offer advice which was useful enough for them to ask me to become involved.

On my return to Dublin in the spring of 1976 I joined Neil, Des and others at meetings of the Irish Writers' Co-operative. These were informal occasions: sometimes rambling and sometimes hurried, they were mostly held in chaotic rehearsal rooms at first, many of the writers being involved in theatre groups, especially the Children's T Company. Between meetings a good deal of work was quietly done, especially by Neil Jordan. Peter Sheridan, who was working for a sports magazine at the time, contributed some knowledge of copy-editing and production, while others, like Ronan Sheehan, had some experience of student magazines.

Des Hogan had written a novel but had lost the only copy of the manuscript in an accident when it had flown out of the front basket of his bike into the canal near Leeson Street, the sole copy of this first would-be opus quickly becoming sodden as it mingled with the waters of the Kavanagh canal. But this was a different era from Kavanagh's time of impossibility, in which the breadth of the creative imagination battered like some self-destructive butterfly against the constraints of the practical world. Recovering from this disaster with remarkable rapidity, Des Hogan had written another novel, *The Ikon Maker*, which Neil now edited. We succeeded in securing a promise of a grant of £300 from the Arts Council, identified a designer, Larry Bennet, and a printer in Kilkenny. Meanwhile, I toured bookshops and wholesalers, convincing them to take a chance on a book by an unknown author from an unknown publisher. Before long we took proud delivery of a consignment of finished copies of the book, and Neil and I toured the Dublin shops in his car making deliveries, while others posted out books to shops outside Dublin; our warehouse was under Neil's bed in his Clontarf house.

The Ikon Maker struck a chord, especially amongst its author's own generation, and contributed a striking new voice to Irish writing. Its allusive prose, with rhythms and a style that was innovative, was something new and interesting; its bisexuality and its general social reference reflected a world which had not previously been explored in the novel in Ireland. This was writing which made no apologies for itself. There was also a certain public responsiveness to the positive belief in ourselves expressed in the whole idea of the Co-op. Many readers shared the reaction to our first book of Kevin O'Connor, who wrote in the *Sunday Independent:* "Desmond Hogan has made an auspicious debut in painfully twanging the umbilical cord of a generation."

Our modest first print-run of 1,500 in paperback sold out and we reprinted. Our second book, published late the same year, was Neil Jordan's short story collection, *Night in Tunisia*. Neil's work, which had been published in David Marcus's "New Irish Writing" page in the *Irish Press*, was admired by his contemporaries and now also elicited the admiration of a wider audience, including Seán Ó Fáolain, the doyen of Irish short story writers. Again, the book sold well and was reprinted.

Both Neil and Des were new writers who had attempted to interest London publishers in their work without success, but they were of a generation which was not about to accept rejection passively. London houses were wary of new authors, unwilling to recognise the exceptional talent that these authors represented.

The Co-op succeeded in hitting a high note from the start and generated a mood, particularly in the media but also in the book trade and amongst a broad readership, that was overwhelmingly positive towards new Irish writing from Irish publishers. At the same time Poolbeg Press, under the editorship of David Marcus, was beginning to publish fiction, with a particular emphasis on short story collections, many of them by women writers. Wolfhound Press and the O'Brien Press were also beginning to develop smaller fiction lists.

The Co-op's progress after its first year was uneven, but we did not confine ourselves to publishing books. We promoted readings of prose and poetry and sought to encourage the involvement of our audiences in the readings. In schools we often succeeded in stimulating excellent discussions and we were pleased to be able to breach, in admittedly small ways, the separation between writer and reader. I read in Galway schools with Des Hogan. The response of the children thrilled us with its directness and lively intelligence. We also initiated a magazine, which published fiction and poetry but which also included an element of political comment, as was reflected in its name, *The Mongrel Fox*, a term used by leader of Fine Gael, Liam Cosgrave, to categorise party dissidents.

There was remarkably little debate and discussion at Co-op meetings as to what we were and where we were going. Several years later some members told me what their thoughts and feelings had been at the time, but by and large most members came late to meetings and left early, and it proved extremely difficult to maintain any kind of discussion above the level of chat and gossip.

The virtues of the Co-op lay in the spontaneous energy of some of its members. Sometimes individuals' energies combined to great effect, sometimes they conflicted or evaporated on contact. For the most part it was one or two people who made each activity or project work; rarely, if ever, was there a real collective feeling about the Co-op. Inevitably some of the original members went on to other things, taking their energies with them. Some new members joined, but the spontaneity and vigour of the early days tended to drain away.

By publishing new Irish writers the Co-op had sought to create an alternative to reliance upon the established London publishing houses. However, while we could launch writers, there was no way in which we could, with our slender resources both of finance and of expertise, offer services to writers which would compare favourably with what was available from larger, professional, long-established and adequately capitalised houses in London. British publishers of fiction had failed to pick up new writers like Neil Jordan and Des Hogan, and had turned down their books, but it was British publishers that happily picked them up once their reputations had begun to be established by the Co-op.

I succeeded through my London contracts in securing British hardback editions of *The Ikon Maker* and *Night in Tunisia*. This brought the authors to the attention of wider audiences and led to the publication of both books in New York; it also made possible the awarding of the Guardian Fiction Prize in 1979 to Neil Jordan, launching him on an international career. George Braziller took both books for the United States, and some translations were published. London houses now took on their subsequent books. The contradiction of our position as a publishing house was that while we were able to launch new writers, we were not able to hold them, and thus we were confined to an area of publishing which was inherently uneconomic.

Arts Council support increased and pushed us quite consciously in the direction of increased emphasis on administration. Des Hogan left for London and Neil Jordan moved on to other priorities. I became chairperson in 1977 and over the next four years attempted to stimulate debate and to develop the Co-op. However, my approach was to some extent out of tune with the rest of the membership, and little debate ensued. I came to be seen as someone who knew the publishing and book world, who was capable of getting things done, and this led increasingly to a situation in which I and our part-time administrator began effectively to substitute ourselves for a co-operative of members. The one respect in which work was genuinely shared out was in the reading of manuscripts and, indeed, a few members devoted a considerable amount of time to this.

Under the initial impetus of playwright Peter Sheridan we began to put out plays, publishing in 1978 four Project Arts

Centre productions: by Peter himself, by his brother Jim, by James Plunkett and by G.P. Galligan. I took over responsibility for the drama publishing then, and as new playwrights emerged at the Abbey and Peacock Theatres we were soon publishing more plays than fiction. Bernard Farrell, Graham Reid and Neil Donnelly were amongst the playwrights first published by Co-op Books, and better-known names included William Trevor and Stewart Parker. Unfortunately, the fiction that was being offered to us in large quantities was by and large mediocre. We had suggested that the conventional British and Irish publishers had been ignoring a well of talent; but as time went on, between our output and that of Poolbeg, Wolfhound and O'Brien Presses, there was little that was excellent, a certain amount that was promising and much that was of dubious quality.

Our membership fluctuated a little but remained small. In 1978 there was about a dozen of us: Neil Jordan, Des Hogan, Ronan Sheehan, Peter Sheridan, Eddie Brazil, Leland Bardwell, Jimmy Brennan, Dermot Healy, Ray Lynott, Brian Lynch and myself. I was keen to develop the Co-op in the direction of becoming a representative organisation, an Irish Writers' Union, which would promote the interests of writers and also be a campaigning body. With the support of some of my fellow Co-op members and the acquiescence of others, I took up freedom of expression issues, which at the time principally concerned the banning of information about contraception and abortion and the suppression of anything supportive of republicanism. We didn't develop far in this direction, since few members shared my appetite for such campaigning, and most new members were interested only in securing publication of their own manuscripts. Anyway, the demands of the fiction and play publishing, added to my continuing paid work as a publishers' representative, were substantial enough to leave me with little time for expanded activities. However, I spoke out on radio against the imprisonment of Eamonn Mac Thomais, the Dublin historian and editor of the republican newspaper, *An Phoblacht*, and against the jailing of people for possession of a banned book entitled *Freedom*

Struggle, the printer of which was also jailed. I also organised, with others, a public meeting to protest the banning of the Ligue Communiste in France, a meeting at which leading members of both wings of the republican movement shared a platform despite their intense mutual hostility (it was perhaps the last time they would share a platform).

Concerned at a deteriorating financial situation in the Co-op, I sought more businesslike approaches to book production and more realistic pricing. Aware of the difficulty of achieving sales for new fiction authors, I proposed that we publish a small book or pamphlet dedicated to arguing against the building of a nuclear power station at Carnsore Point, on the south-east coast. I was convinced that a large sale could be secured for the book and a profit made which would help to underwrite our literary publishing. Ireland had been nuclear-free until this time, and a potentially broad-based movement of opposition to the nuclear option was just beginning to build, with elements from the musical milieu, such as Christy Moore and Moving Hearts, together with avant garde theatre groups and a broad range of cultural, lifestyle and political radicals signing up and involving themselves in the anti-nuclear movement.

Neil Jordan, our former and first chairman, had, it seemed, been uneasy for some time with my attempts to develop the Co-op as a Writers' Union and to take on freedom of expression issues. Now his unease crystallised into opposition to our publishing any radical non-fiction, specifically *Nuclear Ireland?* There were also strong reservations about my later proposal that we commission a book from leading feminist journalist Nell McCafferty. Although Neil's was the most significant voice of opposition, a more public intervention was made by John Feeney, a journalist who had joined the Co-op despite the strong private reservations of members. He published, without reference to his fellow Co-op members, a piece in his gossip column in the *Evening Herald* in which he accused me of turning the Co-op from an outlet for fiction into a propaganda vehicle for "anti-imperialism and feminism".

Members of the Co-op insisted that as chairperson I should expel John from membership of the Co-op. I suggested, however, that any proposal to expel him should be raised at a meeting of the members and discussed, and on a vote he became the first and only Co-op member to be expelled.

Despite the opposition to its publication, *Nuclear Ireland?* by Dr Matthew Hussey, a medical physicist, and Carole Craig, a journalist and the administrator of the Co-op, became an instant bestseller, generating some much-needed income. I wanted to develop a non-fiction series entitled "Focus Ireland", which I felt would fill a widely felt need for radical, critical perspectives on issues in Irish society. I wanted to do so partly because I wanted to see areas opened up to critical perspectives, partly because I believed that the popular demand for such material would enable the Co-op to establish for itself a more reliable financial profile, on the basis of which it would be able to develop and professionalise its publication of new literary fiction and drama.

I also took up international issues on behalf of the Co-op, leading a delegation of writers to the West German embassy to protest the prosecution of a bookseller in Bochum for selling a magazine entitled *Revolutionäre Zorn*. The West German law (Paragraph 88a) held that, because the magazine advocated the overthrow of the state, the bookseller was therefore part of an actual criminal conspiracy to overthrow the state by violent means. I had corresponded with Heinrich Böll on the issue and was delighted when the authorities eventually dropped the proceedings, clearly influenced by international interventions. During the republican hunger strikes I organised a petition by Irish writers and artists in support of the recognition of political status, and amongst those who signed were Robert Ballagh, Benedict Kiely, Anthony Cronin, Brian Friel, Bryan McMahon, Dermot Healy, Edna O'Brien and Ulick O'Connor.

Dublin choked in the smog from coal fires as 1980 ended. Attempts to bring the Co-op a qualitative step forward seemed to have failed. I was exhausted. Most of my time and thoughts were devoted to the Co-op, yet I was not being paid: on the contrary, I was privately subsidising it with my meagre earnings from representing other publishers. Participation by members was low and we were not acquiring new blood with new ideas and energies. In January 1981 I became seriously ill for the first time in my life, with pneumonia.

I went to the Dingle Peninsula to recuperate. Although I had been advised to rest on my release from hospital, nothing had prepared me for the weakness and tiredness I felt. It was an appropriate time to think and to assess. Friends had long criticised me for being a spendthrift with my energies, for thinking that because I could see that something should be done I should therefore do it. Now they asked, what use was my commitment to the Co-op, to my ideas about writing, literature and freedom of expression if I only burnt myself out?

I stayed, alone, in an isolated house on a bay about ten miles east of Dingle town. The house itself was an old coastguards' boathouse perched on the edge of the sea above a storm beach of boulders beside the ruins of a sixteenth century towerhouse, Minard Castle. From its large picture window I had an uninterrupted view of Kilmurry Bay and, beyond it, of Dingle Bay and the Iveragh Peninsula. Gannets, great northern divers and arctic terns dived for fish only a few hundred yards away; seals and cormorants bobbed in the water, while herons and gulls flew overhead and Brent geese passed the mouth of the bay. From the headland came the distinctive evening cries of curlews.

I had first visited the Dingle Peninsula on holiday ten years before and had returned at least once in every year since then. The area exerted a compelling attraction from the start; I walked the hills and pathways and found that everywhere I went there were archaeological sites of many ages of life on the peninsula. The physical beauty of the place alone, with its mountains and cliffs, its lakes and streams, would not have captivated me, but the evidence of so many centuries of human occupation combined with the extraordinary scenic beauty to make me want to spend more time there. Even on my first visit I met people of the area and began to encounter a deeper richness than even that of scenery and history.

It took time, of course, and many visits, but I came to feel strangely at home. I listened and learned, and the more I did so the more I felt drawn. For some years I suspected that my attraction to the place was that of a summer visitor, but as the years went by I found myself spending more time in and around Dingle during the winter and I began to get to know more people and gain a deeper appreciation of its qualities.

There was no particular reason why Dingle should assume such a significance in my life. True, my father had spent some of his happiest times in and around Dún Chaoin and the Blasket Islands, to the west of Dingle, but I had never heard him speak of those times, nor of the fact that he had been offered the post of vicar of Dingle some few years after moving to Rugby. Also, he had never made any attempt to pass on to me the Irish language in which he was fluent. I had grown up in England, had spent time in and identified with Dublin and Donegal, and I had lived most of my life in large towns or cities. I possessed none of the skills of life in a small rural town; I was never likely to make a capable farmer or a fisherman; and I lacked my father's connection through the Irish language with the area. Yet, without sentimentalising or romanticising the place, I was coming to appreciate it more and more.

I was not alone in my appreciation. Quite a number of outsiders had moved to live in the Dingle area: a German and a Corkman had set up a bookshop/cafe; another German was an electrician, and a Danish woman worked as a weaver; Dubliners had established restaurants; there were Belgians and Americans living and working in the area. Many visitors, too, had visited once and returned regularly since, finding in Dingle something uniquely attractive which could not be put down simply to the visual beauty of the surroundings but which had much more to do with atmosphere and the people.

I returned to Dublin, having suggested to my colleagues of the Co-op that it should be wound up unless other members were prepared to take on substantial shares of the work. One or two of the members did put in time, one in particular doing a fair share of proofreading, but we lacked members with sufficient accuracy, reliability and skill in the various aspects of publishing. As our 1981 programme developed, I found myself again doing the bulk of the editing, copy-editing, proofreading, commissioning of design, marketing and promotion, while I also had to maintain my only paid employment as a sales agent. Yet I was still feeling far from a hundred per cent fit.

I returned to the boathouse in Kilmurry Bay in March, bring-ing manuscripts and notes with me. I also brought with me my own manuscript, which I had been working on for some years, about the history, archaeology and folklore of the Dingle Penin-sula. I began to venture out again on long walks to explore and research areas I had not yet adequately covered. In particular, I wished to test a growing feeling that, while the most notable period of the peninsula's history was generally regarded as having been the early Christian period, the Iron Age had been a time of remarkable development.

Every coastal promontory on the peninsula had been fortified with an Iron Age fort. These had been studied and described by both the Ordnance Survey and archaeologist T.J. Westropp in the last century; yet recently a local amateur archaeologist had recog-nised an additional promontory fort at Bull's Head and I had recognised another previously unnoted one at Minard West. I felt that more evidence of the Iron Age might have passed unnoticed, and so I embarked on a plan of seeking to identify and visit what I considered might be Iron Age sites.

I drew a number of blanks as I walked in the mountains in search of inland evidence of Iron Age occupation and I came across several inconclusive possible sites. But one Sunday in March after a lunchtime jazz session in Tralee, I prevailed on my six companions to set out from the foot of Mount Brandon,

Ireland's second highest mountain, in pursuit of what must have seemed a figment of my imagination. Projecting from the main mass of the mountain, I explained, was a narrow arête or knife-edge ridge at just over 2,500 feet, and this, I claimed, was an appropriate situation for a hilltop promontory fort. In addition, I had come across a reference – in a manuscript in the archives of the Folklore Commission – to two strong walls on the top of this peak.

My companions' scepticism was understandable, and gradually they abandoned the climb at various stages so that, despite being still hampered considerably in my breathing by the aftermath of pneumonia, I reached the arête alone. It was almost as if I had seen it before in a dream. In fact, in a sense I felt I had seen it before, at Caherconree. The hilltop promontory fort of Caherconree, which stands at the eastern border of the Dingle Peninsula, had provided a primary impetus for my search of the mountains. The highest Iron Age promontory fort then known in Ireland, it commands from its height of 2,000 feet a view of most of the Dingle Peninsula, of Dingle and Tralee Bays, and of the northern aspect of the Iveragh Peninsula. And now as I stood on this peak in the north-west of the peninsula I was looking at two stone walls and I was struck by the immediate impression that these had been constructed by the same hands that had built the single wall of Caherconree.

The gentle, majestic mountains with their dark corrie lakes, the rugged headlands, soft sweeps of grassland bordered by the rich red and green of fuchsia, massive cliffs north of Brandon and thick stone walls around tiny rough fields facing out to the Blaskets and, beyond them, to the vast Atlantic: these were part of the resource that Dingle came to be for me. And every place had its associations, each field and laneway its name. At a lake the story might be of a serpent that would rear up from the water and devour everything in the countryside; a cairn on a hill carried a legend of Cuchulainn or Fionn Mac Cumhaill. The richness in archaeological remains was at least equalled by the richness of legend and folk tale.

The atmosphere of the place had, however, more to do with the present than with the past. A certain laid-back social ease, an appreciation of the small virtues of conversation of no particular significance, the enjoyment of company for its own sake and not for anything that might be achieved by it: these were just some of the elements that made up the unique ambience of Dingle. It was no Utopia, and it wasn't that the people were all full of virtue and lacking vices, but people hailed each other in the street or on the open road, bicycles and car doors could be left unlocked, pickpockets appeared only on special occasions and muggings were unknown. The special quality of the place was just that: special; attempts to define were like a fly trying to describe an elephant.

I had become particularly friendly with Bernie Goggin, the Dingle postmaster, who was a limitless fund of knowledge about flora and fauna in particular, but also about the archaeology and history of the area. I jokingly remarked to him that I would love to be able to live and work in Dingle, but that Dingle was hardly a centre of the book trade. About a year later Bernie came up with a suggestion that took me quite by surprise.

He had been postmaster for years, had even been born in the post office, but soon the manual telephone system, which was the principal source of his income, would be rendered redundant by automation. He felt he would have to get into another line of business and had been considering various options for some time. He was aware of my frustration with the situation at the Co-op and he suggested that we set up a publishing company together in Dingle.

In July I had again recommended the winding up of the Co-op. The members' response had been to appeal to me to stay on and to say that I should receive some kind of payment for my work. However, the company's ability to pay had been unequal to their intentions.

In response to declining sales for our fiction and the fact that our publication of plays was consistently subverted by wholesale photocopying on the part of drama groups and schools and colleges, I had sought to originate some non-fiction titles which might have the effect of paying more bills than the fiction or drama. However, I had run into considerable opposition from members, in spite of the fact that *Nuclear Ireland?* had performed well. In 1981 the process was revived and I edited and published the first book by feminist journalist Nell McCafferty. *The Armagh Women* was a best-seller within a week of publication but soon after that had to be withdrawn in response to the threat of libel action. It had seemed destined to generate healthy profit for the Co-op but the libel threat put paid to that, though the strong early sale meant that losses were, in fact, small. Amongst the three other non-fiction titles, *Prisoners' Rights: A Study in Irish Prison Law* performed well, as did one of the two novels published in the year.

Although I had twice counselled winding up the Co-op, my announcement that I was leaving it to set up a new company came as a considerable shock to members. Some, principally those who had been involved for some time, viewed the move positively, but others reacted with immediate recriminations. I was one of two directors of Co-op Books, and both of us were in favour of winding up the Co-op, principally because we felt that it had been fairly clearly established that the resources did not exist amongst the membership to continue it viably on my departure. However, we proposed that we would set aside our rights as directors in order that the members should decide the matter. After much unfortunate acrimony the members voted by a majority of one to keep Co-op Books in existence as a publishing company, on the strength of an offer by one member to inject the sum of £10,000, which would provide a significant basis for development.

The fates of the new Co-op and Brandon were entwined for a while. As far as most Co-op members were concerned, my new company represented a welcome development and improvement upon what had been achieved with the Co-op, and most of those who had manuscripts ready for publication chose to be published by me rather than by the new Co-op. Soon I had books scheduled for publication by Brandon from Anthony Cronin, new chairman of the Co-op, Leland Bardwell, new vice-chairman, and other Co-op members and authors Philip Davison, Neil Jordan and Ronan Sheehan. The committee of the Co-op expressed the hope that both the Co-op and the new company would be supported by the Arts Council. As things turned out, the promised injection of £10,000 never materialised, but the Arts Council decided to devote an unprecedentedly high level of subsidy to the Co-op for 1982, while at the same time choosing to make zero subsidy available to my new company.

Despite its enormous subsidy, Co-op Books nosedived with quite extraordinary rapidity. I no longer had any involvement in the Co-op, but due to my long association I was contacted by a number of people who asked me to intervene. I felt that I could not do so directly, but I did undertake to contact the Arts Council's literature officer. He, however, warned me to steer well clear; perhaps understandably, he felt that I was showing an inability to let go of an organisation I had put so much into. For himself, in approaching publishing he was trying to relate to a world he was relatively unfamiliar with. For whatever reasons, he expressed his complete confidence in the Co-op's new administration.

It ceased publishing in 1983 in circumstances of some confusion. It was a sad end, as copies of Co-op books were hawked from door to door in Dublin at one pound each in a brave attempt to rescue some kind of return.

The Co-op had, at its best, been remarkably successful in providing a stimulus and a launching pad for several writers of real ability. It had also provided a remarkable showcase for new Irish drama. The responsibility for the fact that the drama publishing came to an end certainly rested more with the teachers and drama groups that bought one copy of a play in order to photocopy twenty than with any inadequacy of the Co-op. It was never likely that a small co-operative of writers would be able to offer authors the kind of international promotion and rights marketing that the best could achieve with established London houses, but at least we had succeeded in projecting Des Hogan and Neil

Jordan on international publishing careers. The Co-op was the kind of enterprise that illuminates the sky briefly and is gone; for a while, at least, it was a bright star in the firmament of Irish writing and publishing.

As for myself, I had dedicated all my energies to the Co-op and its books, and I was left drained and dismayed. However, I had not lost my commitment to publishing, and at least I had a new direction to pursue.

Chapter Three

A NEW BEGINNING

THE PROCESS BY which the new company, Brandon, came to be associated with controversy is quite easy to trace. That the controversy should come to involve a battle of wits with the British government was not predictable from the start, but I did set out to ensure that at least a few of our books would make waves.

Once the decision had been taken to set up a new publishing company in Dingle, the essential priority was to build a list – to acquire manuscripts and commission projects. The emphasis I wanted to establish was a dual one: innovative fiction and challenging non-fiction. Most of the Co-op authors, and others, saw Brandon as offering a more professional extension of the Co-op's publishing, and building a fiction list posed, in a sense, no problem; soon we had books scheduled from Anthony Cronin, Leland Bardwell, Ronan Sheehan and Philip Davison – all authors previously published by the Co-op. We also soon acquired the rights to reissue Neil Jordan's *Night in Tunisia*, and we took over from the Co-op, by mutual agreement, the project of publishing Dermot Healy.

Healy had long been regarded by contemporaries as an outstandingly promising writer, but he showed many of the symptoms of a man whose promise would not be realised. He spread his energies between editing and publishing a lively local magazine in Cavan, directing amateur drama, writing a few startling short stories and leading a rather chaotic life. In the Co-op we had hoped for a collection of short stories from him and we were aware that he was working on a novel, but as the years passed he was still not generating enough for a book.

In 1980 he had moved to London, and I had seen this as an opportunity for him to begin to realise his potential away from the distractions of his way of life in Ireland. I saw in Bill Swainson, of the London publisher Allison and Busby, an editor with the contrasting temperament that could complement Dermot's chaotic energy and help to develop some much-needed discipline. The relationship flourished, and Dermot became one of our first fiction authors when we published his short story collection, *Banished Misfortune,* in June 1982. Meanwhile his novel, retitled from *Sciamachy* to *Fighting With Shadows,* was undergoing radical changes in rewriting.

Anthony Cronin was the most established writer to have been published by the Co-op and he succeeded me as chairperson when it was decided to keep the Co-op going. In August we published his *Heritage Now: Irish Literature in the English Language* on the same day as our official opening. Later we would publish a reprint of his classic comic novel, *The Life of Riley,* and a collection of essays, *An Irish Eye.*

The then taoiseach, Charles J. Haughey, performed the official opening of our Dingle offices, to the surprise of my friends and colleagues. I was known for both political and cultural radicalism, and here I was associating myself with the establishment, with the prime minister of the state. It was a tough time for Mr Haughey, and his opening of our offices provided him with a rare opportunity for positive publicity in a period when he was beleaguered by a whole series of scandals and other adverse publicity. The attorney-general had just been forced to resign after an accused murderer had been arrested at his apartment, and this was only the latest in a succession of extraordinary events which threatened to bring down the government. As he left our offices the taoiseach remarked that perhaps he would soon be offering me his memoirs. I said I thought there were another ten years in him.

My motives in asking Charlie Haughey were mixed. Our author, Anthony Cronin, was his cultural and artistic adviser and was working, with Charles Haughey's active support, to introduce a scheme which would – amongst other things – provide a certain number of writers, artists and musicians with a wage from the state. It was a concept I applauded, even though I was aware that compromises along the way would inevitably mean that it would fall short of being ideal.

His interest in the scheme was no sudden affectation for Haughey, for he had earlier been responsible for introducing the tax exemption provision for writers living in Ireland. He had also removed VAT from books, a practical move of considerable significance for the book trade. I was influenced as well by the fact that there was some confusion in Dingle about what Brandon was all about: publishing was something very new in the area and I, as the public front-man of the company, was an outsider. Dingle people are not particularly hostile to outsiders, but it is a town which mass-produces rumours, and the opening by Charles Haughey could have the effect of allaying some fears, suspicions and misapprehensions.

In approaching the task of building a non-fiction list I was aware that almost no radical or socially critical books had come from Irish publishers, for reasons, I felt, of general conservatism. I was convinced that there existed a gap in the market for books of this kind. A number of notable books had succeeded in exposing the nature of the Northern Ireland state and specific abuses and situations, and all of these had been published in Britain. Penguin, where Neil Middleton was a particularly effective editor in terms of Irish-interest titles, had, for example, published *Guinea Pigs* by John McGuffin, *Political Murder in Northern Ireland* by Dillon and Lehane, *War and an Irish Town* by Eamonn McCann. Pluto Press had published *Northern Ireland, the Orange State* by Michael Farrell, *The Protestants of Ulster* by Geoff Bell and *Tell*

Them Everything by Margaretta D'Arcy. These kinds of books could, I felt, be effectively published by Brandon, but I also wished to address the general dearth of critical books about life, society and politics in the southern 26 Counties of Ireland.

A friend who was a television producer had made a programme about Father McDyer, the almost legendary priest in Glencolumb-kille in County Donegal, who had done much for the development of his parish. As a reviewer was later to put it, McDyer was "a socialist, a radical, a Catholic priest, that strange combination which even Peadar O'Donnell found it difficult to understand". She mentioned to me that he was working on his autobiography and that she had been assisting him with it. It was a manuscript which said much about the fabric of life in the west of Ireland, the problems of economic underdevelopment and consequent emigration, and about the responses of central government; and through it all ran a sense of the extraordinary, individualistic character of its author.

I noticed an article in the republican paper, *An Phoblacht*, by Gerry Adams, one of the two vice-presidents of Sinn Féin. It was a double-page feature about growing up on the Falls Road, called "Falls Memories", and it was well written. I commissioned him to write a book on similar lines. At the same time I became aware that Zed Press, a London publisher of anti-imperialist and developing world studies, had two Irish-interest titles in preparation, and I negotiated arrangements whereby we would co-publish *The Longest War* by Kevin Kelley and *British Military Strategy in Northern Ireland* by Roger Falligot.

In the book business most people thought that there was no way I could succeed in building and operating a publishing company from Dingle. Frankly, they thought I was mad. I was convinced that it could be done, but I was concerned about how to staff it. The movement of skilled labour was from places like Dingle towards Dublin, London and New York. There had never been any book publishing in Dingle, and there was no pool of available publishing skills anywhere in Ireland. I recruited in Dublin a secretary, Dee Counihan, who was happy to move to Dingle; she lacked publishing experience but she had a capability and an energy which I thought would make a good contribution. In the company's outline proposal, drafted jointly by our consultant and myself, we proposed as a priority to hire an experienced production manager, and I met publishing recruitment agencies in London with a view to identifying and hiring someone. But it was important to allocate and define the working role of my partner, so it was resolved that instead of hiring a production manager from outside, Bernie would fill the position.

Training was a key element in our application to the local authority, Údarás na Gaeltachta, and their provision of rent allowance and training grants made a significant contribution in our early years.

The process of building an initial publishing programme, begun in December 1981, advanced rapidly. Our first books were published in June 1982, and by December we had ten in the shops. It was, I think, the fastest start ever made by an Irish publisher, and it had an impact. I had negotiated sales and warehousing agreements, had attended the London and Frankfurt Book Fairs and the American Library Association convention. I had sold US rights in one book and was actively promoting rights in others. In the New Year we compared our performance with our advance projections and were well satisfied.

Books Ireland editorialised:

Who doesn't warm to frankness? Brandon Book Publishers admit that they viewed their first year's publishing schedule with scepticism, particularly their detailed financial projections. Now they report that they published one more title than planned, distributed several less than planned, and averaged a month late on intended publication dates. At the end of the year, the value of books invoiced was within 2% of the projected total, and the only black spot they will identify is a "resounding zilch" in the Arts Council column.

Of our strategy of marking out a separate Irish-rights territory and pursuing co-editions and the sale and purchasing of British rights, they wrote:

> Such wheeling and dealing may sound like sleight-of-hand, but not only is it straight and enterprising (and we suppose reasonably profitable), but it also points to how Irish publishers can most easily and usefully make their mark in the world at large. Maybe our future in world publishing is as enterprising brokers; maybe it's only a step on the way to greater things. Either way it makes good sense.

Our first six months were something of a false dawn. We succeeded in the following years in building a very interesting list and in earning substantial praise for our professionalism and the quality of our publishing in general. But circumstances in the book trade were difficult, and we were not alone amongst publishers in encountering severe financial difficulties. In particular, sales of fiction declined disastrously in both Britain and Ireland, and our own fiction list, although its design and production standards won for it good display in bookshops, generated substantial losses.

We were disappointed, too, to find that our fiction did not receive the level of Arts Council support that comparable books from other publishers did. The council had, just as we came into existence, adopted a policy of reserving substantial support for those companies that were publishing only literary work and for those companies in need of improvement in design, production and editorial standards; from the start our standards were regarded as exceptionally high, so we satisfied neither of these criteria. I felt far from happy at being penalised on the basis of such questionable, if not ludicrous, criteria. Although no stranger to conflict, I was disappointed to find myself engaged in a conflict with the Arts Council, which had been such an important and sympathetic source of support when I had been with the Co-op. But sadly it was the Arts Council's choice and judgement to devote an exceptionally high grant to the Co-op, and none to Brandon.

A small controversy arose when the *Phoenix* carried a piece pointing out how many of the Co-op's best-known authors, including its new chairman and vice-chairman, had opted to submit their new works to Brandon rather than to the Co-op. Joe Ambrose responded:

> When I was Administrator of the Irish Writer's Co-op I never published books by Anthony Cronin, Leland Bardwell, or Philip Davison. They cannot be regarded, therefore, as writers who had anything to do with my period in that organisation, I was neither dismayed nor surprised nor regretful when they displayed an interest in Brandon Books, the firm that Steve MacDonogh invented in Kerry.

He then listed eight authors published by the Co-op.

> None of these people went to Brandon and several of them had the most profound contempt for Steve MacDonogh. . . The serious animosity between myself and MacDonogh, therefore, has nothing to do with the exit of a few writers to the calm shores of Brandon and its ruler, the gouty MacDonogh. It has to do with serious differences which arose within IWCO some two years ago, when MacDonogh was establishing Brandon. He wished to incorporate the entire IWCO back catalogue into Brandon and, in effect, to disband a writers co-operative . . . The members of the Co-op, strongly advised by me, rejected MacDonogh's suggestion, and he went off to Kerry with his tail between his legs. The differences caused by that fracas were serious, bitter, and personal.

A reply came to the *Phoenix* from Desmond Hogan, who referred to his "minimal" contact with Joe Ambrose before saying that

> Steve MacDonogh is someone of whom I have bountiful regard, to whom I am greatly indebted, who has shown considerable patience towards me. I have never had occasion to make even marginal criticisms of him.

Reply came also from the board of the Irish Writers Co-operative, disassociating themselves from the comments of Joe Ambrose:

> The administrator of the Co-op has, as such, no role in relation to the choice of authors published. . . As it happens, both Leland Bardwell and Philip Davison were published while Ambrose was administrator. . . . The Board have no reason to believe that any of the authors cited by Ambrose take the view of Steve MacDonogh that Ambrose alleges.

They went on to remark upon the amicable relationships between the board of the Co-op and myself.

Another individual who sought to tilt at both the Co-op and me was Fred Johnston. Attacking (in the *Connacht Tribune*) an anthology published by the Co-op after my departure, he complained of the inclusion of Nell McCafferty:

> Under Steve MacDonogh – now Brandon Books – Nell was typical of left-wing writing which was marked down for publication by the Co-op; neither the Arts Council nor the Co-op approved, and MacDonogh, at the beginning of 1982, was quietly removed.

Johnston was unaware that it was at my own happy initiative that I had left. His remarks about writers included in the anthology were similarly misjudged; as, for example: "Sebastian Barry I have never heard of – does he review?"

The relatively controversial nature of a few of our books at Brandon provoked early criticism of a kind for which I was quite prepared and about which I was unworried. Inevitably, there were those who attacked us for publishing *Falls Memories* by Gerry Adams. But I was pleased to note that his book was quite favourably mentioned in the main unionist newspaper, the *Belfast Telegraph,* and that it was well received by many reviewers who were hostile to the politics of its author. One journalist, however, used a book of my own poems to explain why he considered ours a "strange list". After referring to my "raunchy love poems", John

Boland quoted a four-line poem called "At the Match", which he dubbed an "incredible piece of sloganising":

> The eminent don knew nothing of soccer;
> All the same, he yelled wildly for the underdogs.
> "It's the British sense of fair play," he explained.
> "Yes," I said, "we have some experience of that."

My Tribe, a book of my poetry, was published in 1982 by Beaver Row Press of Dublin and was so poorly produced that I felt embarrassed. It rated a few reviews, which were modestly kind, and sold very few copies. Somewhat daunted, I nevertheless continued to write poetry, much of which found its way into magazines in Ireland, Britain and the US.

I also turned to writing prose non-fiction. I had long been working on a study of the folklore, archaeology, history and topography of the Dingle Peninsula, built around my exploration of the area on foot, mostly on old, disused roads. Now I embarked on a study of the folk custom known as "the Wren" which is celebrated in Dingle on St Stephen's Day, 26 December. *Green and Gold:The Wrenboys of Dingle* was published in 1983 and launched by a large crowd of Dingle people at a function in the Hillgrove Hotel, after the fife and drum band of the Green and Gold had marched the town over to the hotel. Later I made a radio documentary for Radio Ulster on "The Wrenboys of Dingle", but as the demands of publishing intensified, it became less and less possible to pursue my own writing.

These were difficult times in the publishing industry, and difficult times for business in general, but we had succeeded in making a mark, in establishing remarkably quickly a prominent presence. We were not making a great deal of money, but we were surviving. In my outline proposal for the establishment of Brandon, I had drawn attention to the importance of backlist sales in securing stability for a publishing company. Few companies, I had suggested, could achieve stability before twenty years of relatively successful decision-making. Viewed from this perspective, I felt that our early years were establishing a reasonably good foundation. Our investment of money and effort was reaping rewards more quickly than I had reason to anticipate in terms of public perception:

"They do seem to be delivering all they promise – and they promised a lot." *Books Ireland*

"An ambitious list." *The Irish Times*

"A very serious new publisher has hit the scene." *Aspect*

"The list is varied and adventurous." *Evening Herald*

"Brandon's peak is already reaching skywards during its first year of publication." *Longford Leader*

"Exciting list. . . the future looks bright." *The Kerryman*

"Welcome and congratulations." *Cork Examiner*

"The best thing that has happened in Irish publishing for many a year." *Irish Observer*

One of the most telling limitations experienced in our publishing was the small size of our home market. I had innovated by engaging in co-editions with British publishers for many of our books, but for greater commercial success I needed to identify, commission and publish titles with greater potential in both the Irish and British markets, and further afield. Britain was our nearest, most accessible market outside Ireland, and I resolved to turn my attention towards commissioning some titles from authors in Britain.

Chapter Four

TELLING A TALE: *BRITISH INTELLIGENCE AND COVERT ACTION*

O UR FIRST BOOK to cause controversy in Britain had quite unsensational origins. In the spring of 1982 I heard from London about a manuscript dealing with British foreign policy since World War II, principally in Africa. It seemed a long shot for Brandon, but I visited the two authors and took away a copy. It had already been turned down by eight British publishers, and it made rather heavy reading as it described in detail the role of the intelligence services in the conduct of foreign policy, particularly in operations to destabilise African governments and to develop middle-class nationalist leaderships which could take over after independence. But it had the potential to provide a well-informed insight into the methods and strategies both of British intelligence and the Foreign Office.

The manuscript also suffered from a definite imbalance, with far too much about Africa as compared with other arenas of British intelligence operations abroad. In order to reach a useful analysis of Britain's post-war foreign policy, it would be necessary both to expand its range and to edit down the African material. However, the authors, Jonathan Bloch and Patrick Fitzgerald, seemed to be aware of the shortcomings and prepared to work to improve the manuscript, and I decided in principle to go ahead.

I worked at some length on it myself and retained a London editor for liaison with the authors.

As Jonathan and Pat carried out their rewrites, I approached British publishers with a view to a co-publication deal. We had no British marketing adequate to the task of achieving reasonable British sales, and it was clear that a British imprint could do much better with it than we could. Amongst those who declined to take it on were publishers who had considered it before but had baulked at the amount of editing that would be needed. However, Junction Books, despite having themselves turned it down when offered it by the authors, expressed interest in the context of our editing of it, and a deal was worked out. Ann Beech for Junction joined in on the final editing and liaised with the authors and legal advisors.

The principal legal question posed in the main text was one of libel, but the authors had sourced their material meticulously enough, and it was possible to cite previously published sources in most cases. However, there were a few instances where names had to be removed to avoid the risk of actions for defamation and other instances where words were slightly changed, as, for example, changing "lied" to "misled".

The Official Secrets Act was also of some relevance, especially in relation to the appendix, in which the authors listed the brief biographical details of about 120 people who had associations of one kind or another with British intelligence. For a prosecution under the act to succeed, the government would have to prove that the authors had come by their information about people listed in an unlawful way, and it was highly unlikely that they could do so.

Although I knew that Whitehall would be unhappy about the whole book's publication on the grounds that the less anyone outside intelligence and government circles knew about intelligence matters the better, I was aware that it was the listing of names which would particularly upset them. But with a careful choice of words in presenting the list I felt confident enough that we could proceed to publish without significant risk of prosecution.

I was engaged in seeking to sell the US rights to the book, and our New York rights agent was able to have discussions with a number of interested publishers. There is a tendency in the US to regard only the CIA as a serious intelligence service; nevertheless, the book was admired by several US publishers, and it seemed certain that we would get a rights deal. The question was just how substantial it would be.

One publisher forwarded a reader's report:

> This book is unique in setting forth in readable form the structure and history of British intelligence and covert action. I found it gripping and a book that I wanted to study at leisure and have in hand over a more extended time. Rival books. . . have less breadth, readability, and (for most) quality.

With a firm offer from a relatively small publishing house and more substantial offers under discussion with some of the largest New York houses, we felt very confident of securing a good US deal as publication date in Britain and Ireland approached.

Books were already in the warehouses of both Brandon and Junction when Junction received a letter from Rear Admiral Ash of the D-Notice Committee at the Ministry of Defence requesting a copy of the book. The D-Notice Committee had no legal power to prevent the publication of anything; rather, it acted on behalf of the intelligence and security services to keep a watching brief on anything that might be published or broadcast with a view to "suggesting" to publishers and broadcasters that they should change or abandon their planned publication or programme. But conservatism ran so deep and wide that it was a system of self-censorship with which almost all elements of the British media complied. Publishers of books dealing with intelligence and security matters voluntarily submitted their manuscripts for vetting and implemented whatever changes the committee suggested. No doubt the underlying assumption was that if such co-operation were not forthcoming then the publisher in question would experience difficulties when seeking co-operation of one kind or another from government agencies. Presumably, also, a publisher who dissented from this system of self-censorship would be bidding farewell to the chances of a knighthood or other such honour or preferment.

Such considerations did not weigh with me and so I saw no reason to co-operate with the self-censorship tradition of the British media, any more than I would have chosen voluntarily to submit to the wishes of the KGB. Had Brandon been a British company I would have acted no differently, and Junction, our British co-publisher, to their credit simply ignored the D-Notice Committee.

In early May Rear-Admiral Ash wrote to Junction complaining about the fact that they were going ahead with publication of the book which, in his words, "constitute[d] an extensive and serious breach of D-Notice No 6 in publishing detailed information about the activities and methods of the security and intelligence services". He had provided us with excellent copy for a pre-publication press release about the book, and the *Guardian* "Diary" carried a piece reporting on his impotent concern.

Philip Agee, former CIA agent and author of the best-selling *Inside the Company*, had provided an introduction, in which he wrote that:

> It is a tale of terror, murder, bribery, cheating, lying and torture, which have been practised in varying combinations from Malaya in the early 1950s to Ireland in the 1980s.
>
> The authors have brought together an excellent historical survey of secret British operations in the Far East, Middle and Near East, Africa and Europe over the past thirty years. Their sources are well-documented and extremely broad. Without doubt this book is a significant contribution to understanding of Britain's role in the aborted century of "Pax Americana".

He agreed to come to Dublin to assist in promoting the book, and I succeeded in interesting *The Late Late Show* in having him on as a guest.

Philip Agee had been deported from Britain and banned from re-entering (there was strong evidence that the British government had acted against him at the behest of the US government and the CIA). As there existed a free travel zone between Ireland and Britain, the question was raised as to whether he would be permitted to enter Ireland. I discussed the situation with Kader Asmal, international law lecturer and chairman of the Irish Council for Civil Liberties, and with Seán MacBride, senior counsel and Nobel and Lenin Peace Prize winner. I wrote to the minister for justice in Dublin, undertaking that Seán MacBride, Kader Asmal and I would act as guarantors that Philip Agee would not use his visit to Ireland to enter Britain, and the minister gave his approval.

In Buswells Hotel in Dublin in late May Philip Agee met the media and launched the book, appearing later on *The Late Late Show* where he gave a good account of the nature of intelligence work. Considerable further media coverage followed in Ireland, but apart from the *Guardian* and the *Observer*, the British media ignored the book. No review appeared in any major British newspaper or magazine, despite the fact that it was of central relevance to British politics. The D-Notice Committee had conveyed its disapproval.

Shortly after Irish and British publication we were surprised to learn that all the US publishers with whom we had been negotiating had suddenly decided to abandon plans for a US edition. We were also very surprised to learn that *An Cosantóir*, the magazine of the Irish defence forces, were refusing to publish an advertisement for another book we had published in the previous month. The book was *In Time of War*, Robert Fisk's magnificent study of Ireland during World War II. No official reason was given for the refusal, and I caught a heavy scent of embarrassment when I sought a reason. However, two journalists with strong army contacts told me that the decision was connected with our publication of *British Intelligence and Covert Action*. This explanation seemed surprising to me, but collaboration between British and Irish military intelligence had become extremely close and had been supported by the general direction of Dublin government policy, and it may well be that elements in the Irish defence forces wished to take some action, however petty, in support of what they regarded as their British colleagues. Another journalistic contact went further and suggested that Brandon was to be regarded henceforth as being on a par with a subversive organisation.

From sources in London I learned that *British Intelligence and Covert Action* proved a severe embarrassment to the intelligence services and to the government. We had expected that the appendix listing biographies would infuriate Whitehall and the intelligence establishment, but apparently, much to our surprise, there was also material in the book which must have had the effect of compromising current operations.

The prime minister, Margaret Thatcher, expressed her fury that our book had slipped through the net of the D-Notice system and had, in fact, exposed the fatal flaw of that system. I had acted on the principle that there was a positive value in establishing a clear picture of the methods and activities of British intelligence; I considered that it was a matter of simple democratic right that the British people should know what was being perpetrated in their name, especially when that included murder, torture, corruption and subversion of democratically elected governments. And we had ignored the cosy system of self-censorship that had served British governments so well in the past.

It was claimed on a number of occasions, in a number of circumstances, that our publication of the book had placed "Servants of the Crown" – intelligence officers – at risk. Quite apart from the fact that the whole area of intelligence operations and covert action is an inherently risky one, with intelligence officers engaging in shootings, bombings and the setting up of "pseudo-gangs" to carry out assassinations and the like, the claim was demonstrably spurious.

Jonathan Bloch and Patrick Fitzgerald were journalists who had used available reference material and published sources to build up their list in the appendix and to create their main text. Any intelligence agency or other group hostile to the British government possessed far greater resources to conduct such research than Bloch and Fitzgerald. It was a relatively simple matter for any counter-espionage agency in any country to identify those in British embassies who were genuine diplomats and those who were intelligence officers on embassy staffs. The intelligence services operated then – as they still do – as an essential element in the implementation of British foreign policy, and the authors would have offered a less than full analysis if they had not satisfactorily demonstrated, by naming names, precisely how intelligence gathering and covert actions formed an integral part of that foreign policy.

The book breached no existing legislation, and there was, and remains, not a single case of a British intelligence officer having been the victim of an assassination attempt as a result of his or her name having been published. It has been alleged that two CIA officers, Welch and Kinsman, were attacked as a result of publication of their identities in an American magazine; however, their identities would almost certainly have already been known to their attackers long before their names appeared in the magazine.

It was absurd to suggest that the KGB, with the immense resources that it devoted to counter-intelligence, would have learned anything new from the book. As for the IRA, as a non-governmental enemy of the British government, any journalist or author with particular knowledge of that organisation would have been able to confirm that it already possessed detailed information about the operations of British intelligence in its area of concern.

The government's real objection to the publication of *British Intelligence and Covert Action* was that it informed the British public about what was being done by "their" intelligence services. A subsidiary objection was that it breached the D-Notice system and so opened the way for further information to be made available to the public.

Some additional discomfort was occasioned in Whitehall by the consequences of a visit I paid to Moscow some three months after the book's publication, in early September 1983. I went not just on behalf of Brandon but also to represent the Irish Book Publishers' Association, CLÉ, at the Moscow International Book Fair.

On the first day of the book fair I was approached as I set up the stand by a professor from the Institute for Foreign Affairs, who spoke enthusiastically about *British Intelligence and Covert Action*, which he had already read and had recommended for publication in Russian by Progress House. I was delighted by such early interest, and as the days went by this was the book that attracted the most attention of all the books on the stand.

Wishing to hedge my bets, I discussed translation rights with both Progress House and Politizdat, another major publisher of political books, and it was with Politizdat that I eventually signed an option agreement, after negotiating the unfamiliar bureaucracy of VAAP, the Soviet copyright agency.

The senior editor at Politizdat with whom I discussed the book, after an initial meeting with the director and three senior editors, was an engaging and unpretentious man who smoked cheap cigarettes with massive cardboard filters. Wreathed in the strong-smelling smoke and surrounded by plates of sweets and cups of strong coffee, we discussed our respective publishing programmes, and I talked to him about political books from other Irish publishers. We were, I think, equally entertained by some small examples of cultural differences as between East and West.

I could not but find amusing, especially in an Irish context, his business card on which, underneath his name, was printed:

CANDIDATE OF PHILOSOPHY
EDITOR, LITERATURE ON ATHEISM
"POLITIZDAT" PUBLISHING HOUSE
CPSU CENTRAL COMMITTEE
RSFSR MERITED WORKER OF CULTURE

He, for his part, found it astonishing that a person of my comparative youth could be not only editorial director of a publishing company but also the national representative of the Irish Book

Publishers' Association at the Moscow Book Fair. In the Soviet Union I would have to have reached the age of at least sixty.

I signed option agreements in relation to many more Irish-published books and joined my colleague, Harold Clarke of Easons, in discussions with the state book import and export agency. In the evenings I took the opportunity to talk with interpreters and other Moscow people, wanting to learn as much about everyday life in the Soviet Union as I could in the course of my short visit.

I was staying in a western-style tourist hotel which Soviet citizens were not encouraged to enter. Nevertheless, two of the interpreters joined me there for several nights of entertaining and interesting chat about everything under the sun and moon.

One night, after a visit with a young lawyer to the Moscow State Circus and a Georgian restaurant, I stayed over at the lawyer's apartment several miles from the city centre. There I saw apartment blocks identical to blocks in Dublin, and in the morning experienced the ease of thumbing a lift.

Moscow was an international meeting point and a vantage point from which the shape of the world differed enormously from the shape projected in the mainstream media of the west. I joined a group of publishers, authors and translators in a trip to a folk-dance performance at the 5,000-seater Kremlin Theatre. In our party a Bolivian spoke Chaqua, translating it into Spanish; an East European Jew brought up in Zimbabwe spoke Swahili with a Tanzanian; and Natasha, my interpreter, who had recently returned from Kazakhstan, mediated in Russian, French, Spanish and English. Eventually we discovered that German allowed the greatest shared vocabulary between us all.

In the Writers' Club of the Soviet Writers' Union – the location of the ballroom scene in *War and Peace*, with its carved wooden staircase and gallery – caviar, herrings and potatoes provided the perfect combination with vodka. A big bowl of fresh vegetables, sturgeon and chips made up the main course. My host, Georgi Andjaparidzhe of Raduga publishing house, spoke with broad gestures of visits to the Reform Club and the Garrick Club in London.

At first I did not recognise Yevtushenko, my image, from a 1960s reading in London, being of a frail, tense, lithe figure. He stood now in in a black leather coat, solid as a monument. Having just returned from East Germany he was in the midst of making a movie. We discussed the prospect of his visiting Ireland, and then he moved on, returning to his role as a literary ship of state on a tour of duty.

At a production of *Giselle* in the Bolshoi with Ilya, my second interpreter, a young man from Novosibirsk, I learned that Moscow people had virtually no chance of securing tickets. At a party later in the Hotel Moscow, overlooking the Kremlin, midnight approached amidst chaotically criss-crossed discussions in multiple languages. On the balcony we raised glasses of vodka as the floodlit Kremlin clock struck the hour; below us the guard was changing at Lenin's tomb.

I had arrived in Moscow a few days after the shooting down of a South Korean airliner over Soviet airspace. Evidence that came to light subsequently suggested that US intelligence cynically used a civilian flight to probe Soviet air defences at their most vulnerable point. But at the time the US government vehemently insisted that the Soviets had committed an act of simple barbarity, and the US line was taken up universally in the western media.

As a reaction to the tragedy, a world-wide boycott by airline pilots of flights from the Soviet Union was promised. The British embassy in Moscow promoted a mild outbreak of hysteria amongst the contingent of British publishers at the book fair who, on attending a reception in the embassy, were handed alarmist leaflets which resulted in hurried cancellations of flight plans and early departures on the long train journey to Helsinki. In a strange way they seemed to be relishing the situation; perhaps it had nostalgic echoes for them of the embattled togetherness of wartime.

I was approached by members of the British party who seemed to assume that as an Irishman I should be taken under the protective wing of the British empire. Their motives may have been generous; however, I gently but firmly insisted that I would seek the advice of my own embassy, where I had already received very efficient assistance from Gabriel McCarrick, the representative of the Export Board, Córas Tráchtála. The Irish embassy were a great deal calmer about the situation and advised me to wait and see. Contradicting the British message, they pointed out that London airport was still open to some airlines' flights from Moscow. However, by the next day the Irish government had adopted the US administration's line: the Soviet Union, the ambassador now insisted over lunch in the embassy, had placed itself outside "the community of civilised nations" by its action in shooting down the airliner.

On the morning after the Dublin government announced the expulsion of two Soviet diplomats, I went to a meeting with the deputy director of Mezhdunarodnaya Kniga, the state organisation controlling the import and export of finished books. I was assured that governmental initiatives would not be allowed to prejudice the trading relationship I was seeking to establish.

The tragic incident was the principal topic of general conversation with those I met, including the Soviet interpreters and publishers. On English-language Radio Moscow news, which I listened to each morning, it was the lead item, and I saw what seemed to be extensive television and newspaper coverage. (When I returned home I learned that it had been widely reported in the western media that the incident had not been reported at all in the Soviet Union!) Amongst those I talked to, the response seemed to be one of regret, and there was some defensiveness; a few suggested that there may have been an element of US provocation, but most summed it up as a tragedy which could and should have been avoided.

On my return to Ireland I was pleased to receive confirmation of the agreement for Politizdat to publish an edition of 100,000 copies of *British Intelligence and Covert Action*. However, bad news came as a bolt from the blue when a month later at the

Frankfurt International Book Fair I learned that Junction Books, our British co-publishers of the book, were about to go into liquidation. Despite various promises and excuses, Junction had still not paid the considerable amount due for their part in the co-publication deal. I consulted with some British publishers who also had associations with Junction; we phoned and persuaded Junction to delay until a meeting could be held in London of interested parties. Although they did delay a short while, the company was in such a poor financial state that not only could liquidation not be avoided but it was clear that we would never see any of the money we were owed by them. It was a crushing blow for a company as small and young as Brandon. We had sold out our first printing of *British Intelligence and Covert Action* and had been about to reprint; now, however, we were not sure we could afford to reprint.

The prime minister, Margaret Thatcher, had responded to our publication of *British Intelligence and Covert Action* by commissioning a report on possible new legislation, the report to be drafted jointly by the Prime Minister's Office and the Ministries of Foreign Affairs and Defence. But this question of new legislation posed problems in Whitehall. In order to bring in a new law to make books such as ours illegal, it seemed it would be necessary to admit in the legislation the existence of the intelligence services. Absurd as it might seem to pretend that they did not exist, the difficulty was that if MI5 and MI6 were to be named in legislation they might then become more subject to the law themselves; illegal actions were, of course, essential to the nature of their business.

News of the drafting of the new legislation was carried in newspapers in March and April 1984 and on 9 April *The Times* published an editorial under the headline "Secrets Which Should Be Kept", supporting the introduction of new legislation and referring specifically to *British Intelligence and Covert Action*:

There are some areas of government activity into which even the most convinced advocate of freedom of information thinks it improper to pry. One of these is the specific operations of MI5 and MI6 and the personnel engaged in them . . . D Notice No 6, which asks the press to refrain from naming intelligence personnel, is entirely voluntary. It is utterly ignored by those who seem to disapprove of the very existence of MI5 and MI6, as shown last year by the publication of *British Intelligence and Covert Action*. . .

I read the editorial at 9.30 that morning, having just stepped off a flight from Dublin at Heathrow. Behind me in Dublin I had left presses rolling with our second printing of the book. Aware of the drafting of new legislation, we had with some care given the impression in appropriate circles that we would not be reprinting. We knew that a new law could be rushed through parliament in Westminster in a matter of days on the grounds that it was a matter relating to national security. We had taken a hammering with the collapse of Junction; we could not stand the further consequences of investing in a reprint only to be prevented from selling the book by a new law.

At the London Book Fair in the Barbican I was the first of the Irish publishers to arrive and I set up our books on the national stand before sitting down to make phone calls. Peter Malone, my newly appointed editorial assistant, joined me, and after we had discussed our plans he went to the House of Commons to make appointments which we were reluctant to arrange on the phone. In the afternoon I met Jonathan Bloch at the Barbican to review our plans for launching the reprint.

Tony Benn poured the tea and Jeremy Corbyn made the introductions when we met in the House of Commons on 12 April. I outlined our position and the reasons why I felt that our publication of *British Intelligence and Covert Action* was in the public interest. Jeremy Corbyn agreed to book a room in the House for a press reception to launch the reprint. Tony Benn expressed his general agreement with the proposition that the book should be freely available, took away a copy and undertook to get back to me to let me know what form of support he would offer.

We left the precincts of the House of Commons pleased with our meeting and impressed with the responses of the two MPs. I had been prepared for prevarication but had found them straightforward and helpful. It was not easy to organise book promotion in London from our base in Dingle, but I felt that now everything was in place for my return the following month, and I was able to concentrate on other aspects of our publishing.

Outside the business of the Book Fair I met Dermot Healy and Aidan Higgins and Bill Swainson of Allison and Busby, with whom we were co-publishing both authors. I visited bookshops in the Charing Cross Road and met editor Tim O'Grady and Neil Jordan. Neil, who was working on his second film, *Company of Wolves*, jokingly asked what kind of trouble I was getting myself into these days.

British Intelligence and Covert Action, which should have been financially successful, had registered substantial losses as a result of the collapse of Junction Books. The reprint, I hoped, would recoup the losses with the aid of the hype surrounding the House of Commons launch.

On 8 May I attended a reception in the National Concert Hall in Dublin for the unfortunately named "Top of the Irish" promotion, in which one of our authors, Neil Jordan, figured in the baker's dozen of chosen writers. At a breakfast with British journalists the next morning there was some interest in *British Intelligence and Covert Action*. The following night, after another press reception – this time to announce details of Listowel Writers' Week, at which we would launch John B. Keane's *Man of the Triple Name* – I flew to London and met Pat Fitzgerald, co-author of *British Intelligence and Covert Action*.

Next day, 11 May, Jeremy Corbyn chaired the press conference in the House of Commons to launch the reprint. Jonathan Bloch, Patrick Fitzgerald and I spoke, and Tony Benn provided a statement for the press. The general theme was our shared insistence on the right to publish the book and our contention that publication was in the public interest. As Tony Benn put it:

The most important lesson to be drawn from the book is that the work of British Intelligence is directed primarily to safeguard the commercial and financial interests of British and western business and has precious little to do with the maintenance of Freedom and Human Rights here or abroad. Indeed, it confirms the widely held view that the security services actually threaten our freedom and democracy, as may be demonstrated by an attempt to suppress this book.

Copies were already in bookshops all over Britain and I had lunch just off the Charing Cross Road with the buyer for Collets bookshop, where it was prominently displayed in the window. At the same time urgent enquiries were being made in Whitehall as to how our reprint was in the shops when all indications had been that we had abandoned our plans to reprint. I had planned to stay on in London to continue my promotional efforts, but in response to an anguished call about a friend in deep trouble at home I got on the next plane to Dublin.

As I read the next day's newspapers it became clear that despite the fact that journalists representing nine newspapers and magazines had been present at the press conference, no major newspaper carried any report, and the story was the same on Sunday. We might have driven a horse and coaches through the D Notice system, but the British media remained committed to self-censorship.

We had secured reasonably good orders for *British Intelligence and Covert Action*, but the continued failure of the British media to review and report on the book kept sales considerably below what we had hoped for. Also inhibiting sales was the fact that many booksellers and members of the public were under the impression that the disapproval of the D-Notice Committee – the only aspect of the book that had been reported – amounted to a legal ban. It was neither the first nor the last time I encountered the almost instinctive inclination in Britain to assume, if in doubt, that something is not allowed.

The British government had failed to prevent publication of *British Intelligence and Covert Action* and had failed to move against its republication. The frustration of the Prime Minister's Office was complete: the D-Notice system had been rendered largely irrelevant and, bitterly as Margaret Thatcher might complain of Rear-Admiral Ash's inability to stop the book, it was the system rather than its implementation that had failed. Consider the matter as they might, no one in Whitehall was able to demonstrate any way in which the book had breached any law. Certainly they felt that it *should* have been illegal to publish the appendix in particular, with its 120 biographies, but no existing law prohibited publication, and the consequences of introducing a new law were simply not acceptable to the intelligence establishment itself.

Whitehall was not, however, inclined either to forget or to forgive. On 20 December 1983, seven months after the book's first publication, the Home Office, in an unprecedented move, refused Jonathan Bloch indefinite leave to remain in Britain. A South African citizen, Jonathan had arrived in London in July 1976 and had, in May 1978, been granted refugee status. Having been involved in student and trade union politics, it was obvious that he faced persecution if he returned to his home country. In the normal course of events he should have been granted permanent residency in July 1982.

In a letter to his solicitors the Home Office wrote:

As you know, Mr Bloch is the co-author of a book entitled *British Intelligence and Covert Action* which, inter alia, names individuals allegedly working for British Intelligence authorities. Such an action is, in the view of the Secretary of State, bound to place servants of the Crown at greater risk of harm whether or not the allegations are well founded, than had the book not been published.

For Jonathan Bloch it was the beginning of a Kafkaesque experience. First he was advised that he could appeal the decision to an Immigration Appeals Adjudicator. He organised support for his position, and by May 1984 nearly 100 MPs, including former Labour leader Michael Foot, had signed an Early Day Motion:

> This House asks the Home Secretary to reconsider his refusal to grant Jonathan Bloch, a South African refugee who has lived in Britain for eight years and was granted refugee status in 1978, permanent residency on the basis of his co-authorship of the book, *British Intelligence and Covert Action* despite the fact that the book was checked by a barrister for libel and breaches of the Official Secrets Act and that no prosecutions have been initiated under this or any other law, and that no action has been taken against his co-author, Patrick Fitzgerald, a British citizen, and therefore we consider this an infringement of Freedom of Expression which sets a dangerous precedent for the treatment of refugees exercising their lawful rights: and we further draw attention to the fact that as the law now stands, although Mr Bloch has the right to appeal, the adjudicator does not have the authority to reverse the Home Secretary's decision and this is a further derogation of justice.

The adjudicator did not, indeed, have the authority to reverse the decision and, on 6 June, he dismissed the appeal not on the merits of the case but because he considered that he had no power to allow an appeal outside the terms of the immigration rules. It had been a bizarre, no-win situation: he could appeal but he could not succeed in his appeal irrespective of the merits of his case.

A second application for indefinite leave to remain was made by Jonathan Bloch in November 1984 and was refused a whole year later, though he was granted leave to remain for a further six months. The Home Office wrote:

> You will recall that your client's application in 1982 for indefinite leave to remain was refused because of his co-authorship of the book *British Intelligence and Covert Action*. The Secretary of State understands that since your client was refused indefinite leave to remain on the 22 December 1983, the book has been [re]published in England and a Russian edition of 100,000 copies was to

be published by the Soviet Politsdat [*sic*] Publishing House. The Secretary of State continues to take the view that your client's co-authorship of the book was bound to place at greater risk of harm, servants of the Crown whether or not the allegations in the book are well founded. In the view of the Secretary of State, this risk is increased by the greater circulation the book will now enjoy. Further, the Secretary of State has taken into account information about your client's associations with persons whose activities are, in the opinion of the Secretary of State, prejudicial to the interests of the United Kingdom.

Totally unsubstantiated allegations were being made about Jonathan's "associations" with unnamed people, yet he was denied access to a hearing at any court of law or even administrative tribunal at which the truth or otherwise of the allegations could be tested. And still they maintained the line that the book had placed servants of the Crown at risk, despite the fact that it had been compiled from published sources.

The state was not required to argue its case in any way. Prior to publication legal advice had been obtained and this advice was that no breaches of the law would be committed by publishing the book; the state never indicated that it disagreed with this legal opinion. Jonathan Bloch was never interviewed by the police or any other state authority about the publication of the book, or even about any alleged "associations". The Russian edition of the book had not, in fact, been published, although I had exchanged contracts with Politizdat. Had the book appeared, as it did some months later, the Home Office's point would have been equally absurd, for the book could not conceivably have contained information of which the Soviet intelligence services, with their massive resources, were not already aware.

Jonathan Bloch was placed in a decidedly awkward position. He had never been charged, let alone convicted, of any offence. What rights of appeal he had appeared to possess had proved to be illusory. He had settled in England, had bought a home and, having lived in the UK since mid-1976, was attempting to live and work in London. Yet he was threatened with deportation and was denied the basic security of knowing where he would be in the immediate future. The authorities took an inordinate amount of time to consider his applications and appeals, meanwhile granting him only short periods of leave to remain. He was for whole periods denied travel documentation which was essential for his work. The fact that he was suffering from cancer of the hand, had had two operations and faced more, certainly did not help ease the considerable stress imposed on him by the actions of the authorities.

He appealed the November 1985 decision to refuse him indefinite leave to remain in the UK and he received support from members of the House of Lords. Lord Kilbracken wrote:

> I would hold that such refusal should be confined in any case to persons who have been duly convicted in courts of law of crimes. The law of the land and the due process of law, rather than any kind of special measures, should invariably be used in such cases.
>
> Yet so far from being so convicted, Mr Bloch has never been alleged to have been involved in any illegal activity nor to have threatened national security, in which case it would have been open to the Secretary of State to initiate deportation proceedings against him. This he has not done, which cannot have been for reason of political convenience.
>
> I understand that it may have been Mr Bloch's co-authorship of a book, *British Intelligence and Covert Action*, that has been held against him. Yet at no time has he been interviewed by the police or the security service about this book. Nor has his co-author, Patrick Fitzgerald, who has in contrast been left free to live an absolutely normal life, with none of the insecurity and uncertainty suffered by Mr Bloch.

Lord Hatch of Lusby wrote:

> I understand that Mr Bloch's solicitors wrote to the Home Office to point out that their client has been placed in a position in which

the Home Office had made serious allegations against him which could not be answered before any court or administrative tribunal. The Home Office was requested to approach the appellate authorities to enquire whether they would be prepared to review their decision on the same basis as decisions have been reviewed in the case of extra-statutory appeals. The Home Office, I understand, declined to take this stop.

It appears to me that a number of serious allegations have been made against Mr Bloch. It is traditional in this country that every person accused has the right of refutation. This does not seem to have been accorded to Mr Bloch.

On 18 May, Mr M. Patey MBE, the chief adjudicator, Immigration Appeals, delivered his decision, dismissing the appeal and refusing to make any recommendation. Following this decision, Jonathan Bloch was constrained within an uneasy compromise, on the basis of which he remained in England while having to renew his residency documents every three months. Eventually it was agreed that his situation could be normalised on the understanding that he would never again write about the security services.

It is difficult to see his treatment as being inspired by anything other than a desire for revenge on the part of the intelligence service and the Conservative governments of Margaret Thatcher. His treatment throws light on what most British citizens would regard as cherished traditions of freedom and justice. Lord Hatch suggested that "It is traditional in this country that every person accused has the right of refutation"; yet Jonathan Bloch had effectively no avenues of appeal and he was denied the natural justice of a hearing. Had he not organised support for his position in the House of Commons and the House of Lords, and amongst British and international organisations, it is likely that he would have been deported. It seems that where the intelligence service is concerned, the considerations of democracy, freedom and justice which are said to be characteristic of the British way of life are simply set aside. Or, as Tony Benn remarked, "The intelligence services actually threaten our freedom and democracy."

For myself I felt pleased that we had done a good job in publishing the book effectively, despite the collapse of Junction and despite media reluctance to report on or review the book. I had no doubt that the British people had a democratic right to information about the actions of the intelligence services, which worked, allegedly, in their interests. I was only concerned at the paucity of any agitation for freedom of expression in this regard. Britain had many civil liberties organisations, freedom of expression groups and well-established unions of media workers, and yet they seemed to be tied in for the most part to the reactionary consensus which denied the citizen the right to know.

Some friends and associates in Britain suggested that the Home Office had me in mind when they referred to Jonathan Bloch's "associations with persons whose activities are, in the opinion of the Secretary of State, prejudicial to the interests of the United Kingdom". However, I could not believe that that was the case, for I was engaged in nothing beyond my role as a publisher.

Chapter Five

A FORCED CONFESSION

IN 1984 AN extraordinary story hit the headlines and generated more media coverage in Ireland than any other in living memory, while also being strongly and extensively covered in the British media. A young woman named Joanne Hayes had apparently confessed under questioning to having killed a newborn baby; members of her family had also confessed to involvement in the crime. However, it subsequently emerged that she could not have committed the crime, and questions were being asked as to how she and her family could have been induced to sign statements confessing in detail to a horrific murder with which they had no connection.

A newborn baby was found at Cahirciveen in south Kerry: it had been stabbed twenty-eight times and its neck was broken. Police investigators sought information in the area regarding women who had been but were no longer pregnant and yet who did not appear to have their newborn babies. Their suspicions fell on Joanne Hayes, who lived in Abbeydorney in north Kerry.

She was brought to Tralee Garda Station for questioning, and members of her family were also questioned. The baby found at Cahirciveen was not Joanne's, neither had she had anything to do with its death or the disposal of its body. However, she had given birth to a baby, which had probably been stillborn, or had perhaps died at birth, and she had disposed of its body in a corner of the family farm.

The gynaecologist who had examined her indicated that Joanne Hayes had probably given birth secretly at home. Joanne herself insisted that she could show them on the farm where she had disposed of the baby's body. Nevertheless, the police, having found a young woman who seemed in some respects to fit the bill, were absolutely convinced in their own minds that they had the culprit and that she would, sooner or later, confess to the crime.

Joanne Hayes and her family were neither tough nor criminals. There was little to distinguish them, particularly from any other family living on a sixty-acre farm anywhere. Joanne's uncle, to whom she had been particularly attached and for whom she had cared in his last years, had been a peace commissioner and a pillar of the local community, with a particular dedication to sport in the area. Her sister, Kathleen, was a member of the local young farmers' association and of CARE, a voluntary group that looked after old people and arranged outings for them. One of her brothers, Ned, was secretary of the local Gaelic Athletic Association and an active member of the local drama group. One of her aunts was a nun; another a former British army nurse who had served with distinction in Malaya; another a priest's housekeeper.

They were a quiet, conservative family, with a tradition of involvement in the life of the local community. Joanne herself, like the rest of her family, and perhaps more so than some, was a committed Roman Catholic with a particular devotion to Our Lady of Knock. She had been socially somewhat behind most of her contemporaries on account of staying at home to care for her uncle; she had been a late entrant into the local disco scene and was regarded as rather quiet. When her uncle died she began to socialise more and she developed a relationship at work with a married man, coming quite quickly to believe his protestations that he would leave his wife and live with her. He was only her second boyfriend.

She became pregnant by her married lover and had a miscarriage. Her family was upset about her relationship with him, especially when three of his wife's relations came to the house demanding that she end it. But she was a strong-willed young woman and believed that her lover was genuinely committed to her. She became pregnant by him again and gave birth to a baby girl. Despite some initial awkwardness, the child was wholeheartedly welcomed into the community of family and friends.

Overwhelmed by her image of herself as the true lover of a man with whom she would soon be living, she took no contraceptive precautions nor asked that he should, and soon she became pregnant again. When, however, she discovered that his wife was simultaneously pregnant, her emotional world collapsed, leaving her in a state of complete, isolated confusion. She tried to pretend that her pregnancy was not happening to her, and such was her strength of will that she managed to repel any attempts by her family or friends to talk about her pregnancy, even when it became evident.

Right up to the day she gave birth, she had succeeded in denying to others and, crucially, to herself, what was happening to her. In a distracted state, either in the house or in a field beside the house, she gave birth and the child was either born dead or died in childbirth. Much was made at the tribunal, in newspapers, magazines and books of the question as to whether she gave birth in the house or in the field.

Joanne had, with her resolute will, sought to deny to herself that she was approaching the enormous, overwhelming experience of giving birth at all; what was more, she had intimidated all around her into silence on the matter. She had proved a loving and attentive mother to her daughter, yet – faced with the confusing circumstances of this pregnancy – she may have walked out of the house to avoid the knowledge of her family and given birth in the field.

She said that she feared afterwards that she might have contributed to the death of her baby by placing her hand over its mouth as it emerged from her body to prevent any cries being heard. She seems to have displayed distress about this possibility when brought to psychiatric hospital in Limerick shortly after her arrest, and she also took considerable comfort from forensic evidence that the baby's lungs had never, in fact, become inflated – in other words, that she had not smothered it with her hand.

Having given birth to a baby whose imminence she had been seeking to deny all along, she placed the baby's body in a bag and hid it under brambles beside a pool on the farm. She later went to hospital where she was examined.

She was not the only young woman who had given birth secretly and then disposed of the body of her baby. The gynaecologist who examined her, Mr Creedon, remarked that in eight years he had had personal experience of five secret births at home of babies who had died, and in none of the five cases had he felt it necessary to refer to the police the question of how the baby had died. It was likely that the experience of this gynaecologist would be replicated by that of gynaecologists and doctors in cities and towns throughout Ireland and in other countries. In normal circumstances the death of Joanne's baby would have passed unnoticed. However, at the time it occurred there had also been the gruesome discovery of the Cahirciveen baby.

Mr Creedon advised the policemen who investigated with understandable vigour the killing of the Cahirciveen baby that Joanne Hayes was not the kind of person who would be likely to go berserk and stab her baby to death, that they were "on the wrong track".

Precisely what happened when she was brought to Tralee Garda Station for questioning about the death of a baby is a matter of dispute, but by the time four members of the Hayes family emerged from interrogation they had all confessed to involvement in the murder of a baby by stabbing and the disposal of the body. They had signed their names to statements giving detailed accounts concerning a bathbrush and a kitchen knife, various plastic bags and a trip to a place over forty miles away to dispose of the corpse.

The apparent fact that she and her family had signed statements confessing in detail to a crime with which they had no connection led to considerable public controversy; as a consequence a tribunal of inquiry was established. It was thought that the tribunal would concentrate on certain serious contradictions in the handling of the case and that Joanne Hayes would give evidence for just about twenty minutes. But to a great many people it seemed that the proceedings centred more upon the intimate details of her private life and sexual behaviour, and that while she was on the stand giving evidence for five days, during which she answered a total of 2,216 personal questions, she was subjected to an appalling and unwarranted public pillorying.

Complaints about the oppressive questioning of Joanne were expressed by, among others, Charles Haughey, leader of Fianna Fáil, the Council for the Status of Women, Senator Brendan Ryan, and the secretary-general of the Conference of Major Religious orders. As Marianne Heron wrote in the *Irish Independent*:

> We have been made fully and graphically aware of the realities of women's biology. No fact of female sexuality has been spared; menstruation, birth, bleeding, lactation, pregnancy. Through Joanne's treatment at the Tribunal we have seen clearly just how the law deals with women where a sexual element is involved, and how the sexual history of a woman can be used against her in an attempt to make her the guilty party.

It occurred to me that I should commission a book on the affair, but I soon became aware that many books were probably going to be written. I concluded that the one story that would be most interesting to publish would be one written from the point of view of the woman at the centre of it. We made enquiries but gained the distinct impression that we would get nowhere with that line of approach. The case had attracted the attention of a women's group in Tralee, the nearest town to Abbeydorney, and, as the story snowballed in the media, we discussed with them the possibility of a book from their perspective. Again, it appeared that we could make no progress in that direction and I approached the journalist whose coverage of the case I considered to have been the best, visiting Deirdre Purcell at her home and discussing a proposal with her. By that time I was aware that between four and six other authors were planning books on the same subject, but I felt that we might still be able to come up with the best.

Then, one Saturday, I received a message at home asking me to contact a John Barrett in Abbeydorney about the autobiography of Joanne Hayes. I thought that there was a confusion between biography and autobiography, but I made a phone call to Abbeydorney and set up a meeting for the next day. John Barrett was a neighbour of the Hayes family, a former *Irish Press* and *Kerryman* journalist, former bookie and constant greyhound and Gaelic football enthusiast. A middle-aged, married man, he had been sufficiently outraged by the public humiliation of this young unmarried mother to become involved in organising a demonstration outside the tribunal of inquiry. About thirty men and thirty women from Abbeydorney had left their farms to travel the icy roads in January to picket the tribunal in support of Joanne; it had been something quite new in Irish life, a quite remarkable instance of neighbourly concern and solidarity.

Unknown to anyone else, even to her solicitor, Joanne had been working with John Barrett on a book which would allow her to tell her own story. She had broken down while giving evidence on the fourth day of the tribunal and had been able to continue only with the help of sedatives. But the questions she had answered had been the questions asked by lawyers representing members of the police force in an attempt to portray her in a bad light; she had not had an opportunity to give her own account of herself, and this she sought to remedy through collaborating on a book. Fearful that she would earn the wrath of the tribunal judge, she had sworn John Barrett to secrecy. Now, however, at our Sunday meeting they wanted a book contract by the following day.

From the very beginning I involved our lawyers in the project. Serious allegations had been made in relation to the case, and I was aware that the libel laws represented a minefield. It seemed, however, that if we were able to bear in mind the legal constraints from the start, this was a book which could tell a fascinating story of enormous public interest, without running a substantial risk of giving rise to legal action. Joanne, keen as she was to tell her own story, was a little taken aback when I explained to her how careful we would have to be, but on reflection she accepted my point.

I worked closely with John Barrett over the following months, and Joanne reviewed everything he wrote. At a certain point, when we had a substantial amount of the manuscript, I approached Easons with a view to persuading them to order large quantities, while also wanting to sort out the question of any libel risk. They insisted that they would handle the book only if we indemnified them against the costs of any libel action. Beyond that, they insisted that we pay not only for our own legal advice but also for their separate legal advice, including their solicitor's costs and the cost of counsel's opinion. The two legal teams ran a fine-toothed comb through the manuscript, and I had a succession of meetings with them and with John Barrett to decide on revisions and redrafting of sensitive material.

The final chapter of the book could only be completed once the tribunal report was published, but the rest of the book was carefully vetted. Our senior counsel observed:

> The book itself is relatively innocuous. I see no danger of it being necessary to remove the book from public shelves when it goes on sale. In fact, I would make the comment that the book is too mild. . .

Despite such advice, we took the cautious approach of implementing changes in any instances which the lawyers suggested might offer opportunities for action for defamation.

One of the things I found fascinating about the tribunal was the ironic twist of history expressed in the different political backgrounds of the families of Joanne Hayes and Judge Kevin Lynch. The fact was that Joanne's uncle, a member of the anti-Treaty IRA, had been the sole survivor of the infamous Ballyseedy massacre in

1922, when the pro-Treaty National Army tied eight men to a landmine; a commander of pro-Treaty forces in Munster had been Fionán Lynch, father of Judge Kevin Lynch. Obviously the judge brought nothing of that history into his conduct of the tribunal, but the clash of culture between his Dublin bar council upper-middle-class manner and the Hayes family's small-farming Fianna Fáil rural character could scarcely have been more pronounced.

As we awaited the tribunal report, I prepared a strategy to protect Joanne from the worst aspects of the inevitable media frenzy.

The judge's findings came as an enormous shock to Joanne, reducing her to a state of howling, hysterical collapse. He declared that Joanne Hayes struck and choked her baby, appallingly serious charges. Yet the state pathologist, Dr John Harbison, had testified that there was no damage to the baby's larynx and no sign of strangulation.

As to the question of how the confessions had been obtained, answer came there none from the judge, except that they were suffering from guilty consciences about the Abbeydorney baby. He accused the Hayes family of lying and criticised them strongly for it, while describing the police as having merely "gilded the lily", because they were accustomed to doing so and "familiarity breeds contempt".

The Irish Council for Civil Liberties said of the report that it "reinforces through its use of misogynistic terminology, attitudes which demean and trivialise the reality of women's lives in Ireland today".

Once the tribunal report was published, on 3 October, the legal advice we received was suddenly different. "It should be stated," reported one senior counsel, "that law is not divorced from emotion. Judicial attitudes will henceforth be strongly against Joanne Hayes."

Substantial changes were suggested by the two legal teams. Although we were in a race with the publishers of the other books being written, we held up printing in order to implement all the lawyers' suggestions. Our own lawyers cleared it on 6 October,

Easons' lawyers on 9 October. Remarking to one of the lawyers upon the costs we were incurring by delaying production while typesetters and printers stood by, he replied that at least the rigorousness of the legal checks by two solicitors and two barristers, all four fully conversant with the text and the issues involved, would ensure that we would never run into legal difficulties.

The book had been ordered in exceptional quantities by the book trade, despite the fact that three other books on the case were also due out within days. With pre-publication orders of 20,000 copies, we had printed 25,000 in all. However, the public atmosphere had been crucially changed by the judge's report: sympathy for Joanne shrank and the judge's extraordinary characterisation of her, without benefit of trial, struck home.

I arranged and negotiated on Joanne's appearance on *The Late Late Show* on publication day, 18 October 1985. Feeling that she had been subjected to an obscene ordeal by the tribunal, I wanted to ensure that she would not have to undergo a repeat performance on television. I had a responsibility as her publisher to promote the book, but also to protect her from being abused in the process. I was satisfied with the assurances given by *The Late Late Show*, but at the last minute an unexpected and unwelcome crisis was precipitated by the BBC. They had recorded an "Out of Court" special with the co-operation of Joanne and her family. It had been scheduled to go out immediately after the tribunal report's publication. The BBC contract granted them exclusivity, but agreed that Joanne's appearance on *The Late Late Show* would not be considered in breach of that exclusivity. For reasons of their own they were unable to broadcast as soon as intended, and now *The Late Late Show* would occur earlier than their broadcast. As I approached RTÉ, I learned that the BBC were trying to have *The Late Late Show* appearance cancelled and had been ringing RTÉ all day threatening all kinds of dire consequences if the programme went ahead, and legal action to prevent its going ahead. It emerged that their reaction was due to the fact that when they had agreed that *The Late Late Show* would not conflict with their contract, they had not been aware that edited extracts from *The Late Late Show* were as a matter of regular practice rebroadcast on Channel Four. BBC representatives berated RTÉ staff with an arrogance which succeeded only in getting backs up.

In the event *The Late Late Show* interview went ahead, and Joanne gave a brave and effective response to Gay Byrne's sensitive, sympathetic questioning, in the course of which Joanne firmly repudiated the judge's finding: "I did not kill my baby." In a contribution from the audience I strongly criticised the findings of the tribunal and their impact on the Hayes family.

Reaction to Joanne's appearance on the show was largely positive; while it probably didn't change minds, it did go some way to lessen the very negative impact of the tribunal report.

The BBC, however, decided to take revenge against Joanne and her family for their misunderstanding of the situation regarding *The Late Late Show*. They broadcast their "Out of Court" special. It was, as the producer of the programme said, "well received", but they insisted on reneging on paying the small fees they had agreed to pay the members of the Hayes family for the several days of disruption involved in filming the programme. I wrote to the programme's producer expressing my disgust, but he sought to evade responsibility. "Any dispute," he wrote, "over the details of the contract between Joanne and the BBC is a matter for yourself and the BBC's Contracts Department. . . I have very limited knowledge of the legalities of contract law and negotiation." I felt it was a pathetic response, and I replied:

> Dear Charles,
> Auntie BBC clearly wears a skirt behind which her little charges can hide when they've been caught swinging the cat by its tail. And the name of the skirt is the Contracts Department. Your letter is a contemptible piece of evasion. . . The behaviour of the BBC, of which you were the prime representative, stinks.

To the Contracts Department I wrote asking them to reconsider. They insisted on maintaining their cheap and vindictive stance.

As things turned out, we sold about twice as many copies of Joanne's *My Story* as were sold of any of the other books about the case. Still, many of the copies sent out to the wholesalers were returned, and the eventual sales fell well short of our initial advance orders.

My own involvement in publishing the book was a more emotional one than most. I was used to the emotions associated with fighting for a book and defending our freedom to publish, but in this case the story touched, moved and disturbed me for personal reasons. At the time that I became involved in discussions with Joanne Hayes and John Barrett, I was also involved in trying to help a friend who was having great difficulty in coming to terms with an unwanted pregnancy. Her strength of character made it difficult to get through to her, and she veered between fierce denial and threats of suicide, all steaming in the pressure cooker of family relations, allied with a general social context in which abortion was the unspeakable crime, even though availed of in secret by thousands every year who travelled to clinics in England.

Joanne Hayes had reacted to her own unwise pregnancy with a mixture of panic, denial and confusion. I felt I understood something of the confusion she had experienced, the collision of unrealistic aspiration and desperate reality. I also felt that "there but for the grace of God go I" – not, obviously, that I could find myself in the same situation, but any mistakes, it seemed to me, that Joanne had made were mistakes of a human order which I could easily imagine making myself, without having any malign motivation. It therefore came as a considerable shock to me when I found that many people I knew were proud to express and wallow in the most hateful attitudes towards this unfortunate young woman.

In Dublin I had friends and acquaintances who were member or supporters of left-wing and progressive organisations such as Official Sinn Féin and the Communist Party, who were trade union militants and working-class community activists. But when I heard them talk about Joanne I was devastated that such people

of broadly progressive views could react with such violent contempt towards her suffering. They expressed themselves with a
grossly sexist hostility towards rural women as a whole. And their
prejudice, I found, was remarkably widespread in Dublin.

Indeed, although some feminists strove energetically to
mobilise opinion around her case, the greatest support Joanne
received, as expressed in countless letters and mass cards, and in
the demonstrations in support of her by her neighbours, came
from devout Roman Catholic country people.

Joanne had written in her preface to *My Story* of watching her
daughter playing with her toys:

> In the years to come I will have a complex and harrowing story
> to tell her of love and tears, joy and heartache and immense
> suffering. . .
>
> I do not plead for sympathy now, nor seek to justify my actions,
> and most of all I want to avoid causing any further hurt to inno-
> cent victims of my behaviour. I acted recklessly and selfishly and I
> am deeply sorry for all the trouble that I have caused for so many
> people.

Yet as I saw it, unwise and reckless as her actions may have
been, she had a great deal less to be ashamed of than had the state
and the legal process.

Within a week of publication we received a solicitor's letter
demanding on behalf of three of the gardaí involved in the case
that we withdraw the book and pay them damages for defamation. Our lawyers advised us we could safely ignore it because
every angle had been covered by the legal vetting. So we neither
withdrew the book nor offered to make any payment.

We heard no more until, about a year and a half later, just after
newspapers had carried reports that a film was to be made based
on the book, we received a solicitor's letter. Three gardaí -- two
of those who had threatened action earlier, plus another --
claimed that the book defamed them by identifying them as
members of the "Heavy Gang" and attributing to the "Heavy

Gang" the practice of extracting confessions by illegal and oppressive means. They announced their intention of suing us for libel in an action which, our lawyers advised us, would generate very substantial costs.

The "Heavy Gang" operated during the Fine Gael/Labour coalition government of 1973-1977. Its attentions had been focused particularly upon members of republican organisations and its most publicised activity related to the robbery of a mail train near Sallins, County Kildare. Over thirty members and associates of the Irish Republican Socialist Party (IRSP) had been questioned about the robbery and eight of them had been beaten up, one so severely that he had to be ordered by the high court to be released to a hospital where he could undergo checks for a suspected fractured skull.

The existence of the "Heavy Gang" was no secret, having been extensively documented in the media. Indeed, in the course of the tribunal of inquiry in relation to the Hayes family confessions, a police superintendent had confirmed their existence in evidence. What the guards who proposed to sue us for libel complained of, however, was that they had individually been tarred with the brush of the "Heavy Gang", especially because Joanne had quoted a song by Christy Moore about Nicky Kelly, an IRSP member railroaded for the Sallins robbery. None of the lawyers who had advised us had raised the issue of the mentioning of Nicky Kelly, or the quoting of the song.

When gardaí had first sought damages and threatened action in the courts for defamation, we had been advised by our lawyers to ignore them. By the time they came back at us again we had new lawyers, while other parties to the action – principally Easons, the wholesalers, and Powers Supermarkets – also had their legal teams.

Now the legal opinion was quite different from the legal opinion we had received when working on the book, but as a small, young company battling for survival in a harsh economic climate, we were in no condition to offer to settle. Our financial position was so precarious that even if a small payout to each of the gardaí would have satisfied them, we would not have been able to make it. The company was threatened with liquidation, my business partner Bernie Goggin with losing the properties which had provided the collateral for the bank loans which were keeping us afloat. Settlement was not an option, and for some time it seemed that we had good grounds on which to contest the action. Consultations dragged on, complicated by difficulties of communication between various legal teams.

I felt under enormous pressure. I was aware that Bernie was positively transfixed with horror at the very real prospect of ruin facing him. While it would be serious enough for me if the company went into liquidation, I would at least expect little difficulty in securing employment elsewhere in the publishing industry. For Bernie, he stood to lose not only his investment in the company but his properties. I felt that there was an immense onus on me to get us out of the mess we were in.

First of all, I had to remedy our poor general trading position. I had to come up with books which would generate substantial income and I had to cut costs drastically. I took more and more work on myself. Rather than pay someone else to design, to promote, to create display material, I would do it myself. I decided to reduce my average hours of sleep from seven to five hours.

For two years we tottered on the brink of extinction. I woke up each morning wondering if this was the day we would finally be forced to fold. I worked feverishly to trade us out of the hole we were in. And at the same time I tried to appeal to friends and contacts to support us on what was to my mind an issue of freedom of expression. There was no organisation campaigning on freedom of expression, and the general culture was not particularly sympathetic. Yet there were those who had taken stands and who were known to be broadly liberal. I decided to approach Christy Moore, author and singer of the song "The Wicklow Boy" which was such an important element in the claims of defamation against us. Christy was a friend; he had come to me in 1983 with a request that I publish a book of songs from his repertoire. He had become aware of people producing scrappy pirated pamphlets of some of these songs; his concern was not to make any money for himself but to have a professionally produced songbook published. The publication had not been without its problems, particularly in relation to clearing permissions for all the songs and music. But we had done a good job and had reaped the rewards in unprecedented sales, for the first time ever getting a songbook into the number one best-selling non-fiction paperback slot and earning for Christy some significant income. The book differed from most songbooks in presenting the words and music of far more songs (over a hundred) than was usual; it was illustrated with an excellent and appropriate collection of photographs; and it was a handy pocketbook size at a popular price. When Christy performed in Dingle I wound up on several occasions drinking with him late into the night in the Hillgrove Hotel. On one occasion I brought him for a swim in Mount Eagle lake; he cursed me as we laboured up the stony track to the lake, sweating in the midday sun, but he was delighted once we got into the water, and the swim proved the perfect cure for his hangover. I was frankly proud of our achievement in making *The Christy Moore Songbook* such a success, and given his generally progressive political views and our friendship I felt that he would be well disposed to express some kind of solidarity with our plight, so I asked him if he could suggest the names of any people who might assist with the organisation of a benefit concert. However, Christy had recently been ill, and in the end I am sure that it was his ill-health that caused him not to reply to my letters. He was a man who gave of himself more wholeheartedly in performance than anyone else I knew, and illness had left him for the moment with no more to give.

In the circumstances it was not surprising that we were up to three months late in paying some of our authors royalties they were due, and we were later still in paying some of our suppliers. What was surprising was that we survived in business at all. In settling defamation claims, we paid out over £100,000 in damages and legal fees. Indeed, we paid out more than our total turnover for the year in which we had originally published the book.

We were by no means alone in experiencing the perilous effects of the libel laws. In the 1970s and 1980s a number of Irish publishers brought out exciting, interesting and controversial books which set the pace in contributing to debate on issues of current affairs. But in very many cases the libel laws were invoked, the books were withdrawn from circulation or never reprinted to meet public demand, and several publishers had to pay out tens of thousands of pounds in damages and costs. In addition, as the largest book wholesaler, Easons had to pay damages on numerous occasions and in order to defend its own position refrained from distributing some books which it felt carried a libel risk. This led naturally to assertions that Easons were engaged in censorship. Publishers, some of whom faced bankruptcy in the face of libel actions, cancelled plans for controversial books and ceased looking for the kind of best-selling titles that had the potential to benefit the whole trade while also contributing to informed public debate.

It was a widespread view in the circumstances that the libel laws had become unbalanced in practice, with amounts awarded in damages rising all the time.

Extremely conscious from my own experience of the very restrictive nature of the defamation laws, and painfully conscious too of the difficulty of coping in isolation with a situation such as we had endured, I turned my attention to working within the publishing industry to increase consciousness of the dangers posed and to begin a campaign to change the laws. I had for several years been a member of the committee of CLÉ, the Irish Book Publishers' Association, and early in 1987 I was elected president of CLÉ for a two-year term. I set up a sub-committee of CLÉ to pursue law reform. We canvassed politicians on the need for reform in the defamation laws, our efforts complementing those of the National Newspapers of Ireland, who were also campaigning on the issue.

In January 1989 the attorney-general requested the Law Reform Commission to undertake an examination of, and submit proposals for the reform of, the law of defamation. The Book Publishers' Working Group, made up of myself, Michael Gill (Gill and Macmillan) and Harold Clarke (Easons), made representations on behalf of the book trade to the Law Reform Commission after taking legal advice from Marie McGonagle of UCG. We also discussed the situation with the National Newspapers of Ireland, and in May 1989 we met with the commission, under the chairmanship of Justice Ronan Keane, at its offices, giving a full account of our perspective on the issue and answering questions posed by the commission members. In November, when Brandon's settlement of damages in relation to Joanne Hayes was in the news, I held a joint press conference with CLÉ (represented by its new chairman, Alex Miller, and by Michael Gill) and with Harold Clarke of Easons, who had joined our working group in recognition of the special risk run by wholesalers in relation to the defamation issue.

In March 1991 the commission published its *Consultation Paper on the Civil Law of Defamation* containing seventy-two preliminary proposals, and in April 1991 at an open seminar held by the commission I made verbal submissions, together with representatives of the newspapers and RTÉ. I stressed that the context was one in which the present state of the law was intimidating publishers into avoiding dealing with important matters of public interest. The law had to strike a balance between competing constitutional rights, but the current situation was unbalanced against freedom of expression and freedom of information.

I was concerned that courts and juries had in their minds an image of publishers as large corporations wielding power and influence, to whom a large libel settlement was small in terms of their turnover. Yet the truth was that the Irish publishing industry was made up of small companies, each of which could be put out of business by a single large libel settlement.

In my criticism of the report I regretted the proposal to retain aggravated damages where there was an unsuccessful defence of justification. The defendant should not, I felt, be penalised for exercising the right to plead justification.

Shortly after the seminar I prepared a detailed written submission to the Law Reform Commission, which my colleagues endorsed.

In March 1992 the commission published its final report and we were pleased to find that the submissions we had made, both verbal and written, were well represented in the report, and many of the points I had made were incorporated in the final recommendations. There were some aspects of the report with which I disagreed, most notably the recommendation regarding defamation of the dead. However, on balance I felt that the recommendations were not only favourable but that they represented a historic opportunity for the book trade and the media. The recommendations were submitted to the relevant government departments, and the joint programme of the Fianna Fáil/Labour coalition government referred to law reform in the area of freedom of expression.

I wrote to publishers, wholesalers and booksellers:

While the recommendations of the Law Reform Commission have now been submitted to the relevant government departments, it is unlikely that they will be given any legislative effect without consistent and sustained pressure from the electorate. Everyone will have their own views regarding the joint programme of the new Government, but one can certainly welcome the fact that it refers to law reform in the area of freedom of expression. One can also reasonably conclude that the priority given to such reform is likely to depend upon consistent and sustained pressure being brought to bear. Legislation will only follow if there is sufficient demand and pressure.

It is therefore essential that a programme of vigorous and sustained action be mounted within the book trade to ensure that public representatives are made aware of our concern that the Law Reform Commission proposals be implemented. We would therefore suggest that you (your organisation/society/group, etc.) would write to your local representatives and to the local organisations of all the political parties, drawing attention to the Law Reform Commission's Report on the Civil Law of Defamation and expressing the opinion that its recommendations should be given legislative effect. Most importantly, representations should be made to members of the parties in government.

However, no campaign developed, no pressure was put on, and no legislation followed.

Perhaps we should not be surprised. Those in positions of power, including some politicians, are the ones who benefit the most from the defamation laws as they stand – laws which have provided a source of tax-free income in damages and a shield for corruption.

Chapter Six

ONE GIRL'S WAR

I WAS NOT led by the experience of publishing *British Intelligence and Covert Action* to seek other manuscripts on the same subject. I was more concerned that we should generate books which offered new and critical perspectives on Irish society. This arose not out of any narrow parochialism but because there had been a general lack of such material from Irish publishers, and I was convinced that there existed a public interest in it. At the same time I wanted to maintain a lively fiction programme.

From both editorial and marketing points of view there were good reasons why we could not expect to build our list on the basis of books of British interest. I was rarely in Britain and was not in touch with the nuances of British political and social life. But the crucial factor was that we lacked adequate marketing and distribution in Britain. I had been trying since our first year to achieve a link with an appropriate British publisher which would allow us to have a real presence in the British market, and I had also researched and approached a number of distribution companies, but our list had always seemed too small and too Irish oriented to interest potential partners. Discussions with Pluto Press and Allison and Busby extended intermittently over several years, but in the end we found ourselves with only the most peripheral access to the British market. If a representative sample of British booksellers had been asked then if they were aware of our existence, I doubt if even one in a hundred would have answered yes.

Although we had escaped the attention of most British book-sellers, our publication of *British Intelligence and Covert Action* had not passed unnoticed by a number of authors, and several manuscripts dealing with various aspects of intelligence landed on my desk in Dingle. Of these only one really interested me: it was *One Girl's War: Personal Exploits in MI5's Most Secret Station* by Joan Miller.

British Intelligence and Covert Action had provided a well-documented and well-sourced account of the methods and activities of the intelligence services. The manuscript of *One Girl's War*, however, added nothing of any substance to the understanding of wartime British intelligence. It contained no new revelations and did not go beyond what had already been well covered in other books. Nevertheless, it did possess a certain charm and interest in the way in which it conveyed not matters of substance but a sense of atmosphere: the atmosphere within the section of MI5 in which she had worked, and the general social atmosphere surrounding a young woman from the "right kind" of school in wartime London.

Joan Miller had been recruited at the age of twenty-one more on account of her social background than for any particular skills or abilities she possessed, and also on account of her striking good looks. She breezed through London and the world of intelligence with an extraordinary insouciance, and I was struck on reading and rereading the manuscript by a particular paradox. She showed no real understanding of the intelligence world, and she came across as a flighty young woman determined to have a jolly good time between tea in the Savoy, dodging bombs in the Blitz, and occasional acts of officially sanctioned burglary and spying in the furtherance of her employment.

She described her relationship with a Spanish diplomat without showing any consciousness of the implications of a British intelligence officer having for a lover a representative of a pro-German Fascist government. She naively believed that the reason why her relationship as "mistress" of Maxwell Knight, her boss, remained unconsummated after two years was due to some inadequacy of her own, only to discover eventually that he was homosexual. Her innocence was at times almost breathtaking. Yet, and this was where the paradox lay, she had played a key role in securing the conviction of a number of pro-Fascists in the first major spy trial of the war. Almost despite itself, the manuscript did, I felt, tell the reader something about wartime intelligence, for its author was seemingly the least eccentric of the bunch of upper class oddballs working in the counter-subversion B5(b) section of MI5.

Whatever else it was, the book was not an exposé of British intelligence by a person critical of its basic assumptions. Joan Miller came across as a patriotic woman who was proud of what she had done in MI5. Indeed, I found it hard to imagine a less subversive book on its subject. There was, it seemed to me, no likelihood that it would provoke the kind of hostility in Whitehall that had been occasioned by *British Intelligence and Covert Action.*

I felt we could make a modest success of publishing it because I knew that there was a considerable appetite amongst the British public for yet more about wartime Britain. Many people of all classes harked back sentimentally to the war years, despite their many tragedies and deprivations, as some kind of golden age of social consensus, of uncomplicated togetherness in the face of the enemy.

This background would, I felt, ensure a certain sale for the book, though our print-run would have to be quite small. It would not make a great deal money for us, but it might do a useful job of drawing our list to wider attention in Britain, might off-set and qualify our overwhelmingly Irish-interest image amongst booksellers. I also had a sneaking feeling that we might interest someone in making a film of it.

One Girl's War had originally been scheduled for publication by Weidenfeld and Nicolson, the London publisher. However, in May 1984, only ten days after we had launched the reprint of *British Intelligence and Covert Action* in the House of Commons, Weidenfeld had received a letter from the office of the treasury solicitor, who acts for the British government in legal matters:

Those who instruct me understand that you are in possession of the text of a typescript written by Miss Joan Miller which includes confidential information obtained by her in the course of her employment as a servant of the Crown. As a potential publisher of this typescript, I think you should be aware that Miss Miller has not obtained the consent of the Crown to the publication of such confidential information and that she may be in breach of the relevant provisions of the Official Secrets Act 1911 if the work were to be published. I should also point out that Miss Miller would be in breach of a duty of confidence owed to the Crown under the general common law.

In the light of the foregoing, I should be grateful to receive your assurance that you will not proceed with the publication of the typescript.

Weidenfeld must have been genuinely surprised to receive such a letter. They had, after all, submitted the manuscript to Rear-Admiral Ash, secretary of the D-Notice Committee, and he had indicated in writing that he had no objection to its publication. In addition Joan Miller understood that she had received verbal clearance from the appropriate intelligence authorities to go ahead with her memoirs. And she had further reason to believe that there would be no objection: she had been quoted and acknowledged as a major source for Anthony Masters' book *The Man Who Was M*; she had also given a substantial interview to Barrie Penrose, which had been published, with extensive attributed quotes, in *The Sunday Times Magazine* in 1981. She had received no representations or complaints from the intelligence service or any other government agency in relation to these published recollections of her wartime career in MI5. In reporting on the letter from the treasury solicitor's office, a front-page *Observer* article described the references to possible breaches of the law as "legally bogus". However, Weidenfeld promptly and supinely decided to drop their plans to publish the book.

One month later Joan Miller died at her home in Malta.

However, her literary agent in London submitted the manuscript to me, in the hope that an Irish publisher, who had already breached the D-Notice system, might be willing to take it on, despite the British government's disapproval.

Before taking a decision to publish the book at Brandon, it was obviously necessary to seek legal advice. I sent the manuscript to a London solicitor, who instructed a barrister with specialist knowledge of the relevant areas of the law. In London again for the London Book Fair in April 1985, I met the solicitor and barrister to hear their advice about the legal implications of publication, and later the barrister forwarded me a written opinion.

In essence their advice was that legal action to prevent publication or for any breach of the law would be unprecedented, unlikely to occur, and, if it should occur, unlikely to succeed. I decided to go ahead with publication and agreed a contract with Joan Miller's daughter, Jonquil Hepper, who lived in Rome, and the book's ghost writer, Patricia Craig.

By the summer of 1985 we had artwork for the jacket and we had completed editing, copy-editing and internal design. My only worry was that our distribution arrangements in Britain were inadequate. There was some delay in typesetting and then, just as we were packing the camera-ready copy and the jacket artwork to be dispatched to the printer, I learned that the British government was due to embark on unprecedented legal proceedings in Australia, seeking to prevent publication of Peter Wright's MI5 memoirs.

One Girl's War was entirely free, I knew, of the kind of sensitive material that was presumed to be contained in Peter Wright's manuscript. Nevertheless, I felt that we should be cautious. Brandon was a very small company struggling to survive in difficult trading circumstances. The previous year had been an unsatisfactory one for us, and 1985 had so far been no better; our fiction, in particular, was dying a death in the bookshops, despite eliciting good critical responses. Not only could we not afford the expenses of legal action but also we could not afford to publish the book and then find ourselves prevented from selling it in its principal market,

Britain. I was also concerned that Patricia Craig, as a British citizen living within the jurisdiction, could find herself exposed to prosecution or harassment by the British authorities. The literary agent had been keen to avoid involvement in any possible legal consequences, but the chain of responsibility placed Patricia Craig in a potentially more difficult position

I decided to postpone publication and meanwhile offer ample opportunity for any British government office, department or agency to express its objections to our proceeding with publication. I was deliberately inviting a response from British government or intelligence sources. We carried out an extensive mailing to foreign publishers, offering the book for US and foreign language rights; we offered paperback rights to major British publishers. We mailed British libraries and library suppliers, and pre-publication orders started to come in, together with requests for review copies. *Intelligence Quarterly* magazine not only requested a review copy twice but also carried a notice of our intention to publish. If British intelligence personnel did not read *Intelligence Quarterly*, I reasoned, then they did not read at all.

In October we exhibited the book's cover at the Frankfurt International Book Fair and advertised the book's impending publication in September's Frankfurt supplement to *The Bookseller*. At the fair itself I discussed the book with a number of British publishers and with Heinemann Australia. Heinemann were unable for legal reasons to talk about their own Peter Wright book, but I gathered that the British government seemed to be serious in their intention of pursuing the suppression of that particular book in Australia or wherever else it might be sought to publish it.

In the succeeding months various dates were given as to when the Australian case would come to a head, and I delayed in the hope that an outcome in Australia might clarify our position. A number of British journalists challenged or otherwise discussed with me our delay, and without exception they ridiculed the notion that we stood in any legal danger whatsoever. But what convinced me most of all that it was entirely safe to proceed was the fact that there had not been the slightest communication from or press item inspired by British government or intelligence sources. I was aware of claims that British intelligence was incompetent; I did not believe them. But even if I had, it was inconceivable that they could be so spectacularly incompetent as to be unaware of the fact that we had been planning to publish *One Girl's War* for quite some time.

In August 1986 I finally sent the book to be printed, and it is a measure of our confidence that we would not run into legal objections from the government that we decided to print it in Britain rather than in Ireland or anywhere else outside that jurisdiction. By the end of October finished copies had been delivered to the warehouse of Turnaround Distribution, our London-based British distributor, and by the first few days of November copies were in both our Dublin warehouse and our Dingle offices. Review copies went out immediately, bookshop orders from the end of the first week in November.

On 14 November the *Guardian* carried a report of the book's imminent publication. On the same day, hurrying between appointments, I did a live radio interview from a coin box in the Abbey Theatre in Dublin with RTÉ's Pat Kenny, in which I stated that the book was already on sale in both Britain and Ireland. On 15 November the *Daily Telegraph* carried a report. Later the British government was to claim that the first it knew of the book's publication by Brandon was on 21 November.

On 21 November, six days before the official publication date, Turnaround phoned in an urgent order for a further 500 copies, having sold out the first 500 already. Later the same day I received a call in Dingle from the Press Association in the House of Commons: Sir Michael Havers, attorney-general of England and Wales, had just stated that legal action against us in the Irish courts was "under consideration". I was frankly amazed.

I phoned legal, political and journalistic contacts in London for a reading on the statement from Sir Michael Havers. The majority opinion was that Sir Michael was bluffing, that there was no legal basis for the suppression of our book, and that it was just a question of making noises that would cover the government's position in relation to the Peter Wright case in Australia. However, amongst MPs and other political contacts there was a feeling that if the government was determined it would press ahead, however little sense it seemed to make.

I was in no position to act on the matter. At the end of September we had published John B. Keane's first novel, *The Bodhrán Makers*, and it had become a best-seller. The day of the attorney-general's bombshell was the day after we had organised exceptionally rapid delivery of the second printing; rather than being thanked for our speed we were receiving complaints about differences in mere hours between deliveries to one shop and another and one wholesaler and another. It was the kind of problem any publisher likes to have. We were faced with the prospect of having to decide rapidly on whether to order another reprint.

Phone calls were coming in from the British and Irish media in numbers that were beginning to make concentration on other work impossible, and they continued to my home at night. Disruptive as such concentrated media attention may be, no publisher can afford to take the phone off the hook or otherwise be unavailable. However, in a situation of controversy with a threat of legal action, it was necessary to combine caution with comment and information. While some journalists and some newspapers were relatively accurate in reporting the general tenor of their phone conversations with me, some were clearly not going to let the truth interfere with a good story, and I found my Nos reported as Yeses, but I was fortunate enough in that none of the misrepresentation was too serious. Most journalists, indeed, were entirely sympathetic to our position, their errors having more to do with sloppiness than with any antagonism or malice.

On 25 November I heard from London that Sir Michael Havers would make an announcement regarding legal action in two days. I drafted a press release and issued it by telex the next day:

We wish to make clear that over 500 copies of this book have already been sold in Britain during the last week to ten days, and it is our intention to ensure the continued availability of this book to the British book trade. The enormous demand for the book has meant that we, as a small publisher with limited marketing resources, have been unable to keep booksellers adequately supplied but we have taken steps to remedy this situation and we would ask members of the public and booksellers to be patient meanwhile.

As regards the threat of legal action against Brandon we feel we have no reason to be intimidated. We emphatically deny that the publication of the book constitutes any genuine threat to national security. It is a lively, fascinating account of the author's activities in MI5 during World War II and as such there is no question of it compromising current intelligence operations.

We appreciate that its publication at this time may, and indeed does, constitute a considerable political embarrassment to the government in the context of its legal action in Australia re Peter Wright. However, to equate political embarrassment with a threat to national security would be to engage in a blatant abuse of language, would constitute a dangerous and undemocratic suppression of freedom of information, and would be against the public interest.

In London that day a retired senior officer of the British armed forces purchased five copies of *One Girl's War* at Hatchards, a central London bookshop. Within an hour of returning home he was visited by two members of MI5 who demanded that he hand over the copies he had bought. He declined; they appealed to him again to do so "as an officer and a gentleman"; he again declined.

I had offered serial rights in the book to several Sunday and daily newspapers, but there had been no takers. The *New Statesman,* however, had expressed an interest, and on the book's official publication date, 27 November, two pages of extracts appeared in the *New Statesman,* much to the chagrin of Sir Michael Havers and his Whitehall associates.

And it was on 27 November that the action really started. A Dublin firm of solicitors, McCann, Fitzgerald, Dudley and Roche – a name I shortened to a more manageable McCann-Fitz for my own use – phoned me in Dingle in the middle of the day and demanded on behalf of their client, the attorney-general for England and Wales, that we refrain from publishing the book. I pointed out, to the apparently great surprise of the solicitor, that the book was already on sale and had been on sale for two weeks, and so there could be no question of refraining from publishing it. Nevertheless, she wanted an immediate undertaking; I gave her a provisional "No" and told her that I would consult my solicitor.

Billy Keane was a young Listowel, County Kerry, solicitor who, although showing no literary bent himself, had grown up in an environment richly coloured by the preoccupations of his father, the playwright, storyteller, poet and novelist, John B. Keane. When I called him that day to tell him that we had "a small bit of trouble with our MI5 book", he reacted with great speed in securing and conveying the best of advice. He confirmed to McCann-Fitz our refusal to withdraw the book and asked them to inform him if they were going to seek an injunction restraining us from selling the book. They undertook to do so. But at 10pm that night they sought and obtained, without notice to us, an injunction at the Dublin home of high court judge Justice Blayney.

The phone rang at my home at 8.00 the next morning: it was McCann-Fitz for the attorney-general, but I was already out. I knew that this was the day on which I could expect concentrated media and legal attention to be focused on *One Girl's War,* but I also knew that it was essential that I deal with other matters before my life was entirely taken over by the twin tribes of lawyers and journalists. I took my notes from my desk and settled down in an alternative office well away from the phones.

We were to publish two new books on 9 and 10 December: *Des O' Malley, a Political Profile* by Dick Walsh, and *The Politics of Irish Freedom* by Gerry Adams. It is hard to imagine two more contrasting sets of politics than those of Adams and O'Malley, but both were revealing about the state of politics and society in Ireland. O'Malley, a former Fianna Fáil minister, had founded the Progressive Democrats only months before and he and his party were expected to face the first electoral test of their new departure almost any day, as pre-election fever had been sustained at a high pitch since October. Gerry Adams, president of Sinn Féin and Westminster MP for West Belfast, was regarded as *persona non grata* by the establishment, but he represented a developing republican politics and enjoyed substantial support in the north.

The Irish Times was to run an extract from the book on Des O'Malley in its Saturday supplement, and I felt that general political interest would ensure reviews for the book. I considered a formal launch for the book but discovered that both the author and his subject shared our view of the limited usefulness of such an exercise, and so I opted instead for a signing session in a Dublin bookshop.

The Adams book, however, posed particular problems in promotional terms. He was banned from Irish radio and television by the political censorship law, Section 31 of the Broadcasting Act; he was also regarded with general hostility by the entire Irish and British media. I had offered extracts from his book, a work of some objective political importance given his position, but even the more liberal elements of the mainstream British press seemed to consider that while they might report his statements and speeches, they could not have him offering his opinions in their columns. However, *City Limits* in London was interested in running an extract. In Ireland the *Irish Press*, edited by Tim Pat Coogan, would also run an extract. Meanwhile, detailed arrangements had to be made in respect of launches of the book at which I would need to preside in both Belfast and Dublin.

I returned to my own office to find that the phones were busy with media enquiries and to learn that McCann-Fitz had called to dictate to us the terms of the injunction granted the previous night; they had also been busy ringing booksellers to tell them that they were required by the terms of the injunction to take the book off their shelves. Meanwhile, Ireland's largest book retailer and wholesaler, Easons, had anticipated the British government action and had already, even without being asked, taken the book off their shelves of their own accord. They had done so, indeed, before the injunction had even been sought and without reference to us. Some booksellers complied with the demand that they withdraw the book from sale and some did not. One outraged bookseller remarked: "To hell with them! I'm not having the British bloody government telling me what I can and cannot sell in my shop!" The general response amongst those in Ireland who took any particular notice of the situation was one of outrage at the arrogance of the British government in seeking apparently to dictate to the Irish courts and people. Some unsolicited expressions of support for us were coming in from lawyers and journalists, and I found that my defiant line in response to press enquiries was well reported and seemed to be broadly welcomed.

The priority was to prepare our legal position. Billy Keane had secured the services of highly respected Senior Counsel Hugh O'Flaherty. The high court hearing of our case would be held on Monday, which gave us only the weekend to prepare. The phones were still ringing on Friday as I left Dingle at 4.30pm with Bernie Goggin, and at 6.00 we began a meeting in Listowel with Billy Keane. I ran through a full account of the background to our publication of the book, which Billy taped, and I showed him relevant documents I had pulled hastily from my files before leaving. I had thought I would be returning to Dingle that night, but Billy had set up a meeting with our legal team in Dublin for 1.00pm the next day, and so Bernie set off back to Dingle to collect clothes for me and further files from my filing cabinet for Billy. After I had given the basic outline of our position, Billy explained the legal situation as he saw it, stressing that the further advice of senior counsel would be vital. I had already adopted a fighting stance in refusing to withdraw the book and in attacking the British government's action in media interviews. There were good grounds for contesting the action in the courts. Yet we had to consider seriously the option of cutting our losses and accepting the situation as a *de facto* ban on our book which we would not fight. We had enough problems as it was without becoming entangled in legal difficulties; earlier in the year our financial position had been so disastrous that we had been within a hair's breadth of bankruptcy. Every day was a struggle to find the money to meet the most pressing bills, and we had only been able to keep going with the greatest difficulty. If we fought the case it would, whether we won or lost, take considerable time and energy from our publishing work; the case might drag on and might precipitate the collapse of our company, leaving us, as directors, in a state of financial ruin. The British government possessed limitless resources with which to pursue us to the ends of the law and all the avenues of appeal if necessary.

I also had to consider for myself whether I could take the strain of fighting to defend our right to publish.

"It's a war," commented Bernie soberly and with evident distaste.

Why, after all, should we have to become involved in a battle with a government when all we were trying to do was publish books? Yet I found that I had an appetite for the fight.

I had long believed in the importance of the written word, of freedom of expression, and I had an abiding belief in the positive power of literature and books to extend the boundaries of thought and imagination and to inform and enrich people's lives. *One Girl's War* was not the most important book I had ever been associated with: it was not of outstanding quality, nor did it contain vital information of great public concern; but I had long ago concluded that battles are rarely, if ever, neat and simple matters fought on grounds of one's own choosing. What weighed with me most was the conviction that if the British government was to succeed in suppressing this book, then their hand would be significantly strengthened in seeking to suppress other books of greater consequence. However, I also weighed a more pragmatic consideration: our character as a publisher, as I had developed it, was a radical and creative one, and this had marked us out from other publishers, earning respect and attention amongst writers, the book trade and the media. If we were to fight to defend our right to publish, we would attract positive media attention in both Britain and Ireland. Given the way the media were shaping up, the principal problem was whether we could cope with the amount of attention.

Billy Keane's parents, John and Mary, have a famous pub in Listowel, and it was there I went after Bernie had set out on his journey back to Dingle and Billy and I had continued with our work for a couple of hours. Mary's meal in an oasis of calm provided a welcome respite, and the pint of Guinness eased the tension of remaining worries. Billy's staff at the office had rallied at short notice and he carried on working away with them until, just before closing time, he managed to escape to join me for a pint.

The next morning Billy and I set out from Listowel in his car, arriving at the Herbert Park, Dublin, home of Hugh O'Flaherty at 1.30. We started in immediately to discuss the case.

Our two senior counsels, Hugh O'Flaherty and Richard (Ricky) Johnson, represented a considerable contrast in temperaments and styles. Hugh O'Flaherty presided over our deliberations and directed them in a way which kept the focus always on the practical realities of the case and which kept in the forefront of our minds Brandon's need for a quick and favourable resolution of the situation. Ricky Johnson, son of a celebrated district justice and playwright from County Kerry, was a man for the flamboyant phrase and the erudite quotation, and he was clearly keenly interested in the potential for establishing new legal precedent. He provided a kind of breadth which admirably complemented Hugh's rigorous, focused approach. Junior Counsel Felix McElroy was a model of applied diligence, a man who knew what to look for and where to find it, and it was clear that he would be putting in many hours of research after we had concluded our discussions for the day.

I was concerned to listen carefully: I had been fully wrapped up in the publishing aspects of the book, but what I needed to understand was the legal framework and context, which were quite different things. Indeed, so intent was I on hearing the matter discussed by the lawyers that Hugh turned to me after a while and suggested that, as the person at the heart of the matter, it was about time I put my view.

I stressed the fact that our aim was to be able to sell the book freely, and to be able to do so without delay. Legal principle might be very interesting and important in its way, but if we were prevented from selling the book, in the production of which we had invested time, energy and money, the consequences could be serious for my company, and in particular for my partner, who was its financial backer, and for those who worked there. I was also very concerned at the prospect of long drawn-out proceedings which would tie up my time and energies, which were relied upon for our publishing activities.

As regards the points at issue in the case, I felt that the principal element was that the claim that the book threatened Britain's national security defied common sense. As I understood it, there existed a legal recourse to the concept of the public interest, in relation to which the onus was on the attorney-general to establish good reason for setting aside the general public interest as regards freedom of expression and freedom to carry on one's business. The fact that the book related to events which had occurred over forty years before and that it contained no revelations of substance about the workings of British intelligence made it seem to me unlikely that he could prevail in seeking its suppression. I was unclear about the relationship between British and Irish law and between the two jurisdictions: I had assumed initially that the British government could take no action against us in Ireland, but the Peter Wright case in Australia had given pause for thought. Could they really claim that it was the business of the Irish courts to defend the interests of British political expediency?

There were, I was informed, questions of the law relating to confidentiality which were at least potentially applicable irrespective of the fact that we were in a separate jurisdiction. Moreover, many high court judges were inclined to be very conservative where a question of national security was involved; we were entering uncharted territory and it was difficult to say what view would be taken of the fact that it was not Ireland's but Britain's national security which was claimed to be threatened. However, the principal element of our case could be expressed in the question, "What is it to us?" Whether or not the British could make a case for the proposition that their national security was threatened, the point for an Irish court to consider was whether or not any threat was posed to the Irish public interest. If the British were unable to keep the lid on their own former intelligence officers, then that was their problem, not ours and not the court's.

That night, after leaving Hugh O'Flaherty's, Billy and I experienced one of the small coincidences that are characteristic of a small country like Ireland: in a Donnybrook pub we met friends of Billy's, and it happened by the merest accident that in their company was a solicitor working for the opposition, for McCann-Fitz, Dublin solicitors for the attorney-general. It posed no problem: we simply avoided any mention of the case.

I had arranged to have background documents sent by fax from London to Dublin and Billy and I went into the city centre to collect them. In the Mount Herbert guesthouse I read Nigel West's book, *MI5*. I made notes on the book's contents as they related to our case and had them typed up and photocopied. I spoke on the phone with Joan Miller's daughter, Jonquil, in Rome and made further notes into the early hours of the morning in an effort to organise my thoughts thoroughly for the following day.

At 9.30 on Sunday morning Billy picked me up from the guesthouse and we went to Hugh O'Flaherty's for further discussions followed by lunch. I found Hugh O'Flaherty to be not only focussed and effective in discussing legal issues and strategy, but also enthusiastic about his native county, Kerry, and very affable. Both he and his wife Kay made a difficult and tense time for me feel a good deal less fraught than one might have expected. In the evening I met friends in the city centre but, with my mind on the case, was poor company and left soon enough to scribble more notes back in the guesthouse. With the high court hearing scheduled for the next morning, my mood was one of less than perfect equanimity, and I hardly slept at all.

In high court Number 5 in the Four Courts a man sat beside me clutching a green leather briefcase embossed with the British royal insignia: ER and the crown. It reminded me immediately of the seats in the room in the House of Commons where we had launched our reprint of *British Intelligence and Covert Action*.

As I adjusted to the cramped and shuffling ambience of the proceedings, I was surprised to find that there was no real element of cut and thrust. Each side chose its precedents, its case histories, its reference books; court ushers came and went with volumes requested by the judge, Justice Mella Carroll. The forms of address of the lawyers were predictably stilted, but they were also more indistinct and cryptic than I had expected and inevitably much passed over my head. Others in the crowded courtroom were, I noticed, listening intently; the case had attracted other lawyers and students of law as one which would set precedent.

Although much detail escaped me, the general drift of the arguments was clear enough. The British government claimed that the first they had known of our intention to publish the book was when they had seen the item that had appeared in *The Bookseller* of 21 November. For this contention to be true, MI5 would, of course, have had to have been incredibly incompetent; but anyway it seemed to me to have no real bearing on the matter. Perhaps, I reasoned, they simply wanted to disguise the fact that the motivation for their legal action was political rather than having anything genuinely to do with the interests of national security.

Niall Fennelly, senior counsel for the attorney-general of England and Wales, sought to make much of the book's subtitle, *Personal Exploits in MI5's Most Secret Station*, twice misstating it – no doubt inadvertently – as *"Secret Exploits. . ."*. Our two senior counsels contended that there was nothing of a sensitive, secret nature in the book, while he sought to establish that the book was all about revealing official secrets. Yet later it became clear that it was not actually the contents of the book that concerned his clients. In this area of the case, at least, I felt reasonably confident that our lawyers' contentions would prevail.

Joan Miller's insights into the wartime activities of MI5's B5(b) Section had in essence already been published elsewhere prior to the publication of *One Girl's War*. They had appeared in an extensive interview in *The Sunday Times Magazine* in 1981 and in the book *The Man Who Was M* by Anthony Masters. No government action had been taken in relation either to the magazine article or the book. By being published, they had passed into the public domain and could no longer be regarded as secrets.

On the question of confidentiality I found it almost impossible to assess the respective merits of the opposing arguments. Lawyers for the attorney-general cited cases seeming to support the contention that her employment had imposed on Joan Miller a duty of confidentiality which the court should uphold. I was prejudiced against their contention, of course, but I could gain no impression of the judge's view. For our side cases were also cited, including an Australian case which seemed to me to offer convincing precedent for rejecting the British case; but I was unclear as to how heavily an Australian precedent would weigh with an Irish judge.

With no verbal pyrotechnics or other drama the arguments ran their course, the judge periodically asking lawyers to clarify or elaborate. And then it was over for the day: she announced that she would give her judgement the next morning and the court rose. The press were waiting outside the courtroom but I could not talk to them about the case.

That night British television carried reports from the Four Courts. At the guesthouse I received calls from journalists but could not discuss the case. Again I hardly slept, yet in the morning I felt a strange, irrational and overwhelming confidence. I even felt remarkably unperturbed when Billy Keane took me aside and gently prepared me for the worst: the legal team all felt that we would lose in the high court, that the decision would go against us. I should be aware that this was their unanimous and considered opinion, but I should not be too depressed when the judge handed down her judgement. We would immediately appeal to the Supreme Court, and it was in the Supreme Court that we would stand a better chance of winning. The high court was often, it seemed, inclined to take a conservative position, effectively passing the matter on to the Supreme Court.

Nevertheless, my confidence had not deserted me when I entered the courtroom at 10.30; I chatted away and shared a few jokes with journalists. I was smiling broadly when I chanced to glance across the courtroom and see the man with the green leather briefcase: he was looking straight at me, a notably unhappy expression on his face.

Crisply and clearly Justice Mella Carroll summed up her judgement, carefully going over the legal issues which were raised by the case. She concluded by outlining the considerations which should be considered to apply:

(a) the Defendant has a constitutional right to publish information which does not involve any breach of copyright
(b) the public interest in this jurisdiction is not affected by the publication
(c) there is no breach of confidentiality in a private or commercial setting and
(d) there is no absolute confidentiality where the parties are a Government and a private individual. . .

In those circumstances I have no doubt that the balance of convenience must lie with the right of the Defendant to exercise its constitutional right to publish. The exercise of a constitutional right cannot be measured in terms of money: what is at stake is the very important constitutional right to communicate *now* and not in a year or more when the case has worked its way through the Courts.

On the steps of the Four Courts I tried to manoeuvre my briefcase in the crush and put it down somewhere while I collected my thoughts and faced the cameras. What was my reaction to the court's judgement? How did I feel? Did I feel vindicated? Was I pleased with the outcome? I don't remember what I said then, apart from the fact that I was delighted. Whatever else I said, the remark that went out on British television news was that I was delighted that the high court had rejected "the British policy of suppression".

Advised that some journalists, including a TV crew from Belfast, were still on their way to the Four Courts, not having expected the hearing to be over so soon, I said that I would be available in the nearby Clarence Hotel. There RTÉ Radio 1's John Bowman phoned me to enquire on air how I was taking the result. "Sitting drinking a glass of Glenpatrick spring water," I answered truthfully if rather literally. Later RTÉ television news recorded an interview at the back of the hotel. Indoors I chatted on for a while with journalists and photographers, winding down in the informal setting. I had phoned the office in Dingle but they had already heard the news on radio and were organising the quick release of copies of the book from the warehouse. There was no great sense of elation, more just of relief that the case was behind us and we could get on with pressing other business. But still, there was laughter amongst the journalists as they and I relished the defeat inflicted on an arrogant British government.

In London news of the judgement had already reached the House of Commons, where Labour MP Dale Campbell-Savours was jeering at a government that had, as he put it, "taken a sound thrashing in the Dublin courts". In Australia the response of Malcolm Turnbull, solicitor for Peter Wright, was "Good on ya, sport!"

In the afternoon I strolled down the Liffey from the Clarence Hotel to Easons' bookshop in O'Connell Street. Easons had earlier come down decisively on the side of the British government and I had considered withholding copies from them in view of their pre-emptive action in withdrawing the book from their shelves in advance of any injunction. However, revenge, I decided, was no reward, and now they were enjoying a sudden sales bonanza. At the front of the shop a large crowd was gathered around a pile of copies of the book, and at the back harassed staff were preparing to put more on the shelves. Shortly beforehand a BBC television news crew had filmed the book being sold, and that night's news programmes gave Easons' substantial publicity. Unfortunately the BBC in their reports suggested that we had increased the price of the book by a pound; perhaps their staff were familiar only with plastic money themselves and were unaware of the currency differential that made the book £8.95 sterling and IR£9.95.

Soon Billy Keane and I set out in his car for Listowel and what we hoped would be a small celebration and some well-earned rest. First the car broke down in Dublin and we were delayed by nearly three hours. Then, on the road near Mountrath we had a freak accident.

The first indication that anything was wrong came when we saw a large articulated truck coming towards us on the wrong side of the road at high speed, flashing all of its numerous lights.

"Some bloody maniac," muttered Billy in alarm as he slowed and moved in towards the verge. And then, as Billy slowed almost to a standstill, we saw what appeared to be the figure of a boy or a small man, standing in the road some yards ahead of us. But it was no boy and it was not standing, for a second later we were hit with sudden force by this object right in the middle of the front of the car.

The giant wheel of an articulated truck had come loose when the truck had been travelling at speed, had bounced across and along the road and had crashed into our car. The quick-thinking driver of a second lorry had overtaken the first, lights flashing, and had caused us to slow down. As it was, the car was a write-off and we were lucky to be alive and unharmed apart from having been badly shaken. Later, the shock having not yet set in, we drank brandy at a nearby hotel and joked about how the accident had obviously been set up by MI5.

The high court judgement represented an outstanding victory for us, a small, independent company which the British government had undoubtedly assumed would just give up in the face of overwhelming odds. It was also something of a victory for freedom of expression generally.

On very few occasions has the Irish Constitution's guarantee of freedom of expression been tested in the courts, and the direction in which the law and precedent had been developing in Ireland was towards limiting freedom of expression rather than expanding it. Thus the British legal journal *Public Law* reported that:

> Brandon Books strikes an important blow for freedom of the press in Ireland. In view of the emphatic manner in which Carroll J. upheld the right to communicate, it would probably be only in exceptional circumstances that the Irish courts would restrain the publication of material which a government found embarrassing or disclosure of which was deemed to be contrary to the public interest.

Now, however, we faced an injunction against our distributors in London.

Turnaround Distribution was a small co-operative based in north London which specialised in representing and distributing radical and community publishers. It had very limited resources of both finances and people, and it felt unable to become involved in a legal fight for the right to be able to distribute our book. Also, the people working in Turnaround were from the start poorly disposed towards investing their energies in a struggle in defence of a book whose perspective was clearly not radical. I was disappointed that the conservatism of the author should strike Turnaround as a significant issue. The point at issue as far as I was concerned was the freedom to publish, irrespective of the extent to which its contents might be radical. They had seriously misunderstood the point in my view, and I couldn't help feeling that it was characteristic of the inability of left and radical opinion to counter effectively the phenomenon of Thatcherism. Thatcher and her allies had clear objectives and an instinctive grasp of power and how it worked; her opponents were hopelessly confused, without coherent strategy, and unable to see the wood for the trees.

The ban remained in place in Britain, though many copies found their way into Britain from Ireland, with Dublin airport reporting particularly good sales. In Scotland a bookseller courageously challenged the ban, seeking recourse in the separate Scottish legal system. But the British situation was at one remove from me, and I felt that to some extent I had to accept the right of Turnaround to take their own decisions, and to respect the fact that their lawyers were very well respected and had a good reputation in terms of civil liberties issues. Nevertheless, I was convinced that the inherent conservatism of British liberals was blinding them to the opportunity to declare that in this instance the emperor was wearing no clothes.

In Ireland we sold large numbers of copies of *One Girl's War*, going quickly into paperback, and then publishing a revised and updated paperback edition in which I summarised the legal battle. The book was successful beyond my greatest expectations. We also sold an option on film rights, but the production company was intimidated by the continuing British high court injunction, and so no film was made.

Some years later, in 1992, having long been frustrated by the continuation of the ban in Britain, convinced that it could and should have been fought, I arranged a meeting with our solicitors and a senior counsel in Dublin and put to them the proposal that we should invoke European legislation regarding the freedom of movement of goods between European countries, with a view to having the ban lifted. *One Girl's War* was available in Ireland, a member state of the EC; the British government, I suggested, was in breach of international law in preventing it from being sold in Britain, another member state. The lawyers considered my proposition and concluded that I was right, so I wrote to Turnaround and Turnaround's lawyers, suggesting that this approach be pursued. They rejected unequivocally my suggestion, clearly feeling that it was irrelevant and ill-considered. I then returned to my lawyers in Dublin and drafted, with their assistance, a letter to the attorney-general of England and Wales. In essence I informed him and those he represented that I proposed to arrive in England with copies of the book and in defiance of the law offer them for sale myself. If they wanted to act upon the injunction, we would pursue them through the European courts. I was even prepared to inform them as to which flight I would arrive on.

The British authorities were caught in a bind. If they knowingly failed to apprehend me on my arrival with the books, or on my attempt to sell them, the injunction restraining the book from being sold would automatically fall. If, on the other hand, they apprehended me and confiscated the book, they would face not only some unfortunate publicity, but they were also very likely in my view to find themselves in bad odour with the European Court.

At first they replied that they would insist upon the injunction but, in the event, a certain limited realism prevailed, and on the day before I flew to London they crumbled and indicated their willingness in principle to discharge the injunction. They conceded that they were, as I had suggested, wrong in law all the time to ban *One Girl's War*. The Treasury Solicitor's Office also agreed to pay £7,000 damages to Turnaround Distribution. But there was a sting in the tail, for after discharging the injunction they issued a new threat to prosecute us, this time under the 1989 Official Secrets legislation which had been introduced since our publication. I responded by informing the British government that I would be going to London shortly, again clutching copies of *One Girl's War*, and offering them the opportunity to apprehend me.

The attorney-general of England and Wales, again one day before I was due to arrive in London, conceded my point and agreed not to invoke the Official Secrets legislation against me. Six years after defeating attempts to suppress the book in Ireland, we finally prevailed in Britain also.

Chapter Seven

PUBLISHING UNDER
POLITICAL CENSORSHIP

MY DECISION TO publish Gerry Adams was prompted by an article I read in late 1981 in *An Phoblacht*, the Sinn Féin newspaper, which impressed me. It was an account by Gerry Adams of growing up on the Falls Road, and it was unusually well written, showing that its author had a finely tuned ear for the dialogue of the streets in which he had been reared. As I began to build Brandon's first year's list I was keen to find material which accorded with my special interest in chronicles of the everyday lives of "ordinary" people. I had little interest in the lives of the famous, still less in "celebrities". Both categories provided the favoured material of most large and successful publishing houses, but the perspectives and voices I wanted to give expression to at Brandon were quite different. Adams was not widely known, and his article expressed well and positively aspects of the life of a community which was by any standards oppressed. I wrote and asked him if he had any more material in a similar vein, and he replied that he had, in fact, been thinking of putting a pamphlet together about the Falls Road area.

"See if you can make it book-length."

He was somewhat daunted when I spelled out how much he would need to write, but we met in Dublin on a fine sunny day, sitting at tables on the pavement outside a pub on Pembroke Street, and we agreed the outlines of a book contract, which included provision for the commissioning of a number of line drawings to complement the text.

He explained that the exigencies of his lifestyle meant that he would have no opportunity to work on the manuscript in a consistent manner. Rather, he would be scribbling snatches of it in the backs of taxis; in the course of political meetings which didn't demand his whole attention; in the early hours of the morning after returning home. It meant that the manuscript would come to me in a scrappy, awkward form. I reckoned I could live with that. As a new, small independent publishing house, Brandon would have to be prepared to develop authors rather than expect to acquire them ready-made, and I would have to put in substantial work remoulding.

A more serious problem was that the author could not be interviewed on television or radio due to political censorship. The promotional potential of an author must inevitably be part of the publisher's considerations, and in seeking to promote any book by Gerry Adams we would be working with both hands tied behind our back.

Section 31 of the Broadcasting Act (1960, amended in 1976) gave the minister for communications the power to order the broadcasting stations not to broadcast any kind of material which he or she believed would tend to undermine the authority of the state, and was targetted specifically at the political representatives of organisations, such as the IRA, which had been proscribed under either Irish or British legislation. It was a measure of the purest authoritarianism, and year after year it was renewed without parliamentary discussion or debate, being supported by all the parties in the Dáil. Year after year it rendered almost completely impossible the making of any balanced, informative programming for television or radio about the political situation in the north of Ireland. Year after year the citizens of the state were denied the truth, by order of the government.

Of particular relevance in our case was the provision banning the spokespersons of organisations with links to paramilitary groups, including Sinn Féin, from being interviewed. As if the legislation were not draconian enough, the broadcasting authorities chose to take it a step further by banning any *member* of any proscribed organisation – and some of these were registered political parties – irrespective of whether they were acting as spokespersons for those organisations, and irrespective of what they might be interviewed about. This meant that whatever Gerry Adams might write about – and the proposed book would combine local history with reminiscence – he could not be interviewed about it on television or radio.

Despite this obstacle, I felt that it would make economic sense in the long run to publish this book if, as I believed, Gerry Adams were to become a public figure of some substance. Also, and more importantly in my perspective, the generally excluded voice of the besieged working class community of West Belfast was one which should be heard. And in his own perspective he seemed to me to be articulating the everyday life and history and world of working people in something of the same way as a writer like Patrick MacGill.

I knew Adams to possess considerable intellect, combined with an intense feeling for the people amongst whom he lived and from whom he sprang. He was, I felt, unusually disciplined, exceptionally capable and highly articulate. Regarded by most as being simply a political activist with a reputation – whether deserved or not – for having reorganised and energised the Belfast Brigade of the IRA during its most crucial period, I saw in him an intelligent observer, a wry commentator and a passionate representative of a newly forged young working-class republicanism. As a writer he possessed a fine sense of humour, especially of irony, and he seemed to have an admirable lack of ego; his interest in the lives of the people around him was not an affectation, nor the tactical manoeuvre of a conventional politician; rather, he was genuinely self-effacing. He also possessed the kind of passion which transforms raw material, rendering it compelling reading.

e editor of *Cosmos*

Producing Artaud's *Pour en finir avec le jugement
de Dieu*

Outside the Irish Writers' Co-operative office with Adrian Kenny, Leland Bardwell, John Meehan a
Brendan Foreman (Derek Spiers)

Steve MacDonogh and Taoiseach Charles J. Haughey at the opening of Brandon's offices in Din
August 1982 (Don MacMonagle)

:án MacBride and Philip Agee (Derek Spiers)

anne Hayes on *The Late Late Show*, October 1985 (Derek Spiers)

Book launch, December 1986 (Derek Spiers)

ice Taylor, photographed by the author on his first visit to her home in Innishannon, January 1988

Press conference with Salman Rushdie, January 16, 1993 (Derek Spiers)

dna O'Brien, Steve MacDonogh and Gerry Adams, at the launch of *Selected Writings* in the Irish 'riters' Centre, September, 1994 (Eamonn Farrell)

ritish Ambassador Veronica Sutherland, Alice Taylor, US Ambassador Jean Kennedy Smith, Steve 1acDonogh; at the National Library, Dublin, April, 1996 (Dave Meehan)

Peter Malone, Tracy Kenna, Linda Kenny, Alice Taylor, President Mary Robinson, Steve MacDonog
Bernie Goggin; at Aras an Uachtarainn, May, 1996 (Dave Meehan)

Launching Mount Eagle, the National Library,
October, 1997 (Eamonn Farrell)

After less delay than I had feared, the manuscript was complete, and we published in November 1982. I had discussed with Neil Middleton of Penguin the possibility of selling them British rights, and he had been interested. We went over the details of a deal in Penguin offices in London, but when I compared my projections with theirs it appeared that we would probably sell just as many as Penguin, despite their vastly superior marketing muscle. As it turned out, sales exceeded projections, and in the spring of 1983 we published a new, revised edition.

The qualities of the writing in *Falls Memories* were in some respects the qualities of fiction. While parts of the book included relatively dry recitations of historical facts, the heart of it showed imagination allied to a sensitive ear and eye. I was therefore very interested when Gerry mentioned that he had written a couple of short stories, one of which he had submitted under an assumed name for a competition, which it had won. I asked him to send me whatever he had in the way of stories, and some months later I received a small bundle, certainly not sufficient to make a book. A number of them, which mixed narrative with political comment and analysis, concerned his experience of internment in Long Kesh, and I advised him that he might like to work up a book-length manuscript offering a portrait of internment.

We had published *Falls Memories* in 1982 and in the following year he was elected both president of Sinn Féin and MP for West Belfast. His schedule had been busy before, but now his life was even less his own, and so I understood that the Long Kesh book was a long-term prospect. Meanwhile, however, I was well aware that what a great many readers wanted was a book outlining his political philosophy. Recognising that himself, he had written in a note at the front of *Falls Memories*: "I trust that those readers who buy this book expecting something else will not be too disappointed."

The political background against which I considered commissioning such a book was generally but not universally hostile. In the context of the continuing armed struggle of the IRA, the demonisation of republicanism, and of Gerry Adams himself, had been intense in both Britain and Ireland for several years. Middle-class opinion in the south was heavily on the side of dismissing republicanism as lying outside the pale of civilisation. Amongst my fellow Irish publishers there had been some evident shock and deep disapproval of the fact that we had published *Falls Memories*; some consoled themselves with the thought that it was a book of local history and that I would not go so far as to publish his polit-ical views; some assumed that no bookseller, wholesaler or dis-tributor would handle such a book. I had no doubt in my own mind that I would like to see his political views given serious and considered ventilation at book-length, but as a publisher I had to consider whether we could achieve a viable sale and whether we might run certain risks as a company if we went ahead with it.

Hostility to republicanism was not universal. In local elections in the south in June 1985, Sinn Féin increased its representation to thirty-six councillors from twenty-eight in 1979. In July the public was graphically reminded of the culture of unionist political vio-lence with which nationalists had to contend in the north when there were a series of clashes in Portadown over Orange marches; in an article in *Universe* Cardinal Tomás Ó Fiaich asserted that 90 per cent of bigotry was Protestant. One of the problems we faced with Gerry Adams as an author was the active opposition to him of the media in Ireland and Britain, which augmented the censorship leg-islation; it was all very well to publish a book, but if the author would not be interviewed in the media, and if reviewers, news edi-tors and features editors were predisposed to be hostile, then the prospects for sales might be poor. A significant political tendency within the media was the Workers' Party, which was engaged in an ideological struggle against nationalism and republicanism. It com-manded limited popular support but had successfully pursued an entrist strategy within the trade unions and media; amongst RTÉ producers and journalists and within *The Irish Times*, it constituted an influential political tendency which complemented the Fine Gael hostility to republicanism and nationalism. At times, as when they classified anyone who did not share their anti-nationalist views as "hush puppies" – a term coined by Eoghan Harris, whose version of leftism was soon to drift to the opposite pole of the far right – their witch-hunting activities seemed laughable. But it was no joke for producers in RTÉ who found threatening messages pinned to noticeboards or slipped under their doors.

Despite the difficulties which I anticipated in terms of the media, I was convinced that the developments within Sinn Féin, of which Gerry Adams was a principal architect, were of immense potential significance and that in spite of extreme establishment hostility there was sufficient public interest to provide a basis for reasonable sales. I was also deeply committed to challenging the culture of censorship which I felt distorted intellectual and political life in Ireland. Specifically in relation to the conflict in Northern Ireland, I felt that censorship provided a substantial barrier to the possibilities for developing the kind of debate and dialogue which might lead eventually towards a negotiated settlement and peace. It stultified political language and encouraged the calcification of the situation in hostile stalemate.

Significantly, too, I was encouraged to seek to develop Gerry as an author by the fact that I liked him and came to regard him very soon as a friend. He and I came from extremely different backgrounds, but I knew very few people who came from similar backgrounds to my own, and I had never approached friendships as things to be sought and found only in one's own social circles. Gerry was lively, intelligent, humorous and considerate, a good listener and an interesting talker. If he said he would do something he would always at least try his best to fulfil that promise, and he always treated other people in Brandon with consideration. Others in the company did not, I knew, share my opinions about the advisability and importance of publishing Gerry, nor did they express any concerns of their own regarding the climate of censorship and suppression. Indeed, they were reluctant to express any opinions on the issues involved, and on any occasion when I returned from a public occasion after which Gerry and I had appeared on television or in newspaper photographs, no remarks were offered or questions asked.

I raised with Gerry the possibility of publishing a book which would constitute a direct personal political statement. He was reluctant, raising immediately two major problems: firstly, he was extremely unwilling to present himself – or seem to present himself – as a "leader", in the sense of someone above and beyond the general membership of the republican movement; secondly, there was no question of his being able to give the necessary time to the project. I countered that he was objectively in a position of leadership as party president; he replied that it was important that I understand that there could be no question of his taking advantage for personal reasons of a position which he owed to the membership of the movement as a whole. Also, he was extremely suspicious of traditional notions of leadership: he wanted political leadership to work from the bottom up, and it was his approach to seek to clarify consensus within the movement, then play his leadership role in articulating that consensus. I countered that, while I had no wish to commission a party political document, I did feel that there was a broad public need and demand for an exposition of Irish republicanism as it stood now. He, I knew, was saying that important changes were in train within the movement, which had taken a decisively political turn; it was time, I suggested, that this be properly exposed to public view. As regards the question of his not having time to write the book, I said that I would collaborate with him, using tapes, transcripts and rewrites. We suspended our discussion on the understanding that he would think about my proposal; he would also need to consult his comrades, because he would not wish to go ahead without their approval in principle.

I had to engage in some gentle badgering in order, first of all, to win his agreement, and, secondly, to get him to assign time in his schedule for us to work together on the projected book. He provided me with some texts which he felt might provide a basis for parts of the book, and I worked out a detailed framework, shaped by my concern that the book should address the questions that an intelligent interested reader would be likely to wish to put to him. My days, nights and weekends were fully taken up with work on other books, but I managed to jot down substantial preliminary notes before becoming submerged in the business of publishing and promoting other books.

In November I was further stimulated to concentrate on the Gerry Adams project when the Anglo-Irish Agreement, also known as the Hillsborough Agreement, was signed by Prime Minister Margaret Thatcher and Taoiseach Garret FitzGerald. Although Gerry Adams took the view that the agreement copperfastened partition and insulated Britain from international criticism, it seemed to me that it suggested crucial new directions in British strategy, and it made all the more relevant the articulation of a clear inside account of contemporary republicanism.

By early 1986 we had the shape of the book, which we had decided to title *The Politics of Irish Freedom*, well worked out, and in February and March I spent time in Belfast working with Gerry, in sessions which lasted up to nine hours non-stop. Tiring as the sessions were for me, I was aware that before joining me in the morning he had probably already held at least one meeting, and that after leaving me in the evening he was going to other meetings, and so I was concerned to make the best possible use of this concentrated time.

In late June, on the day of the first referendum in the south on divorce, he visited me in Dingle, looking tired and drawn and apologising for the fact that he was unable to deliver to me the final draft of the manuscript on schedule. We had lunch, I brought him to visit friends in town, and we went for a drink. I had been keen to publish before year's end, but this now seemed impossible. Simultaneously a very different political book was running late – Dick Walsh's political profile of Des O'Malley.

It always imposed a particular strain to attempt to publish topical books on tight schedules, and now it seemed that for all our extra efforts we would still fail to have them ready on time. It was not until early October that I was able to finalise the manuscript of *The Politics of Irish Freedom* at a final editorial session with Gerry in Belfast. We were now involved in a breakneck rush to publish, and I found myself shuttling in early mornings and late nights between Dingle, Dublin and Belfast. In late October, having delivered proofs to Gerry in Belfast, I met Tim Pat Coogan, editor of the *Irish Press*, in Dublin to discuss running an extract from the book in the newspaper. Not only was our author banned from radio and television in the south, but also most newspapers in Ireland north and south and in Britain would not dream of publishing extracts from any book by him. I was convinced that there was a substantial potential readership for the book, but we would not reach it if no one knew the book existed. Tim Pat, however, recognised the potential interest amongst his readership, and we agreed that he would run an extract.

In Dublin I also met Dick Walsh to put the finishing touches to his book, which as well as running behind schedule was coming out a great deal shorter than intended. Gerry arrived late in Dublin with his corrected proofs, having been delayed en route by the Garda Special Branch. It was a bank holiday weekend, but it was clear that it would take me most of the three days to collate and edit the corrections. On Monday I also collected chapters of Dick Walsh's book and headed for Kerry, reaching home in the early hours of the morning.

Back in the office later the same morning I tried to catch up on other business. Bernie Goggin was at a heritage conference; Peter Malone was working on the desk editing of the Adams and O'Malley books. I was simultaneously acting as publicist for Joan Miller's *One Girl's War*. Although it was difficult to engage in promotion to the London media from Dingle, I had secured commitments for reviews and feature articles in most of the dailies and Sundays.

Two days later I was back in Dublin again to work at the typesetters and to meet with Dick Walsh. I spent Saturday at the Sinn Féin Ard Fheis, where the atmosphere was electric in anticipation of the crucial debate on the constitutional issue of abstentionism, an issue which had split the movement before and which threatened to split it again. Behind the scenes I had a chat with Gerry about the proofs; out front I met several London media people whom I briefed about the book; they were interested, but some of their Irish colleagues reacted with hostility or apparent indifference.

On Sunday I arrived at the Ard Fheis to find that people were being refused entry because there was no room. I got through because I had an appointment with Gerry, and so I was able to witness the historic debate on abstentionism in its entirety. The atmosphere was extraordinary in the packed Mansion House. Circulating before the start of the day's business, I met many people I knew from all over Ireland, exchanging a few words with Mairead Farrell, who had recently been released from Armagh prison. The crowd was vibrant, committed, serious, and the debate as it unfolded was conducted with some passion in circumstances of grave tension. Gerry Adams intervened significantly in the debate, doing everything he could to avoid a split, but in the end the vote fell strongly in favour of dropping abstentionism, and a small rump, led by Ruairi Ó Bradaigh, walked out, despite all appeals to them to respect the decision of the conference. In the evening I ran through final proof checks with Gerry. In the hour between the vote and my meeting with him I had written a postscript to the book, bringing it up to date, which Gerry approved.

First thing Monday morning I had the final corrections to the typesetters, and on Tuesday I was able to give final proofs to lawyers for a libel reading and to the wholesalers and the *Irish Press*.

I had discussions over these two days on the possibility of Gerry Adams, attending a press reception to launch his book in London, but it was eventually ruled out. I had secured the agreement of an MP to host a meeting in the House of Commons to launch the book. But the defeated minority in the Ard Fheis debate on abstentionism had gone off to form a new party (Republican Sinn Féin) and would maintain that the dropping of abstentionism in respect of Dáil Éireann was only a prelude to the recognition of Westminster. For Gerry Adams to enter the House of Commons, even for a book launch, would have seemed to this disaffected rump, which included influential individuals and significant groups of rank-and-filers and local leadership elements, to signal the final betrayal, presaging recognition of the British parliament and, by extension, of its right to rule Ireland.

On Tuesday night I returned home, a week later going up to Dublin again to oversee the finishing touches to the Des O'Malley book.

We prepared for launches of the Gerry Adams and Des O'Malley books, and I travelled to Dublin to join Dick Walsh and Des O'Malley at a signing session in Greene's bookshop, after which I brought Des O'Malley for a leisurely lunch in Buswells Hotel. Taking the afternoon train to Belfast, I met Gerry Adams that night, and in the morning we launched *The Politics of Irish Freedom* in the Art Shop in the Falls Road at a reception attended by most of the Belfast print and broadcasting media. Then we climbed into a large, bullet-proofed Volvo, and drove south. As we reached the countryside the mood in the car lightened.

"One of these days," said Gerry's minder in the front passenger seat; "one of these days I'm going to write my own book."

"Oh, yeah?"

"And what'll you call it?"

"*Confessions of a Republican Window Cleaner* – I've seen some things, boys, I've seen some things!"

"I might write a book too," said our driver.

"You?"

"Sure, you couldn't write to save your life. What'll you call it?"

"*My Drive for Irish Freedom.*"

The importance of *The Politics of Irish Freedom* was that for the first time in many decades a leading republican had set down his beliefs and principles, and that this particular republican was seeking to lead his comrades towards new and more effective political strategies. It had its impact within republicanism and it was read with great interest by members of anti-imperialist and social-ist organisations in many countries. In Britain there was strong interest within the broad black movement, within socialist groups and amongst left-wing elements of the Labour Party. In Spain the book was published in translation by a Basque company. Six months after the publication of *The Politics of Irish Freedom* Sinn Féin themselves, in May 1987, published for the first time in fif-teen years a document setting forth their aims and objectives. Its title, *A Scenario for Peace*, pointed an important new direction.

In the period that followed, Sinn Féin began to develop its peace strategy, engaging in 1988 in talks with the SDLP and pro-ducing a new discussion document. Offered this by Gerry for publication by Brandon, I reluctantly declined. My reasons were twofold: it was a pamphlet rather than a book; I wasn't interested in publishing pamphlets and I felt that it would lack integrity to bulk it out to look like a book; secondly, and perhaps most impor-tantly, I did not want to get involved in publishing party political documents (of any party). *The Politics of Irish Freedom* was a per-sonal political statement. Certainly it was by the president of a political party, but it was not drafted by that party, and it had an openness and a personal quality which was quite different from an official document. This new manuscript had been drafted by the party, and even though it was proposed to publish it under Gerry's name and Gerry had evidently played a leading role in its drafting, I declined to take it on. To me as an independent pub-lisher the distinction, small as it might have seemed to others, between a personal political statement by Gerry and an official party document largely written by him, was a vitally important distinction. I was a member of no political party myself, and I proposed to publish on behalf of no political party. Gerry was dis-appointed, but he understood my reservations and he was imme-diately able to get a commitment from another publisher, Mercier, who were only too delighted to take it on, hoping, I think, that they would thus acquire him as their author for the future. It was published as *A Pathway to Peace*. In 1991 Sinn Féin drafted a more developed document, entitled *Towards a Lasting Peace*, which they published themselves in 1992.

In 1989 I had again discussed with Gerry Adams his short stories, and I felt that he was closest to being able to complete a collection of pieces about internment, many of which already existed in the form of articles he had written in *An Phoblacht/Republican News*. Revision, expansion and development were needed, and I embarked on editorial work, trimming down some of the pieces and looking for Gerry to develop and expand some others. Many of the pieces combined semi-fictional accounts of life in the "cages" of Long Kesh with political polemics. These may have worked well in the context of the particular newspaper at the particular time, but they were laden with references to events of the moment which dated them, and they suffered from a preachiness which would prove tiresome, I felt, in the context of a book. A few of the pieces were simply political essays, while others offered history lessons which, while appropriate to a newspaper column, would look simplistic in a book. For some time I exchanged notes and redrafts with Gerry, and eventually we had a manuscript we were both happy with, and we scheduled it for publication in 1990. We tossed around various ideas for titles, with a front-runner being *A Prisoner's Tale*, which I didn't much like, and in the end we settled on *Cage Eleven*.

I had tried previously to get Gerry Adams over to Britain – for a press reception to launch *The Politics of Irish Freedom*; for the London Irish Book Fair; to speak to a labour history group in Manchester – without success. But now he and his Sinn Féin advisors seemed to be prepared to go along with my plans for a press reception to launch *Cage Eleven*. Again I proposed the House of Commons as a venue, but again there were difficulties: Gerry felt that the media would make a fuss about him being in the House of Commons, a fuss which would distract all attention from the book itself. I could see his point, and anyway I just wanted some kind of a launch in Britain so that I could get my teeth into the business of properly promoting his book in Britain. I had already convinced the *Guardian* to run an extract in a prominent position in their Saturday weekend section. I was happy to agree to a reception in a hotel, and we sent out invitations for 4 June at the New Ambassador Hotel near Euston Station. Then, a week before our planned reception, the IRA shot dead two Australian tourists, Stephen Melrose and Nicholas Spanos, in Holland.

To say that my feelings were varied as I heard the news would be an understatement. Living in a tourist town, I saw many visitors of many nationalities and often enjoyed talking to them. Most of the Australians and New Zealanders I met came in the winter when there was plenty of time to talk to them, the pubs being quiet and uncrowded. I was well aware that most of them were on breaks of about nine months, travelling through the world, rambling around from country to country, many of them working along the way, especially in London. And so I thought of these two people who had been shot in very personal terms, as representing in a way all the Australian visitors I had met over the years in Dingle. Other feelings were quite different and had to do with the fact that, if we went ahead with the planned press reception, it would be used by the media to question our author not about his book but about this latest IRA atrocity. I had already focussed our promotional efforts in Britain on this press reception, and I had to consider whether we should abandon it on the grounds that it would be of no benefit to the book; I also wondered whether Gerry and his people would wish to cancel it for their own reasons.

Decisions had to be taken quickly as I was about to leave to accompany Alice Taylor, whose second book of memoirs, *Quench the Lamp*, had just been published, on a promotional tour of London, Manchester and Liverpool from 30 May to 2 June. I consulted as widely as I could with people in London and Belfast, and it was agreed that we would go ahead, even though we all knew that the book would be largely ignored in the context of the London-based media having an unusual opportunity to question Gerry Adams in the wake of an atrocity.

139

On the morning of 30 May, Alice Taylor, her husband Gabriel Ó Murchú and I flew to London. They were happy to look after themselves for the rest of the day, so I left them in order to go to a series of meetings through the day with our distributors, our film-rights agent, Green Ink bookshop, and the London Sinn Féin people involved in arrangements surrounding the Gerry Adams book launch.

While the launch was entirely organised by Brandon, there were obvious implications which required co-ordination with Sinn Féin. In the evening I met Sylvester Stein, South African author of *Second-Class Taxi*, the anti-apartheid satirical novel which we had published in March, and we went together to a party at the *Guardian*, where I met members of the ANC as well as of the newspaper staff.

On Thursday I accompanied Alice Taylor for a series of media interviews through the day, culminating with an evening signing session at the Willesden Bookshop. Early next morning we left for Manchester where Alice signed books in Dillons at noon, followed by an evening reading at the Liverpool Irish Centre. On Saturday we arrived back in London in time for her 1.00pm appearance at the Irish Book Fair in the Camden Irish Centre, followed by an afternoon session at Claude Gill's in Oxford Street. As Alice and Gabriel flew back to Cork that night, I again met Sinn Féin people in London. On Sunday we had a signing session with Gerry at the Irish Book Fair, and he and I ran over final arrangements for the next day's press conference.

Monday found me in nervous form as I approached the New Ambassador Hotel. Entering the conference room with Gerry I glimpsed an enormous array of media people before turning my attention to negotiating the route to the platform from which we were to speak. But it was sounds rather than sights which registered most strongly with me. From the moment we entered the room there was a noise like that of a sudden, intense hailstorm, and it took me a moment to realise that this was the sound of camera shutters.

Opening the proceedings, I appealed to those present to respect the fact that this was a press reception to mark the publication of a book and that it was organised by Brandon Book Publishers, not by Sinn Féin. I understood, I said, that their principal interest lay in asking Gerry Adams about other matters, and we would open up the press conference to allow for that, but first I asked them to bear with me while we dealt with the matter of the book. And so, the first fifteen minutes concerned the book, which was introduced by Geoff Bell, author of *The Protestants of Ulster* and *The British in Ireland: A Suitable Case for Withdrawal.* Gerry Adams spoke briefly before I invited questions about the book from the floor. Apart from one tabloid journalist who offered up some mild abuse, the assembled media people were patient. And then I opened the reception to any questions they liked to ask, and immediately the questions about the IRA came raining in.

That night I flew back to Kerry and in the following days I was pleased to see that the book had not been entirely lost in the media coverage, though in most cases it constituted little more than a footnote. On Thursday I left Dingle again to travel north for the Belfast launch of *Cage Eleven* on Friday morning. Speaking at the launch, I said:

> The writing shows an ear for dialogue, sensitivity and humour, all of which qualities make this book stand out as something of a departure within the general genre of prison writings. It stands out partly because its author possesses the considerable virtue of not taking himself too seriously. Indeed, he succeeds in establishing a wonderfully effective tension between the seriousness of the circumstances of imprisonment and the frequent levity of his writing about it.
>
> *Cage Eleven*, in brief, offers a compelling insight into a world hidden from public view. It also offers an insight into its author which goes far beyond and, indeed, conflicts with the simplistic battle-cries of certain sections of the media.

In late June I received news from London that the fascist National Front had been plastering copies of *Cage Eleven* in branches of W. H. Smith with stickers. Smith's, to their credit, refused to be intimidated, but in July the DUP took up the campaign against W. H. Smith, insisting that they should "not allow their bookshelves to be used as a propaganda point for the Provisionals". The DUP and the NF enjoyed cordial relations but their joint campaign had no discernible effect. However, there were booksellers in the south of Ireland who refused to stock any of the books of Gerry Adams, and this certainly restricted sales. As regards the north, it was entirely understandable that some booksellers might be unwilling and might feel that it was unsafe to sell his books, and so we had difficulties in achieving sales there. Nevertheless, the critical response to the book was good in both Britain and Ireland, and we had by the end of the year sold a respectable number of copies. We were also selling translation rights, bringing his writings to a sizeable international audience.

In reviewing our publishing of Gerry Adams, which we had begun in 1982, I felt pleased with what we achieved, but angered and offended by the continuing political censorship, which prevented him from being interviewed either about politics or about his various writings. Ireland lacked any culture or history of respect for freedom of expression, and the overwhelming influence of two authoritarian religious traditions had left populations north and south with little expectation that they could successfully insist upon the right to know and be informed. There were no organisations or campaigns dedicated to the pursuit of freedom of expression, and I felt that only the determined practice of freedom – in my case publishing work which challenged the authoritarian consensus – could achieve any enlargement of such freedom. I was convinced that Section 31 would fall, but only if it was pushed.

Chapter Eight

BREACHING THE WALL

I WAS IN Belfast in early August of 1991 for the West Belfast Festival, and Gerry and I started discussing a collection of short stories again. Getting back to him a week or so after returning home, I wrote:

> . . . the important thing is to allow your imagination to be the prime decider, rather than feeling that you "should" cover this issue or that fact or whatever. The important thing about any story is the integrity of the narrative and of the characterisation; when people try to use short stories to illustrate particular points, then it is immediately clear that they are illustrations of points rather than genuine short stories.

I received the manuscript of *The Street and Other Stories* in January 1992 and we published in August. The launch was held in Belfast as part of the West Belfast Festival. Gerry himself had recently contracted hepatitis and was supposed to be confined to bed. In discussing with him prospects for publicity, which included fairly elaborate plans for a London launch, I stressed the fact that I had no wish to put him under pressure which would end up damaging his health. And so we scaled back plans. I met him the evening before the launch and he was notably weak, but he was determined to be at it. As it turned out, he was in good spirits on the day, and I found that I had to reassure him on several occasions that I was happy that he should go straight home at the end of the launch.

Although we had been prevented in the past from advertising *The Politics of Irish Freedom* on RTÉ radio, the situation had changed significantly regarding censorship of Sinn Féin members within the past few months. Larry O'Toole, a Sinn Féin member, had been a shop steward at the Gateau cake factory in Dublin and had been interviewed by RTÉ during a strike there. When RTÉ then banned the broadcasting of interviews with him under Section 31 of the Broadcasting Act, he took a high court action. In July the high court had decided in his favour, holding that RTÉ had been over-restrictive in its interpretation of Section 31.

This, I felt, provided us with an opportunity to advertise *The Street and Other Stories* on RTÉ radio. I was further convinced that we would have no problem when Wesley Boyd, a senior member of RTÉ staff, announced that following the high court judgment in the Larry O'Toole case RTÉ could now interview Gerry Adams about his book of short stories. I drafted a twenty-second ad which I felt would work well.

> This is Gerry Adams speaking. My new book is called *The Street and Other Stories* and it's on sale in good bookshops in the 32 Counties. Most of the stories are about ordinary people and every-day events, and there's a fair bit of craic in them too. That's *The Street and Other Stories* and this is Gerry Adams. I think you might enjoy it. Slán.

We submitted it to RTÉ in the usual fashion through Eason Advertising, with whom I discussed the budget and the timing of the ads.

Then came a call from Eason Advertising that RTÉ were refusing to broadcast the ad. I issued a press release, protesting against the ban in quite trenchant terms. Some in the media picked up on the press release, and on 18 August eighteen independent radio stations broadcast an interview with Gerry Adams about the ban; the interviewer was Conor Lenihan of Independent Radio News, and it was the first ever interview with Gerry Adams on radio in the south; it was broadcast repeatedly on the hour for several hours. Many supporters of censorship, including leading politicians, intellectuals and broadcasters, had insisted that for Gerry Adams to be heard on radio would be a disaster for democracy in Ireland, but no disaster befell the land that night.

I was delighted that this anti-democratic measure, which had poisoned the atmosphere for years, and which I had opposed for years, had now been cracked wide open. Censorship would never be quite the same again in Ireland.

My celebrations were shortlived. The rest of the media took little notice of the breach in the censorship wall; broadcasting journalists and producers and their unions took absolutely no action to press home the advantage; indeed, the unions observed an uncanny silence, not even rising to a statement between them.

Meanwhile, I had submitted the ad to several independent radio stations; if they were prepared to broadcast interviews with him, they would surely broadcast the ad. I also appealed the decision to RTÉ:

> In support of our position we would invoke the remarks of Wesley Boyd, Director of Broadcasting Development in RTÉ, who stated at a recent seminar in Derry that in the light of the high court decision RTÉ *could* interview Gerry Adams about the book. . . We suggest that it defies logic to say that he can be interviewed about it but he cannot simply advertise it in the straightforward words used in our proposed copy.

Word came back from Brian Pierce, manager of radio sales, who indicated that, while they would not broadcast the ad as submitted:

> We have, however, clearly indicated that we would have no difficulty in carrying advertisements for Mr Adams' book so long as they were voiced in the normal way by a member of Irish Actors' Equity who would not be precluded by Section 31 and we would be very pleased to arrange an immediate campaign for such advertisements.

I was surprised by this letter, since the only places in which republicans' words were dubbed by actors were Britain and Northern Ireland; the practice was far from being "the normal way" in RTÉ. Also, I had drafted the ad deliberately to be spoken by the author, since I was quite convinced that this was by far the most effective way to advertise the book. I was by no means certain that another form of ad would be as effective.

Now Michael O'Keeffe, chief executive of the IRTC, advised in a letter to independent station heads that "the advertisement in question should not be broadcast".

I asked our lawyers for advice. At a meeting with solicitors and senior counsel three options were outlined: firstly we could take an action for damages, but this would take a long time and could involve us in large costs. Secondly, we could take an action for an injunction to require RTÉ to broadcast the ad, but we would have to demonstrate that it was a matter of urgency for which no damages could compensate, and we would therefore be unlikely to succeed in getting an injunction. Thirdly, we could go for a judicial review of RTÉ's decision, which we were pretty well guaranteed to win; we could also couple it with a claim for damages.

I informed our lawyers that we could not possibly become involved in any legal process which would make us liable for significant costs. We had had enough experience of the appalling financial risks of legal action, and if there was any chance of having to pay significant costs, we would simply not pursue the matter any further. I was informed, however, that the great advantage of the third option was that it could be pursued at "absolutely minimal" cost. It was almost certain that we would win, and if we did there would then be an inquiry as to damages, and if we could quantify the loss, it would be recoverable. I was immediately asked to prepare documentation which would establish what losses we might have suffered as a result of the refusal of RTÉ to carry the ad. When the IRTC followed suit and also banned our ad, our lawyers advised that we take action for judicial review against them as well, since no extra cost to ourselves would be involved, and we could pursue them for damages as well as RTÉ. When the first senior counsel retained by our solicitors went missing, a second senior counsel, Adrian Hardiman, had to be briefed, provided with the documentation and met.

On 3 September, my birthday, Mr Justice Johnson in the high court heard our application for leave to seek judicial review in respect of both RTÉ's and the IRTC's bans. In stating that he had no hesitation in granting leave, the judge asked:

> If it transpires that the man assigned to commentate on the Derby happened to be a member of Sinn Féin, then he can't commentate on the Derby?

Following this, RTÉ changed the grounds of their refusal to carry our ad. Their director of sales and marketing, Colm P. Molloy, wrote:

> I am writing now to advise you that following further and wider consideration of the matter within RTÉ and on legal advice given to it and in reference to the standing of the writer and particularly to Section 18, as amended, of the Broadcasting Authority Acts 1960–1979 that RTÉ will not accept for broadcast *any* advertisements for the said book. [emphasis added]

At the end of September I laughed out loud when I read a report in *The Irish Times* suggesting that the IRTC would claim that one of the stories in the book, "A Good Confession", advocated support for the IRA. But after a while I realised that these people were actually serious. I wrote to *The Irish Times*:

> ... There is insufficient space in a letter to offer an adequate description of the story in question, which is included in Gerry Adams' new book, *The Street*, but the IRTC view can be briefly placed in a reasonable context by quoting reviews from *The Sunday Times* and the *Sunday Press*. The former states: "Although the setting for the short stories is Northern Ireland, he does not use them to make political propaganda. Instead, he brings a wry humour and a detailed observation to small events... If there is a unifying

strand, it is compassion for people in difficult situations." The latter remarks that "these pieces are in no way didactic, nor do they seek to preach. . . well written and authentic in form and tone".

It seems to me to be dangerously undemocratic that the two broadcasting organisations behave like prisoners with gate fever, insisting upon censoring themselves even far beyond compliance with censorship imposed by the Dáil.

In October we received affidavits from RTÉ in which they indicated their grounds for defence of the action we had brought. Colm Molloy, director of sales and marketing, submitted that

It is. . . the view of RTÉ that to broadcast any statement whatsoever on any subject by Mr Adams would amount in effect to the broadcasting of propaganda on behalf of Sinn Féin. Where his utterances touch on political matters, they are clearly related to the affairs of Sinn Féin. If they touch on other matters, it is clear that they would have the effect of better publicising Gerry Adams and his reputation generally, and thereby making the message which he carries on behalf of Sinn Féin more acceptable to the public at large. In the current context, the publication of a book of short stories can only have (or be reasonably construed as having) the aim of portraying Mr Adams as an artist, a man of culture, and a man who writes stories which by their nature are intended to enable the readers to identify with both the story, and, by inference, the writer and the message he conveys. . .

It is RTÉ's view that. . . the broadcasting of any material of this nature emanating from Mr Adams (or any material whatsoever) must be reasonably regarded as either likely to promote or incite to crime or [a]s tending to undermine the authority of the State. . .

The IRTC took a different approach, standing by its extraordinary view of "A Good Confession".

It considered that certain stories in the book could amount to or be reasonably taken as advocating, offering or inviting support for Sinn Féin, particularly the story entitled "A Good Confession", the implication or tenor of which is that membership, participation in or co-operation with the IRA is understandable and acceptable for practising Roman Catholics, thereby impliedly inviting support for the IRA and Sinn Féin. The commission noted that the back cover of the book proclaims that its author Gerry Adams is the president of Sinn Féin and is also the author of *The Politics of Sinn Féin* [*sic*], a book which is advertised on the last page of *The Street and Other Stories* as emanating from "a leading member of the republication [*sic*] movement clarifying and defending its aims and methods".

Conor Cruise O'Brien, in an affidavit in support of the IRTC ban, submitted that:

. . . the tone of this book is uniformly one of sympathy with the Catholic paramilitaries and of antipathy to the security forces and the police. This is to be expected in a book by Gerry Adams, President of Sinn Féin and chief apologist for the IRA and who is shown in an advertisement at the end of the book as being the author of another book which is plainly a manual and justification of IRA activity [*sic*]. An advertisement for *The Street and Other Stories* would of necessity be an advertisement for this other book which blatantly justifies and seeks support for the IRA and Sinn Féin [*sic*].

When asked by RTÉ Radio News to square his welcome for the recent Supreme Court decision in relation to Larry O'Toole and RTÉ with his opposition to the broadcasting of an ad for a book of short stories, Conor Cruise O'Brien claimed that he could not speak about the upcoming case because it was *sub judice*. It was not, of course.

In April 1993 we heard that our action for judicial review of the ban was to be heard in May. I sought to interest newspapers in running anticipatory stories. However, journalists who might have been expected to be sympathetic to my position insisted that it was not possible to do such pieces for legal reasons. This did not prevent the other side from advancing their argument in the

Sunday Independent in an interview with their regular columnist Conor Cruise O'Brien, who would give evidence as an expert witness against us, and who had clearly revised his opinion that the matter was *sub judice*. They reported, unchallenged by any other view, his opinion that in one story, "A Good Confession":

> There is a bad priest, who tells the penitent that he can't get confession until he renounces IRA membership. And there is a good priest who says forget it.

This, he suggested, meant that the book, seemingly of short stories, was in fact a cunningly disguised book of propaganda for the IRA.

If the story had been as he described it, then that would still have provided no good basis for banning it. However, the story concerned a woman rather than a man. There was no man (or woman) who was told "that he can't get confession . . .". And as for this non-existent man renouncing IRA membership, the question was simply not raised in the story!

I contacted a number of organisations, looking for statements of support. The Irish Writers' Union issued a statement characterising the positions of RTÉ and the IRTC as "invidious and unacceptable". Niall Meehan of the School of Communications, Dublin City University, in a letter to *The Irish Times*, described as "police state type" the views of RTÉ and the IRTC. And the Irish Translators' Association wrote in a press statement that:

> It is nothing short of scandalous that two public institutions should take it upon themselves to exercise a form of private censorship which goes far beyond the already repressive censorship legislation governing the Irish airwaves. Gerry Adams is thus denied not only expression of his political thought on radio and TV but even promotion of his artistic and creative output.

I also wrote to some thirty organisations and individuals outside the country, including Article 19, *Index on Censorship*, and the trade and literary media in Britain.

Meanwhile, no one in the media sympathetic to my point of view would cover the story in advance of the hearing. And just as the day of the hearing approached, all the journalists who had been active in anti-censorship campaigns departed for Cambodia to act as observers of the elections there. It now became clear that our high court hearing would not be covered by any journalists apart from the routine court reporter.

I sent invitations to a large number of organisations and individuals, requesting them to come to the high court proceedings.

On the day of the hearing, the mood and advice of our lawyers were quite different from before. Suddenly it all seemed to depend on the virtual lottery of which judge we got, and now our lawyers scampered like schoolboys through the corridors and courtrooms of the Four Courts, eventually congratulating themselves on succeeding in avoiding two particular judges. "I think the best way I can describe Justice [A] is as a Castle Catholic," said one of them, as he leant against the nicotine-stained wall of the public area outside the Bar Library. "If we get Justice [B], you might as well go away home to Kerry. He's a complete Blueshirt and we wouldn't stand a chance. Carney will consider it on its legal merits, and so he offers us the best chance altogether."

"Yes," said our junior counsel, "if we can't win with Carney we can't win with anyone."

The judge we got was indeed Paul Carney, a recently appointed judge who in presiding over our case confounded the expectations of our lawyers. They had predicted that the hearing would be over within one day, but the proceedings stretched into five days. I had been under the impression that the documents of the case would be taken as having been read, but instead even the stories from the book which were referred to in affidavits were read out. So wigged and black-robed counsel stood before the court reading stories of working-class Belfast in the tones of the south Dublin legal elite.

In Court No. 10 sunlight slanted generously through three large windows. The bewigged men all seemed to have at the tops

151

of their piles of papers not *The Street* but *The Politics of Irish Freedom.*

The principal witness for the IRTC was Conor Cruise O'Brien, the architect of the modern form of political censorship of broadcasting. He proved an illuminating witness, saying that he had read all eighteen stories in the book and that "I would regard ten of them as containing political material." In the context of his evidence, he seemed to be suggesting that this was political material of a kind that he felt should be suppressed.

He even objected to the fact that the book included at the back an advertisement for *The Politics of Irish Freedom.* For RTÉ to advertise the book of short stories would, by extension, he argued, be to advertise this political book.

He explained why he would not like to see Gerry Adams allowed to speak even about roses:

> I could imagine, for example, if the person whom we are speaking of was included in a programme on rose growing, he might be quoting Yeats: said Pearse to Connolly, there is nothing but our own red blood can feed a right rose tree, and I wouldn't want him to have the privilege of reciting that highly motivated statement.

The reaction in the court ranged from puzzled frowns to suppressed laughter.

He was asked if he could explain why so many newspaper reviews of the book differed so starkly from his view that the stories were propaganda; reference was made in particular to reviews in *The Times, The Sunday Times* and *The Times Literary Supplement.*

> The fact is that many people in the journalistic world have at least a sneaking sympathy, not only for Sinn Féin, but the IRA and this applies to writers in Britain as well as here. Many people are taking sympathy into the extremities for Sinn Féin and indeed sometimes for the IRA and I think some of these reviewers are in that general category.

He was leafing through the documents before him, searching for reviews by alleged sympathisers of the IRA lurking in the pages of newspapers such as *The Times*. But soon he was forced to withdraw his suggestion that reviewers of *The Street* were IRA sympathisers.

The questioning moved on to consideration of the claim that to advertise any book on any subject if it was by Gerry Adams would necessarily benefit the political party he represented.

Hardiman: Would you agree that to publish a book by a person who is in a leadership position in a political party on irrelevant subjects is necessarily to benefit the political party?

O'Brien: I think marginally my objection is not to the publication of books. It is the advertising of the books over the national airways.

Hardiman: Would you agree the advertising of a book which is written by a person in a position of leadership in political terms would necessarily benefit the party?

O'Brien: I think so.

Hardiman: On Saturday next my clients are publishing the poetry of Mr Michael D. Higgins, the Minister for Arts, Culture and the Gaeltacht. Do you think that it is likely to benefit the Labour Party?

O'Brien: I think it may. I am no longer a member of the Labour Party.

Hardiman: Are you serious about that? I suggest to you it is far-fetched almost to the point of paranoia to suggest an advertisement for a book by a person will benefit political parties.

O'Brien: I think it will marginally.

The laughter now was less suppressed. O'Brien went on to explain why it was that radio advertisements were crucially more dangerous to the security of the state than newspaper reviews. They would, he feared, be heard by the wrong kind of people.

They include people who are poor and who are not so well educated. That is, . . . less educated people who on the whole are more
likely to be impressed than more educated people. . .

Colm P. Molloy, director of sales and marketing, gave evidence
for RTÉ, and soon had to admit that he had not, in fact, read the
book at the time that he had signed the affidavit defending RTÉ's
decision to ban any advertisement for it.

However, since then he had read the book and as part of his
evidence he informed the court that he had formed the view that
one story in particular was especially "dangerous". This was a story
entitled "Shane", which in his view constituted propaganda for
the IRA because it suggested that British soldiers mistreated dogs.

I attended the first day of the hearing, and on the following day
launched *The Season of Fire* by Michael D. Higgins in Listowel. I
attended none of the subsequent court proceedings, but on 26
May flew out of Shannon airport to Miami via New York. I was
travelling to the American Booksellers' convention in Miami
Beach, where I had been invited by the American Booksellers'
Foundation for Free Expression to speak about the international
campaign in solidarity with Salman Rushdie.

I returned to Ireland in June, and on 16 July I was in the high
court to hear Judge Paul Carney deliver his judgment in relation to
RTÉ. Our lawyers, in common with the lawyers for RTÉ and the
IRTC, were baffled as to why he was giving a ruling in relation only
to RTÉ. After all, the cases had been heard together. However, the
general opinion on all sides was that we would win our action
against RTÉ. It was the IRTC case which might go against us, more
or less for technical reasons. Members of Let in the Light and the
NUJ attended the court, and I had arranged a press conference in
a nearby hotel, at which they would join me in speaking to the press
after the ruling had been given. In the context of confident expectations that we would win, I wanted to provide anti-censorship
campaigners with an opportunity to share the limelight and to use
our victory to add momentum to their own campaigns.

The judge recited selected elements of the evidence that had been presented in the case. And then, suddenly, in a few paragraphs he announced a ruling which no one in all our discussions had ever anticipated.

RTÉ now accept that an ordinary member of Sinn Féin may broadcast on a range of subjects but they say that so far as Mr Adams is concerned his public persona is such that he cannot be divorced in the public mind from advancing the cause of Sinn Féin. As Mr Colm Molloy put it in evidence "You cannot separate Mr Adams from the position he holds".

Whether this is so is a matter of judgment. It is a matter of judgment in relation to image and the projection of same. It is a judgment in relation to public persona. It is a judgment in relation to the probable effect of the broadcasting of particular material by a particular voice and public personality and the holder of a particular office.

In the first instance it seems to me that greater expertise in relation to making a judgment on these matters must lie with the National Broadcasting Authority than the Courts. Secondly, it must be asked whether the exercise of such a judgment by the Broadcasting Authority is reviewable by the Courts. On the facts of the case. . . I do not see that it is proper for the Court to interfere.

In essence he ruled that RTÉ was better qualified to decide the matter than the high court.

I was shocked, and I struggled to hold my feelings in control and balance, aware that I might have to speak to the media within minutes. I was conscious of a need to avoid saying anything insulting about the judge, but at the same time I did not intend to convey a position of meekly accepting defeat.

Emerging from the courtroom to face the microphone of an independent radio station, I expressed myself deeply disappointed that the high court had "failed to vindicate our right to freedom of expression". I suggested that it was about time that broadcasters stopped acting as the "thought police".

Suddenly I saw my solicitor, Michael Farrell, and junior counsel, Shane Murphy, advancing upon me, and I broke off my interview. They were concerned that I might be responding injudiciously to the high court judgment, and they were keen to impress upon me that I should think before I spoke to the media and that I should avoid criticism of the court and of the judge.

Our action against RTÉ and the IRTC was only one element in a wide-ranging but narrowly organised campaign against censorship in Ireland. As it went on, the United Nations Human Rights Committee was hearing the first report by Ireland under Article 40 of the International Covenant on Civil and Political Rights. The committee expressed serious concern about Section 31. In response, Ireland's attorney-general drew attention to the *O'Toole v RTÉ* decision which, he said, represented "a substantial narrowing" of the scope of the Ministerial Order under Section 31.

Now, however, the Executive Committee (EC) of the Irish Council for Civil Liberties sent a supplementary submission to the UN Human Rights Committee, pointing out that the decision in *Brandon v RTÉ* had "undone much of the effect of the O'Toole decision and has once more widened the scope of the Ministerial Order". The decision, the EC said:

> . . . allows RTÉ to continue to operate a blanket ban on prominent or well-known members of [Sinn Féin]. It effectively turns such members of a legal political party into unpersons and not only deprives them of the right of free speech but even of the right to have a private existence distinct from their political role.
>
> We would dispute that even a threat to national security could justify such curtailment of fundamental rights but we think it is frankly ludicrous to maintain that the advertisement of a book of short stories could undermine the authority of the Irish State.

None of the political parties in the Dáil, nor any of the trade unions made any statements about the implications for freedom of expression. RTÉ journalists and producers were silent.

I was in contact with international organisations, including PEN American Center and Article 19, and on 3 August a letter was sent to the taoiseach, the minister for arts, culture and the Gaeltacht and the attorney-general, signed by Louis Begley, Frances FitzGerald, Allen Ginsberg, John Irving, Faith Sale, Susan Sontag and Rose Styron:

> On behalf of the 2,600 writers who are members of American PEN, we write to express our deep concern over a recent high court ruling upholding RTÉ's decision to ban an advertisement for Gerry Adams' fictional book, *The Street and Other Stories*, published by Brandon...
>
> It seems little short of absurd to us that a brief advertisement, merely urging listeners to buy a book of short stories, should be judged a threat to Ireland's national security. Whoever Gerry Adams may be in his public life, and whatever the rights and wrongs of his views, we sincerely believe that the Irish people should have the right to be credited with enough discernment to make up their own minds regarding both the merits of his fiction writing and of his political beliefs...
>
> We therefore urge you to make a public statement questioning RTÉ's decision to refuse to air the advertisement; to redraft or abolish Section 31 so that its potential to undermine the legitimate exercise of free expression is eliminated; and to ensure in future that writers are given full freedom to promote their books and that unfettered debate about the conflict in Northern Ireland is permitted.

Delighted as I was to receive a copy of this letter, I was nevertheless concerned about the comparative lack of response in Ireland. On 10 August I wrote to a number of organisations and individuals, asking them to send similar letters to that from PEN American Center. Amongst those I wrote to were Aosdana, the Arts Council/An Chomhairle Ealaíon, the Arts Council of Northern Ireland, the Association of Artists in Ireland, the Booksellers' Association (Irish Branch), Bord na Gaeilge, CLÉ (the Irish

Publishers' Association), Comhaltas Ceoltóiri Éireann, Conradh na Gaeilge, the Irish Film Centre, the Irish Film Institute, the Irish Museum of Modern Art, Irish PEN, the Irish Translators' Association, the Irish Writers' Union, the National Union of Journalists, Poetry Ireland, SIPTU, the Society of Irish Playwrights, and the Tyrone Guthrie Centre. I also sought the support of the International Federation of Journalists and Article 19, the International Centre Against Censorship.

At the same time I decided to target the International Writers' Festival, which was scheduled to take place in Dublin in late September. Conscious that I was suffering from exhaustion and constant respiratory infections associated with my asthma, I was delighted when the Let in the Light organisation agreed to organise a press conference at the festival; they would do all the work of contacting participating writers and of generating media interest.

My colleagues from CLÉ responded to my 10 August approach with a letter to the taoiseach and the minister for arts, culture and the Gaeltacht, and Article 19 in a similar letter wrote:

> Under international law, any restriction on a fundamental right must be proportionate to the legitimate aim sought to be achieved. Article 19 believes that in this case a mere statement on radio by Mr Adams advertising his book of fiction cannot be seen as supporting terrorism . . .
>
> Article 19 calls on your Government to end the Section 31 ban and to take appropriate steps to compensate Brandon Books for the costs of this action.

However, there was silence from most of the rest I had appealed to. And as the opening of the International Writers' Festival approached, it became clear that Let in the Light had done nothing to organise their promised press conference.

Exhausted though I was, I tried at the last minute to contact writers attending the festival, and I succeeded in organising a reading by Gerry Adams, which was supported by a number of other writers, including Edna O'Brien, Evelyn Conlon and Albyn Leah Hall.

Shortly afterwards, as we published Alice Taylor's new book, *Country Days*, and I made my final preparations to attend the Frankfurt Book Fair, I suffered a collapse from exhaustion.

Out of action for several weeks, I realised that I would have to make plans to take some of the strain off my shoulders. Peter Malone had stalwartly stepped into the Frankfurt breach, but longer-term changes were needed.

Soon after my return to work I travelled to Belfast for the Eigse, or winter school of the West Belfast Festival, where I spoke at the Chultúrlann on the subject of "Cultural Identity and Writing in Ireland". On that day, 4 December, Ireland stood poised tantalisingly before the prospect of an historic breakthrough towards the possibility of lasting peace. A summit between the Irish and British governments, held in Dublin the day before, had failed to arrive at a resolution, but further developments were expected in the next few days. Word was that John Hume, who had staked so much on his joint initiative with Gerry Adams, was feeling the pressure; I was aware that Gerry was also under pressure. That night a reception was held in Belfast City Hall involving many who had attended the West Belfast Festival. The nationalists had at last penetrated the citadel of unionist power and there was a carnival atmosphere amongst the Union Jacks, imposing ceilings, portraits and statuary.

I found myself sitting quietly with Gerry discussing the political situation under a bust of Edward Carson. I could tell that he was under strain, but there was an aura of urgent determination about him, almost of confidence – not confidence about the outcome of current deliberations but about the potential for progress; a sense perhaps of excitement. We talked about how things hung in the balance. He could not know, and no one could know, how things would turn out, but we sat there in that stone niche on the brink of enormous possibility. A City Hall porter, a stern opponent of anything nationalist, let alone republican, came over, his hand held out in greeting.

"Pleased to shake your hand, Mr Adams."

"And I pleased to shake yours; how are you doing?" he said.

That night I went on to a party at the Felons' Club in West Belfast, and in the early hours of the morning I wrote my first notes towards a proposal for an autobiography by Gerry Adams. I noted that Gerry's role in developing the Irish peace initiative would result in his achieving a new public prominence. Already people who had long been dismissive of him were asking me what he was like. Sinn Féin had long been portrayed in the media as a bunch of pathological criminals, its politics ignored; but now, I felt, even antagonistic commentators would begin to write about Sinn Féin political strategy, and would find in dealing with Sinn Féin activists that there was an impressive substance. Above all, they would encounter in Gerry Adams himself a formidable intelligence with a strong and impressive personality. These were circumstances which would establish an expanding momentum, creating conditions in which an autobiography might be able to achieve sales substantially greater than those of any of his previous books. However, I decided to wait for a while before raising the project with him; it would be well to see what progress would be made by the process he and John Hume had initiated.

On 15 December the British and Irish governments released the Downing Street Declaration, a statement which had been argued over and negotiated for many months between the two governments and which had amongst its elements inputs from John Hume, Gerry Adams, and Protestant clergymen. It was a historic document, which addressed the question of Irish national self-determination, while also binding in the question of consent. An ambiguous formulation, it was hailed as a momentous achievement in Dublin, and it was rejected by neither the unionists nor the republicans, though Sinn Féin sought clarification.

British Prime Minister John Major created a logjam which frustrated the development of the peace process by refusing to clarify points for Sinn Féin, insisting against logic that clarification was synonymous with negotiation, and he would not negotiate with Sinn Féin.

It was at this point that I raised the question of the autobiography with Gerry for the first time. He couldn't possibly, he said, find the time to write any book, let alone an autobiography. But as we discussed matters, a chink appeared in his refusal as he conceded that he might be interested in working with someone on an authorised biography. We discussed potential authors and agreed to talk again.

I considered the options, looking in particular at the international potential for a major book by or on Gerry, and got back to him to say that in my view the real publishing potential lay in an autobiography rather than a biography, even one written with his co-operation. I knew that Gerry had never earned any money for himself, receiving only the amount of the dole while out of internment, and that he was conscious of the fact that his wife and son had lived difficult lives on account of his commitment; in addition, they had had to live with the constant danger that he might be killed, a danger which would undoubtedly persist and perhaps intensify through any peace process. All the royalties he had earned from his previous books had been paid to a republican prisoners' charity rather than to him. Now, however, I argued, there was a real opportunity for him to earn some money so that his family could have the prospect of at least some element of security. He pointed to the fact that if the peace initiative developed he would have even less time to himself than he had ever had. The only circumstances he could imagine in which he would be able to write the autobiography would be if everything went wrong and internment was introduced again – a prospect which could quite possibly come about. Though I was discouraged, I had a conviction that I was right to pursue the project, and I got him to agree that we would discuss it again, though meanwhile we would work on a new edition of *The Politics of Irish Freedom*, to be published under the new title of *Free Ireland: Towards a Lasting Peace*.

After five months of delay the British at last responded to Sinn Féin's questions seeking clarification, and Sinn Féin in turn gave its response to the Downing Street Declaration. Speculation had been rife for some time as to whether the IRA would declare a ceasefire and for how long. The best estimate of most commentators was that they might declare as much as a three-month ceasefire; however, in August they declared a "complete cessation" to begin at the end of the month. The unilateral nature of the cessation, and its lack of limiting time-frame, took everyone by surprise. It was widely believed that multi-party talks would begin in about three months, and amongst northern nationalists jubilation and relief mingled in a mellow cocktail. Unionists reacted, ironically, with horror, and soon the leader of the Ulster Unionist Party, James Molyneux, was observing in revealing terms that the cessation had destabilised politics in the north. Southern enemies of northern nationalism and republicanism were confounded, for they had long denounced the process which had brought about the cessation, arguing in often lurid and personally vindictive terms that the Hume-Adams initiative was heading not towards a ceasefire but towards full-scale civil war. That they should castigate Adams was nothing new, but what was new was the vitriol which had been thrown from the *Sunday Independent* and other sources in the face of John Hume.

I met Gerry again in August and September and finally convinced him in principle that he and I would collaborate to create an autobiographical book, if I could generate sufficient international interest to be able to come back to him with a package which would make it worth his while. At Frankfurt in early October I succeeded in eliciting substantial interest, and so a couple of weeks after returning I advised Gerry that I felt we could go ahead.

The peace initiative and the legal precedent established by the Larry O'Toole case, and perhaps also our case against the broadcasting authorities, had created an atmosphere in which Michael D. Higgins, Labour Party minister for arts, culture and the Gaeltacht, suspended the operation of Section 31 of the Broadcasting Act. In late October Gerry Adams appeared for the first time on *The Late Late Show*. I had been in contact for some time with the show about having Gerry on. Gay had always opposed Section 31, and I had particularly raised the question of a first television interview with them at the time of Gerry's independent radio interview about the banning of the ad for *The Street and Other Stories*. They had decided against it at the time, but we had agreed to stay in touch and to review the situation, and when Section 31 was suspended senior researcher Brigid Ruane contacted me to say that the show was definitely interested in having him on. We discussed possible dates and formats, and from the start I argued in favour of a one-to-one interview rather than a panel situation. I then contacted Gerry and Richard McAuley and I arranged for Sinn Féin people to have discussions with the show.

At the final planning meeting I joined Richard McAuley and another Sinn Féin member, and *The Late Late's* Brigid Ruane and John Masterson, in Sinn Féin's Parnell Square headquarters. The show's chosen format reflected a compromise between my strong preference for a one-to-one interview and their interest in setting up a confrontation with a panel; first Gay Byrne would interview Gerry and then after a commercial break a panel of politicians would take Gerry on. Richard McAuley and I both stressed that it would be a mistake for Gay Byrne to try to "take him down": first of all, Gerry would be well able for any ambush Gay might try to launch, and secondly, to give the whole show over to attacks on Gerry, first by Gay and then by the panel, would either make for a poor show or would rebound in their faces. Somewhat to the surprise of *The Late Late Show* people, we made no further or more detailed demands or suggestions, simply stressing again that it would be a mistake for Gay to adopt a confrontational posture from the start; they indicated that Gay would not try "to take Gerry down".

The show fell on the day on which the Forum for Peace and Reconciliation opened with speeches from all the leaders of delegations, including Gerry Adams. Having been up since the early hours and engaged in a plethora of meetings as well as the forum, Gerry was weary.

"My main problem at this stage," said Gerry, "is that I may fall asleep in the middle of it."

Any fear that he might doze off was dispelled in the first moment of the interview when Gay Byrne took up a hostile, accusatory stance, for once refusing to sit with his guest. Gerry gently, skilfully disarmed his interviewer.

"First of all," he responded, "I would dispute your intro that I am the most controversial man in Ireland, and invite you to come and sit beside me and we'll talk this out."

Within moments I knew that he had the audience on his side.

Gay's interview, probing and challenging, continued for twenty-five minutes, concluding with a question about people's animosity towards him.

"What we have to do," Gerry replied, "is try to bring about a situation where we can actually put all of this behind us. And if I'm prepared to sit down with the people who tried to kill me, who tried to kill my wife and who tried to kill my son, who killed my brother-in-law and who killed my cousin, surely it's good enough for me to ask them to reach out the hand of friendship and sit down and talk with me and those that I represent."

The audience responded with loud applause, not just, I felt, for his immediate words but for the way he had come over to them during the interview which had now drawn to a close.

In the second part of the show Gerry was faced by a panel consisting of Austin Currie of Fine Gael, Dermot Ahern of Fianna Fáil, co-chair of the British-Irish Parliamentary Body, Jim Kemmy, chairman of the Labour Party, Michael McDowell of the Progressive Democrats and, as odd man out, the dramatist and newspaper columnist Hugh Leonard, who hit the most bitterly strident note.

"These people in their graves are crying out for retribution, and it's not going to come any more."

The continuing exchanges with Hugh Leonard were greeted finally with sustained applause for Gerry from the studio audience.

"Let's try and be constructive," suggested Gerry, "because what we have here is an opportunity which Mr Reynolds has described as the best opportunity in seventy-five years to bring about peace . . . Of course you can recriminate; we all could. But it's better to try and move the situation forward."

Michael McDowell fulminated about "thugs and savages" and he and Currie engaged in joint haranguing and recriminations. From audience reactions it was clear that their hectoring approach succeeded only in increasing support for Gerry Adams; this heartened me considerably since I knew that the audience had been selected on an entirely random basis.

At the end of the programme members of the audience queued patiently to shake Gerry's hand, ignoring the five panelists who stood in a huddle on the other side of the stage.

In the hospitality room after the show Gay Byrne was already conscious of the fact that his attempt to expose and rattle Gerry had not been well received by the television audience. Phone calls to the programme were strongly critical of his approach. He observed to me that he would have been criticised if he had been too soft. I didn't contest the issue with him, nor did I take up with him or anyone else in the programme the fact that he had departed from the understanding we had had at our last planning meeting. There was no point: Gay's hostile approach had, after all, rebounded to the benefit of Gerry. Over the following days and weeks, public reaction was overwhelmingly favourable to Gerry Adams and critical of Gay Byrne. I saw it as having achieved a quantum leap in the mellowing process which I had anticipated would characterise public attitudes to Gerry in the wake of the IRA cessation, and it was this expectation which underlay my conviction that his autobiography could achieve far greater sales than any of his previous books.

Chapter Nine

BOMBS BEFORE DAWN

THE FRONT OF Waterstones in Charing Cross Road in London was thronged with people at 12.30 on 18 November, television cameras poised high above crash barriers and a couple of bobbies gently moving through the crush of journalists, photographers and the reading public who had bought tickets to hear Gerry speak about his *Selected Writings*. Bill Godber of Turnaround was finding it difficult to get into the shop, where the shutters were being drawn down and irate journalists who had not requested admission in advance were being turned away.

Gerry and I had arrived in London the previous day and had enjoyed an informal private dinner which was attended by Peter Benenson, founder of Amnesty International, Jon Snow, Paul Foot and others.

Now he engaged in a discussion with author Ronan Bennett about his writing and took questions from the floor, and it was characteristic of him that with apparent ease he established a good rapport with his audience. After the session was over we had a cup of coffee in a downstairs office while Gerry signed copies of the book, and by the time we were ready to leave the shop we presumed that the crowd outside would have dispersed.

On emerging from the shop, however, it was obvious that the crowd had grown rather than shrunk, and I was momentarily alarmed. But to my considerable surprise, despite a lone voice raised in protest, the large crowd applauded him as he left the shop and our only problem was to clear a way through the throng and get him into the waiting car. I followed in a second car with Sinn Féin people and remarked that they had organised their supporters extremely well to turn up. However, it was clear that they were as surprised as I was at the size and tenor of the crowd, and they speculated that word of Gerry's presence had percolated through the Irish community after tickets for the event had been sold out, and people had nevertheless just come to catch a glimpse of him.

Gerry was finding it extremely difficult to find any time to work on his autobiography. At the same time Peter Malone and I were working with him on *Free Ireland: Towards a Lasting Peace*. We had already edited a US edition, but we needed to revise and update the final two chapters for our Irish and British edition. During October Gerry and I met for an hour and a half to discuss the autobiography in the midst of his preparations for the opening of the Northern Ireland Forum; in early November we had a working session in Dublin, and two weeks later I was with him in Belfast again. I was working intensively to secure firm deals for international editions, but the incessant demands of his political commitment made me doubt whether Gerry would be able to fulfil his commitment to the book, especially as the process approached a state of crisis.

The initiative launched by John Hume and Gerry Adams matured into a process when it became a three-legged stool, its three legs being nationalist consensus in the north, a stable government led by Fianna Fáil in the south, and US support for the process. Even with these elements of stability in place, progress could not be taken for granted, for opposed to the process were the British government, the British intelligence services, the unionists and the opposition parties in the south, all of whom sought to place barricades across the road of progress towards all-party talks. If any one of the three legs were to be broken or removed, there was little chance of progress, and some form of reversion to violent conflict would be just a matter of time.

All parties involved in the process were aware of the position, yet within months of the IRA cessation the Dublin leg of the stool was chopped off. The Labour Party, junior partner in the coalition government, had seized upon issues arising from the mishandling of a file in the attorney-general's office to exploit a sense of crisis of confidence in the government.

I was in Belfast as the scene unfolded in Dublin and I watched with horror. Visiting both nationalist and unionist people, I was painfully aware of just how high the stakes were. Yet in Dublin the Labour Party seemed to me in the circumstances to be reck-lessly intent upon bringing down the government over an issue which they alleged to be one of principle regarding "trans-parency", yet which I felt was an attempt to secure party advan-tage and to gain revenge for past wounds on their pride inflicted by Albert Reynolds. Whatever the reading, the issue was by no means of such magnitude as to warrant bringing down a govern-ment at any time, let alone at this time when the greatest oppor-tunity for peace in seventy-five years hung precariously in the balance. And the person whose head the Labour Party demanded was none other than the one leading politician in the south who had been most prepared to stick his neck out and take a risk for peace, Albert Reynolds.

I was not so egotistical as to think that my opinion could carry any weight in the situation. But in despair at what I saw as the impending mugging of the peace process, I faxed two Labour TDs I knew, insisting that to bring down the government would be the height of irresponsibility. I was not surprised when I received no reply. The government collapsed, Albert Reynolds was removed from power, and John Bruton of Fine Gael, an avowed opponent of the Hume/Adams initiative, was installed as taoiseach. This facilitated enormously, as almost no other imaginable action in the south could have, the British strategy of frustrating the process, of slowing its momentum, seeking to stall it completely.

John Bruton, after a rhetorical flourish in his first weeks in power, reverted to his deep, inherent convictions, including his intense hostility to republicans and his belief that the hardline sectarianism of the unionists would soften if concessions were made to their demands.

Gerry stood on the steps of Government Buildings after a meeting with Bruton and expressed his fear that the peace process was failing. "The British precondition which has blocked the peace process has the potential to destroy it."

As he was speaking I was sitting in the bar of the Mont Clare Hotel, where I had been waiting for him for almost two hours. I was not surprised that he was late: the meeting with John Bruton was important, and he had been good enough to reschedule a subsequent meeting with US Ambassador Jean Kennedy Smith to accommodate me.

He flopped into the seat beside me, clearly tired and discouraged but not despairing.

"At least I had the pleasure," he said, "that when I left the meeting Bruton was looking even worse than I felt."

We had a drink and a chat and I was struck by the fact that in Gerry the process had one crucial player with the kind of capacity for doggedness, persistence and patience which was undoubtedly going to be needed.

*   *   *   *   *

In early December I left for North Africa to work on editing Gerry's autobiography, to prepare for a longer visit and to recuperate from a minor operation. Under doctor's orders to walk at least five miles a day, I gladly became a daily communicant with the sand and sea of a five-mile-long strand. Since my first visit prior to the publication of *The Rushdie Letters* I had come to feel quite at home in North Africa, and the warm, dry weather suited my respiratory condition far better than the cold dampness of the Irish winter.

Back in Ireland two weeks later, I headed straight for Belfast and spent two days working with Gerry before heading home to Dingle for Christmas. In mid-January 1995 I returned to North

Africa, to a small village which was without running water or telephones but which did have an electrical supply. Here I worked on the book, while also working on other Brandon projects, including novels by Tom Phelan and Vincent McDonnell. I established a regular routine, working in a more intensive way on manuscripts than I could have at home. However, Gerry was finding it impossible in the demanding political circumstances to find time to do the necessary work

I had taken a considerable risk in throwing myself headlong into the project, and I was extremely concerned that it was falling apart in the early stages, because Gerry's schedule, including a three-week visit to the US, seemed to allow no opportunity for him to work on the book. I considered an early return to Ireland and the abandonment of the project. However, this autobiography had been my idea, and I still held the conviction that this was a project which could yield substantial sales worldwide and add significantly to understanding of aspects of the political conflict in the north of Ireland. I decided to persevere and to put pressure on Gerry. I pressed for a session of several days in Belfast on my return to Ireland in mid-March.

On my return Gerry and I conducted a realistic review of how things stood. His schedule, including a three-week visit to the United States, precluded him working on the book until after the end of May. We agreed, however, that he would try to make time available to talk to me in Belfast, though he would be very tired and so the quality of his contribution to interviews with me might be rather rambling. He hoped that in travelling in the United States he would be able to write some pieces of text late at night in his hotel rooms. The idea of the interviews was not to create a ghost-written book, but to create, by a mixture of his talking and my writing up his talk, a draft which he could then work on to make it fully his own.

In Dingle I worked on autumn titles, returning to Belfast in early April with the tape recorder. In early May we travelled to London again, this time to launch *Free Ireland: Towards a Lasting*

Peace in the House of Commons in Westminster. Here we ran into trouble with the Speaker of the House of Commons, Betty Boothroyd, who suddenly discovered an antipathy to book launches, despite the fact that they were commonplace events in Westminster. Jeremy Corbyn MP had booked the room and had agreed to chair the launch, as he had done for several previous Brandon titles, and he now engaged in negotiations with the Speaker's office and with the quaintly named Sergeant-at-Arms, as a consequence of which it was agreed that Gerry Adams should be permitted to hold a press conference but that I should be prevented from holding a book launch or from speaking at the press conference.

On the day Jeremy Corbyn introduced Gerry, sitting beside him, and welcomed me as I stood behind them wearing a lapel badge reading "Don't Mention the Book", and explained the circumstances of the ban on the launch.

"It seems," said Gerry in his opening remarks, "that now it is not me who is the subversive, but that Steve MacDonogh is the last true subversive left in Ireland!"

The controversy resulted in excellent media coverage, and newspapers the following day showed Gerry in the House of Commons holding up his book. What was more, the reviews as they started to come were very positive. Writing in the *Independent* David McKittrick wrote:

> *Free Ireland* is written in an easy, open style. . . His book gives fascinating glimpses of stories yet untold about the peace process. . .
> It gives an insight into the development of the mind of the man who has led his people from the cul-de-sac of violence towards the path of peace.

In Ireland the *Irish Independent* wrote that "*Free Ireland* is frequently more accurate, and better argued, than the work of some mainstream writers."

In May Gerry dictated notes and drafts of pieces for the autobiography on to tape while touring the US, and I received material from him from the Beverly Hilton. In the succeeding months I continued shuttling between Dingle, Dublin and Belfast, juggling the combined demands of our general publishing programme with an obsessive determination to see the autobiography completed. Gerry was available only in brief snatches of time; his schedule was extremely busy and included a political visit to South Africa.

We met on his return from South Africa in June. Although tired after travel and an intensive round of meetings to catch up on his return, he was positively glowing with enthusiasm as he spoke about his trip.

"We met people at every level in the ANC. The Brits had put such pressure on Mandela and the ANC not to meet with us at all that Mandela was determined to ensure that we got every facility, and although he had a terribly busy schedule I had a good long meeting with him which was absolutely wonderful. And you know," he said, smiling and gesticulating, "he was great crack, with a brilliant sense of humour!"

He went on to describe in detail his meeting with this remarkable man whom we both admired so enormously, and to describe his meeting with Kader Asmal, now a government minister, whom I knew from Dublin. In talking of one of his visits to townships to meet ANC activists, he burst into the song with which he had been greeted there. It was some time before I could drag him back to the business at hand of trying to make up for lost time in the writing of the book.

Having more or less abandoned any personal life, I also turned down various invitations to attend and speak at conferences, but I did fulfil one speaking engagement, Peter Van Der Kamp of the Kerry International Summer School in Tralee having already secured my commitment almost a year earlier to speak on "The Art of Publishing" and to give a poetry reading.

Ranging from the impact on publishing of the collapse of the Soviet Union to the suppression in Britain and Ireland of the oppositional voices of Gerry Adams and others, I tried to relate my remarks to the general theme of the conference which, a year after the declaration of the IRA cessation, was "violence and reconciliation".

> I associate the art of publishing with creative innovation and diversity. I believe that reconciliation requires mutual understanding and that mutual understanding requires access to the diverse voices that make up society. The art of publishing is too important to be left to the workings of the free market, and the role of government should not be to engage in acts of suppression but should be to intervene to mediate the effects of the free market by providing support specifically for the art of publishing.
>
> ... The more the conglomerates advance internationally, purveying an ever more bland and narrow range of voices, the more important it becomes that state intervention be employed to support independent, creative publishing and the diversity it is able to foster.
>
> To me as a publisher the suppression of voices is violence; the publishing of diverse voices is reconciliation.

We had promised our partner publishers a finished manuscript of the autobiography by September, but although I had been able to make up for some of the time lost in the early months of the year, I still did not have the input from Gerry which would allow us to bring the manuscript to completion. His schedule remained extremely full and the pressure on him intensified as the peace process became more and more bogged down.

Essential to the success of the autobiography was the achievement of international-rights sales, and I had resolved to bring Gerry to the Frankfurt International Book Fair with a view to enhancing our rights-marketing efforts. In 1994, although there had been strong interest from the US, which had subsequently led to agreement with Morrow, there had been a great deal of nervousness and plain political hostility on the part of British houses. Germany's Volk & Welt had come on board at an early stage, and they would host a press conference in the Frankfurter Hof, while we would bring Gerry around the international publishers of his existing books and introduce him to some of those interested in acquiring rights to the new book. It proved to be an interesting exercise for Gerry, a useful one for me, and in its immediate aftermath I was able to conclude deals for other rights territories, most significant of which was an agreement in respect of Britain, Ireland and the Commonwealth for the book to be published by Heinemann in association with Brandon, an agreement the details of which I concluded with Heinemann on 4 November in London.

At the same time in London I also attended, with writer Albyn Leah Hall, an auction in support of *Index on Censorship*, an auction to which I had donated some of my books and papers in relation to Joan Miller's *One Girl's War*.

Meanwhile, journalists had been busy inventing stories. On 23 November London's *Evening Standard* ran a "Londoner's Diary" piece headlined "Adams Poised to Sign British Publishing Deal", alleging that "Random Century has made a tentative offer to Adams to publish his autobiography. . . the British deal is believed to be worth between £50,000 and £100,00."

There was no truth in the story, Random Century having made no offer, having had no discussions with me, with Gerry, or with anyone representing him, and the figures being an invention. Gail Rebuck of Random Century immediately rang the *Evening Standard*, and at least they published a retraction the following day, but this did not stop *The Sunday Times* running with a story which announced in a front-page article that Gerry Adams was to be paid £100,000 in a British publishing deal for his autobiography.

This was then copied by an agency and turned up in numerous papers in Britain, Ireland and, quite likely, further afield. Neither the agency nor any of the newspapers checked the story with us. I contacted one of the newspapers, the *Cork Examiner*, writing to their news editor a stinging attack on their readiness to publish an invented story without checking, and I demanded a retraction. Far from apologising for getting it wrong, the *Examiner* claimed that they had discharged their journalistic responsibilities by ringing my office at 9pm – when it was, of course, closed – expressed outrage that I should suggest that their standards were questionable and refused to print a retraction. Thereafter newspapers the length and breadth of Britain and Ireland endlessly repeated the invented figures.

In general, newspapers were inclined to regard Gerry Adams as a figure whom they had a duty to denigrate, and they were rarely interested in extending to their coverage of him the standards of professionalism which most of them regarded as important when approaching many other stories. What I found most insidious, however, was not the brash inventions but the cultivated ignorance adopted by the "qualities". To be informed about republican figures in any depth was regarded in media circles as suspect in itself. The "correct" journalistic position was, it seemed, to refuse to progress beyond sweeping dismissal and puerile abuse. Political correspondents wrote ponderous analysis pieces about republicanism and Gerry Adams, referring to his alleged IRA involvement and outmanoeuvring of the republican old guard of Ó Bradaigh and O'Connell, but ignoring entirely his body of published writings. Alone amongst serving political leaders of the 1980s and 1990s in Ireland, Gerry Adams had committed his beliefs to paper in book form, and *The Politics of Irish Freedom* and *Free Ireland: Towards a Lasting Peace* had sold very well despite the refusal of some booksellers to stock them. Yet almost all the political correspondents and columnists refused to engage with his writings, or even to refer to them. Instead they insisted on maintaining the propaganda line that republicans were brainless thugs and gangsters to whom political ideas were a foreign language, an image which did not sit well with the publication of thoughtful books. Rare exceptions such as Mary Holland found themselves castigated, often in gross terms, as crypto-Provos or fellow travellers. Ignorance was a badge of honour where most political journalism about republicanism was concerned, and in the circumstances I felt quite proud of the job we had done in succeeding in selling as many copies as we had. Many people attacked me to my face, many more behind my back, claiming that I was giving credibility to "criminals" and "mindless murderers" by publishing Gerry Adams.

Now, however, as the peace process developed, I observed with wry amusement how so many people suddenly wanted to know him. Mediating some of the media access to him, I was approached by many people who were suddenly eager to talk to him after years of contemptuously dismissing and condemning him. As for Gerry himself, he was happy to meet these people who would not have touched him with a bargepole before because he understood that he was engaged in a process of seeking to win wider acceptance of republican politics. Never a man of rigid, puritan character, he understood that things worked in contradictory ways. He has never liked the idea of himself as a leader, but it was something he would live with and use if it could deliver results. In addition, he approached new experiences, including mixing in new milieux, with curiosity and genuine interest. Nevertheless, he remained always more at home with the kind of people amongst whom he had grown up in West Belfast, and wherever he went he carried in his head a bullshit detector tuned to the integrity of his own native turf.

On 3 January 1996 I picked up Gerry from Kerry airport at 11.00pm and drove him to my home, where we immediately set about work on completing the book. I was under fierce pressure from our international publishing partners, who had expected the manuscript in September. But also I was at the end of my tether personally, having expected to be able to devote myself to other work from September on, and I was seriously concerned about the consequences if I could not finish this book off in short order.

For five days we worked intensively from early morning until late at night. I cooked meals and he washed up the dishes and made cups of tea. Only Colette, his wife, knew where he was, and we were undisturbed by phone calls. My colleagues in Brandon knew that he was in Dingle but were sworn to secrecy, and a few local people became aware of his presence when he took a walk for about forty-five minutes every day. People greeted him in a friendly way which was not at all intrusive, many of them warmly wishing him well. On the Saturday we went for a couple of drinks in a pub, on the Sunday he went to mass in the morning, and in the evening we met a couple of people for a drink in another pub. He enjoyed the opportunity for those quiet drinks, appreciating the fact that people were discreetly friendly towards him, but then it was straight back to work, knowing that this was the only chance we had to polish off the book, his schedule in the weeks and months ahead being simply too full. By Sunday the media had picked up on his presence in Dingle, but as he was to leave on Monday I was not concerned. Having driven him to the airport I returned home to begin the process of drawing together all the new and revised material.

During the rest of the month Gerry and I exchanged notes and drafts, and I met him again in Dublin at the Forum for Peace and Reconciliation in Dublin Castle. On the last day of January he was due to fly out of Dublin for an exceptionally difficult visit to Washington. The peace process was foundering. Major's government had stymied any movement on the political track of the process, and it was an open secret that some form of resumed action by the IRA was imminent unless sudden progress were made. The night before Gerry left he and I ran over final changes to the manuscript in a long session on the phone, and he told me, his voice creaking with exhaustion, that he would rather be going anywhere else, doing anything else than having to be making this very difficult trip. Although he and I agreed at the end of our conversation that we had now concluded our work together on the manuscript, I got another call from him early the next morning as he drove from Belfast to Dublin airport. He wanted to check a couple of points about the foreword and epilogue.

"Gerry," I said, "I am going to have to invoke Section 32. You are hereby banned from phoning me any more. Don't worry; the book is under control and it's fine. So goodbye and good luck in the States!"

At the airport as he left he told journalists: "I'm going to get international support for the peace process." Soon, I thought, he'd need international support to tie his shoelaces.

He took a set of proofs with him and worked on them during the flight. From the Phoenix Park Hotel in Washington the next day he faxed me with fourteen pages of changes. Now it remained only to subject the manuscript to legal consideration. At last able to send a final draft to our international publishing partners, I sought candid opinions from a number of readers and was mightily relieved at their positive responses. There followed for me a process over the next months of responding to long lists of questions from editors and translators of foreign editions, providing them with notes, glossaries and historical introductions.

On his return from the US, Gerry and I discussed the state of the peace process. He had been warning that the British government's stalling would cause the peace process to go into reverse. Yet the only response from politicians in Ireland and Britain had been to accuse him of issuing threats. Now seventeen months had passed since the IRA's cessation, and the British government had not even named a day for the opening of talks. It was inevitable that things would fall apart. Yet the RUC chief constable announced that intelligence reports indicated that there was no threat of a renewed IRA campaign. Media commentators and many politicians said that the peace process was now well established, was, indeed "safe". I found their complacency so evidently misplaced that I wondered whether part at least of it derived from a deliberate strategy on the part of the British and Irish governments.

For my own part I was amazed that the IRA had held off so long from resuming its campaign. I had felt that it might well place a dramatic punctuation mark on the anniversary of the ceasefire, after a year of British refusal to move towards talks. By November I was sure that a resumption of their armed campaign was imminent, but it was widely speculated that, while they had planned to return to armed struggle in November they had been persuaded by Clinton's visit to hold off. Gerry gave me no privileged information, but we discussed issues in a general sense, and through knowing him over the years I was fairly well attuned to his moods. I felt that despite his phenomenal determination and stamina an element of resignation had entered into his feelings: he had come up against the limits of his ability to secure a continuation of the ceasefire; the British had succeeded in frustrating the momentum of the peace process and, inevitably, that momentum was now doubling back on itself. He seemed to me to be braced for the explosion, not knowing quite when and how it would come but knowing nonetheless that it was inevitable.

In February the explosion came as the IRA finally ended its ceasefire, bombing Canary Wharf in London, killing two people and injuring more. The politicians who had blocked progress towards peace talks affected surprise.

Only in the aftermath of the bombing was a date announced for the opening of talks. Sadly it had taken this tragedy to get the governments to move, and sadly it had also illustrated the political lesson that months of peaceful political work could not move them as effectively as a dramatic act of violence. But obstacles to dialogue were kept in place by the British and Irish governments: a date was set at last for the opening of talks, but before these would be held all parties to them would have to go through a bizarre election of a kind never before witnessed.

Sinn Féin contested the elections and garnered a larger vote (15.47 per cent) than any commentators had anticipated, increasing its vote in every constituency. John Major had declared that the elections would provide a "clear, direct and automatic" entry to the all-party talks to all who received a mandate. Yet when the talks finally opened on 10 June, Gerry Adams and Sinn Féin were locked out by the British government.

In London there were understandable jitters in Heinemann and their parent company Reed Books. Everyone had hoped that the book would be published in circumstances of peace or, at least, of ceasefire, and it was understandable that some argued that publication should be delayed in hopes of a renewed cessation. At a somewhat fraught meeting in the Reed offices in Michelin House in March, I argued strongly for sticking by our planned publication date of the end of September. I had no reason to believe that the chances of a renewed ceasefire would be any better if we waited a few months, and I feared that if publication was once postponed it might be abandoned altogether. Also, I was convinced that despite the resumption of hostilities by the IRA the mellowing towards Gerry Adams had not been reversed, and we could still get good sales for the book. What I didn't say, but what I felt most strongly and with a rising sense of panic, was that I might crack up if the prospect of publication was spun out. I desperately needed to be able to see the finishing line of this particular race.

On the day following the meeting it was agreed that publication would, after all, go ahead in September. Heinemann editor Tom Weldon and publisher Sandy Grant had succeeded in holding things steady, and on 1 April Brandon and Heinemann both issued press releases announcing Heinemann's involvement.

In the midst of many agitations I edited in the spring and summer a study of the theological foundation of Ian Paisley's virulently anti-Catholic politics by Methodist minister Dennis Cooke, often moving between meetings with Gerry in the Falls and meetings with Dennis in the leafy surrounds of the theological college off the Malone Road. Later, in the wake of the Orange Order's siege of Drumcree, I was also working at a time of great tension in Belfast with Vivienne Draper on *The Straight Furrow*, her memoir of life as a daughter of a Church of Ireland clergyman.

On 20 September dawn was breaking as I boarded a train for Dublin, where Gerry was due to appear for a second time on *The Late Late Show*. I was satisfied that on this occasion Gay Byrne would take a different approach, and I was confident in Gerry's ability to come across well enough to boost sales of *Before the Dawn*, which was already on its way to number one in the bestseller lists. I met Gerry, Richard McAuley and Eamonn McCaughley for a quiet meal in the Montrose Hotel before the show. All too often Gerry grabbed hurried snacks of sandwiches or burgers and chips, and I wanted to give him the opportunity of a relaxed and leisurely meal for a change. Over coffee we discussed the show, anticipating some of the problems which might arise. Gerry was, as so often, very tired after a very full schedule of meetings during the day, including a lengthy and, I gathered, difficult Ard Chomhairle meeting, and I realised, regretfully, that in his tired state he would be unlikely to open up on the more personal aspects of the book but would retreat to the safer ground of politics. Nevertheless, I was sure that he would give a good account of himself.

As it turned out, a lot of the show was given over to questions from the floor and, true to form, Gerry established an excellent rapport with the studio audience. On the show with him, sitting to the side, were Christy Moore and Mike Murphy, who were a study in contrasts, Mike waffling a good bit while Christy was brief and to the point, expressing his admiration of Gerry and his distaste for Gay's treatment of him back in October 1994.

It was an easy enough ride for Gerry, though a woman in the audience complained that he wasn't answering her question regarding the source of his income. The gulf between his and her world was apparent in her demand to know how he paid his mortgage, for in her world everyone had a mortgage. Gerry, however, did not, though he hoped that income from the book might enable him at last to acquire one. He lingered for a while in hospitality afterwards, the atmosphere pleasant and relaxed, and then some time after midnight he and Richard and Eamonn headed back for Belfast and home.

Three days later I travelled to Belfast, arriving in Andersonstown on the night before the official publication date. With Gerry I talked over our schedule for the next few days in Belfast, Dublin and London. Sitting in the study room where we had spent many hours closeted working on the book, Gerry told me that he would not be able to take much pleasure in the book launch. A young IRA member, Dermot O'Neill, had been killed

in London by a special police unit. He had considered cancelling
the press conferences and launches but felt that they should after
all go ahead.

In the morning I didn't need to accompany Gerry during his
series of interviews about the book with northern radio programmes, so I left the home of the friends I was staying with in
Andersonstown early and took advantage of a beautiful morning
to stroll at my ease down to the Falls Road, past the Falls Park
where six weeks earlier I had enjoyed the opening of the West
Belfast Festival, and down to the Conway Mill, arriving in plenty
of time to have a cup of coffee and a chat before setting up the hall
for an 11.00 o'clock press conference. A number of leading republicans whom I knew started to arrive at about a quarter to, and it
was apparent early on that we would have a good media presence.
The book had already sold out at the nearby Art Shop and only
at the last minute did additional supplies arrive, to be quickly
snapped up.

I introduced Gerry, remarking upon how it took a certain arrogance for me to come from West Kerry to the heart of West Belfast
to introduce Gerry to an audience made up principally of Belfast
people. I expressed my appreciation of Gerry's accomplishments
as a writer and acknowledged the importance of Heinemann's role
in the book's publication. Gerry spoke briefly in a subdued tone,
pointing out that although the publication of the book should be
a happy occasion for him he felt, in the circumstances of the death
of Dermot O'Neill, no sense of celebration.

Our schedule was tight and I chivvied Gerry and Eamonn to
ensure that we left on time for Dublin, where we were due to
arrive in time for him to start a series of interviews with southern
radio programmes at 3.00, and I was congratulating myself in getting everyone moving when, with a sense of foreboding, I realised
that we were in two cars which were due to meet up in Dundalk.
Normally I could be sure of finding myself in Gerry's car, and I
had taken it for granted that this would be the case now, but suddenly I was in another car and Gerry had taken a detour in his

own. It was Colette's birthday and nothing was going to stop him doing something for her, even if it was the publication date of his biggest book. He had earlier looked for a postponement of the launch date to avoid a clash with her birthday, but I had insisted that the plans were in place and should not be disrupted, so no doubt he felt no compunction about stealing a march on me to go shopping with her en route to Dublin. And so it was that Richard McAuley, our driver and I found ourselves stuck in a pub in Dundalk waiting for Gerry as the minutes ticked by past our deadline.

When he arrived with Colette, having completed her birthday purchase, he was clutching in his arms a small cardboard box containing a black and white puppy, offspring of one of his dogs, which now sat at his feet for the ride to Dublin, where it was to be handed over to some friends of his.

Arriving at the Sinn Féin office in Parnell Square thirty minutes later, I whisked him into an upstairs office where Linda Kenny was champing at the bit to get him started on a series of interviews with local radio stations. She had succeeded in organising a magnificent publicity schedule, quite the biggest campaign I had ever witnessed, and these local radio interviews were a small but important part of the campaign. It seemed like only yesterday that the high court had ruled that for his voice to be heard on radio would undermine the stability of the state.

Interviews successfully completed, we walked from Parnell Square to the Gresham Hotel for the official book launch in a crowded room where photographers, camera crews and journalists quickly pressed in on us. Only the briefest of greetings was possible with our co-hosts of the occasion, Tom Weldon and James Holland of Heinemann, as I manoeuvred Gerry and Tom over to the table and chairs set up in front of the display stand. I introduced them both and then Gerry delivered the principal contribution as I struggled to hold back an over-eager journalist who had come around the side of the table and was leaning heavily into me and across me towards Gerry with his tape recorder. The formal pressure of speeches and questions over, a slightly more relaxed period ensued during which Gerry was able to mingle with guests, who included Niall O'Dowd of the *Irish Voice* in New York, author Ulick O'Connor and veteran republican Joe Cahill.

I was soon urging our party of Gerry, Richard and Eamonn to prepare to leave, and by 7.30 I was checking the four of us in at the Aer Lingus desk at Dublin airport for our flight to Heathrow. Sitting in the departures area, we discussed the situation regarding our press conference scheduled for London the next morning.

It had been planned that, as on other occasions, we would hold it in the Jubilee Room of the House of Commons, which had been booked for the purpose by Jeremy Corbyn. However, there had been some problems of co-ordination between Belfast and London and details had gone out too early and in a wording which had posed some problems. In the past Tories had waxed indignant over our book launches and press conferences with Gerry in Westminster, but now Tony Blair was pressing vigorously for the exclusion of Gerry from the hallowed grounds of Westminster and the prevention of the least discussion between Gerry and Labour MPs Jeremy Corbyn and Tony Benn.

Sitting now in Dublin airport and contemplating the storm we were about to fly into, as I outlined how the situation had developed from my perspective, Gerry turned to me with a broad grin and exclaimed: "Well, Steve, this is another fine mess you've got me into!"

Just then a woman came over to shake his hand and wish him well, interrupting our laughter. Agreeing then to discuss the matter again later, we decided provisionally that the best course of action might be to shift not only the press conference but also the private meeting with the MPs away from the House of Commons, a position we had already prepared by announcing the day before that we would hold a press conference in the Camden Irish Centre.

On arrival at Heathrow, Gerry, Eamonn McCaughley and Richard McAuley were met by Sinn Féin people. Later, from my room in the Groucho Club, I talked with Gerry by phone: he was expecting to speak to Jeremy Corbyn later, and we just ran over the schedule for the following day; it was a taxing one and it was important that Gerry should be clear about the type of interviews he would be facing in the morning.

In Broadcasting House we grabbed polystyrene coffees at 7.00, just before Gerry started on the *Today* programme with John Humphreys. Gerry, there a few minutes ahead of me, told me that due to all the discussions over the meeting with Corbyn and Benn, he hadn't got to bed until 4.00 and had had to be up at 6.00. It had been decided in the early hours not to hold their meeting in the House of Commons, since to do so would cause unnecessary trouble.

On the way into Broadcasting House Gerry had held an impromptu press conference for waiting journalists. As we left, the media numbers had grown and we held another press conference. As Gerry went off for his meeting with Tony Benn and Jeremy Corbyn, James Holland and I grabbed a bite of breakfast and perused the newspapers, which were full of reports of the conflict within the Labour Party over our planned presence in the House of Commons. "War on Adams" read one headline.

Our Jubilee Room press conference we had rescheduled for St Stephen's Green just outside the House, where I met up again with Gerry, Richard and Eamonn in front of a substantial media presence. From there we the drove to the Camden Irish Centre, arriving at 11.30 where a crowd of over a hundred media people were waiting.

There had been a small amount of pressure on me as I had sought to mediate and co-ordinate between different elements in the situation, but I was happy at how things had worked out in terms of publicity for the book. But I could see and appreciate that serious pressure was on Gerry. He had no wish to place the two Labour MPs in a difficult situation over a matter which was clearly of little or no substantial political significance. He had been up almost all the night engaged in damage limitation, and then he had had to pitch into intensive media interviews, radio phone-ins and four press conferences, all within the space of the morning.

We had struggled through crowds to get into the Irish Centre and now we struggled again to get out, and as we sat into the car to go to our next media appointment, Gerry snapped – in a small enough way, but it was a rare departure from his normal manner, which just reflected the pressure he was under. We had allowed Maureen Orth, the noted *Vanity Fair* journalist, unprecedented access to Gerry in Belfast, Dublin and, now, London, and here as we left the Irish Centre Gerry found himself unable to wind down because she was in the car with us and putting yet another question to him, while someone else was asking him about arrangements later on in the day.

"Do you not realise," he said to us, "that I need time not to be talking to anyone for a while, just to be on my own?"

It was a mild enough reproof, and well founded. I had generally been at pains while organising busy schedules for him to include moments of quiet seclusion in which he could recharge his batteries. But he had been on the go for the last six hours, through the press conferences, an hour-long phone-in and a meeting with the two Labour MPs.

Now we were on our way to the Groucho Club and a succession of further interviews, but at least in a lull I was able to send him up to lie on the bed in my room there for half an hour and take full advantage of his recent acquisition of yoga relaxation techniques.

We spent a second day in London fulfilling further appointments with the media, including a lunch in Michelin House with members of the provincial press, including Ewan Macaskil of *The Scotsman*, Eric Roberts of the *Yorkshire Post*, Fred Hackworth of the *Manchester Evening News*, Peter Rhodes of the *Wolverhampton Express & Star*, Sarah Vincent of *PA News*, Fergus Shepherd of the *Birmingham Post* and Jim McKillop of the *Glasgow Herald*. In the evening Gerry went to Sky TV for an interview with Adam Boulton before taking a flight to Dublin.

I travelled on a different flight, leaving a hot and sweaty London and arriving to shiver in a suddenly wintry wind on Dublin airport's tarmac. I arrived at Kerry airport at 11.00, and on the midnight road from Farranfore to Dingle I stopped to contemplate the scene at Inch strand, where a full moon illuminated the landscape. Further on, two miles below the road where it veered sharply at a hairpin bend, reflected moonlight winked from the sea behind Minard Castle.

The following day Gerry did a signing session at Waterstones bookshop in Dawson Street, Dublin. Starting at 1.30, it was due to end an hour or so later, when he was expected at a meeting across town. Brandon was represented by Linda Kenny, while I was at home in Dingle working on preparations for the Frankfurt Book Fair. I received a call from Linda at about 2.00 to say that the signing session was going extremely well, with an enormous queue stretching out on to the street. She had rung the media to come down and photograph or film the exceptional queue, but no one had responded.

At 8.30 that night Gerry rang me. "I'm just leaving Waterstones," he said.

"Very funny!" I laughed. "How did it go? Where are you now? Are you back home?"

"No, I'm serious! I'm just driving away from Dawson Street this minute. I've only just left Waterstones."

People had queued for seven hours, the queue stretching up Dawson Street and around the block into Molesworth Street. Waterstones staff had tried to persuade people to leave the queue, saying that Gerry had to leave for other engagements, but they wouldn't leave. Later novelist Robert McLiam Wilson observed that he had spent a lonely time waiting in vain for punters to sign his own new book in a bookshop across the road, and that he had been depressed to see the long queues for his fellow Belfast writer. I was, of course, delighted, but it was clear that Gerry's other signing sessions would have to be rescheduled to allow enough time for the phenomenal public response. Meanwhile, it was already apparent that a reprint was needed.

Three days later, I left Dingle with Peter Malone and by 4.00

o'clock in the afternoon we were setting up our stand in the Frankfurt Book Fair. At lunchtime the following day, after a morning of appointments in the fair, I met Gerry and Richard McAuley off the plane at Frankfurt airport and with a member of the staff of his German publishers brought them to their hotel, where they had some time to settle in before Gerry's first media interview. That night he gave a talk and engaged in a question and answer session at the trade union hall, the DGB Haus, moderated by Paul Ingedaay of the *Frankfurter Algemeine Zeitung*. I brought him over to the hall, and it was clear there that he would have a full house, but before the meeting started I had to leave to go to dinner at the Villa Leonhardi with Gerhard Kurtze, the president of the Börsenverein, the German publishers' association.

On the following day I joined Gerry in the Frankfurter Hof, where he had further media interviews and participated in a low-key press conference. In the afternoon we went to the book fair, where he was interviewed on both the German publisher's stand and our own stand, and that night we had an interesting and very successful dinner in the Frankfurter Hof with senior editors of the principal German media. It transpired later that a British journalist representing a newspaper close to the thinking of the Conservative government had approached a couple of the German editors and had buttonholed them on their way in to the meal, trying to persuade them that they should not sit down to dinner with Gerry Adams and that, if they did, they should be aware that he was a consummate propagandist and they should beware of being taken in by him. These senior German media people were not, it seemed, impressed by the presumption of the British journalist.

On the following day Gerry had a couple more interviews with German media, and at lunchtime I saw him into a taxi to the airport for an afternoon flight back to Ireland.

On 7 October I returned to Ireland myself. *The Times* that day carried a first leader headed: "Adams in Frankfurt: A book to please the publishers – but at what price?" Stung by the international attention accorded to his book, they insisted that the book should not have been published, complaining that:

> There is no acknowledgement that IRA violence also compre-hends. . . the death of children or the murder of men whose fam-ilies have shared Ulster's soil for as long as Mr Adams. . . The judgement of a company prepared to publish for profit an excul-patory and evasive memoir from a man like Mr Adams must be called into question.

In the book Gerry had, in fact, acknowledged "the loss experi-enced by those who have suffered because of the armed actions of the IRA".

I replied to the leader in a letter published on 17 October.

> I have been Mr Adams' editor and publisher since 1982. In none of his seven books published to date is there any recommendation of violence, nor is there any attempt to portray violence as excit-ing, admirable or heroic. . .
>
> I have absolutely no apology to make for publishing the writ-ings of Gerry Adams. On the contrary, I believe that they can con-tribute to understanding, just as censorship worked to frustrate understanding. . .

A week later Gerry left for Paris and the publication in French of *Before the Dawn* by Flammarion. There he was looked after most assiduously by two policemen who usually protected heads of state and prime ministers before they delivered him to his onward flight to Amsterdam, where the Dutch-language edition was being published by Babylon De Geus.

In Ireland he did a very successful series of signing sessions at bookshops in Cork, Belfast, Limerick and Derry, and in Novem-ber he visited Athens to promote the Greek-language edition. A week-long promotional tour had been planned for Australia, but suddenly we heard that the Australian government might refuse him a visa. The British government made a special point of trying to prevent international audiences from hearing what Gerry

Adams had to say. They had mobilised their considerable diplomatic resources to prevent his being granted a visa to visit the United States; they had been shocked when he had been allowed in for the first time for forty-eight hours, but they had mobilised again to try to prevent subsequent US trips.

As the deadline approached for Gerry to leave on a flight I had booked out of Dublin via Amsterdam to Sydney on 7 November, the Australian government gave Sinn Féin a commitment that they would let them know what decision the cabinet had taken about the visa before announcing it to the press. On the day a decision was expected in Australia – it was night-time in Ireland – I stayed at home in order to be available to draft and send a press release in response. Finally, at about 2.30am word came through that, without getting back to Sinn Féin, the Australian government had held a press conference and announced that they were banning Gerry from entering the country to promote the book. By their timing and failure to fulfil their promise to get back to Sinn Féin, I took it that they wanted to outmanoeuvre us in the publicity stakes, but I immediately drafted a press release, went down to the office, and by 3.30 had faxed a statement to all the principal Australian, British and Irish media, which was widely carried.

As was the case with the Westminster press conference, the fact of the ban delivered media headlines, ensuring that few in Australia could be unaware of the publication of *Before the Dawn*. Meanwhile, anyone with any kind of independence of mind was able to draw their own conclusions as to why the British government were so determined to prevent the voice of republicanism being heard internationally.

Ironically, on the day before Gerry's scheduled departure to Australia, Neil Jordan's film *Michael Collins* had its Dublin premiere. Elements of the British and Irish media mounted a hysterical attack on the film, opening their assault before the film had even been completed and denouncing it roundly sight unseen.

Before the Dawn was already a substantial success, riding high in the best-sellers lists when I left Dingle for London again to promote another, very different book, Dennis Cooke's *Persecuting Zeal: A Portrait of Ian Paisley.*

On Thursday 14 November the heart of London was bathed in winter morning sunlight as I strolled down Victoria Street towards Westminster past hundreds of small black crosses protruding from the earth amidst arrays of red poppies while staff were rolling up lengths of red carpet which had covered the paths.

At the Chancellor's Gate entrance to the Houses of Parliament a camera crew manoeuvred to no evident purpose as I entered and pursued my well-trodden path to the Jubilee Room, where colleagues from Turnaround Distribution were preparing to set up the room.

At 11.00 Rev. Martin Smyth joined us and explained that numbers might be low because Northern Ireland MPs would be occupied with delegations from Gallaher's tobacco company and, contradictorily enough, the health services. Grand Master of the Orange Order, the organisation which had for so long orchestrated and maintained anti-Catholic sectarianism, Martin Smyth was courteous as I shook his hand and thanked him for agreeing to chair the press conference.

Martin Smyth opened the proceedings by welcoming the media to "the launch" and explaining his interest in the book. David Trimble, leader of the Ulster Unionist Party, came into the room and perched on the edge of a table near the door. Frontbench Labour spokesman Donald Anderson and another Labour MP penetrated further into the room. Martin Smyth introduced Dennis Cooke, who spoke for a little less than ten minutes about his book, after which he took questions from the floor. I rounded off the book launch by thanking Martin Smyth for chairing and the media and other MPs for attending. Privately I reflected upon the contrast between these unionist politicians and Gerry Adams.

US publication of *Before the Dawn* was scheduled for February, and a two-week coast-to-coast tour of the United States had been carefully planned by William Morrow, the US publishers. Given Gerry's prominence in the States and his media performances there in the past, we were confident that his promotional presence would shift a lot of books. However, in late December I realised that we faced obstacles to pulling off the tour when Gerry and I discussed the approaching British election campaign: once it started Sinn Féin would want him to be in Ireland, and it was Gerry's feeling that the campaign would have started by mid-February, and so it would be impossible for him to go to the US. I had anticipated that this problem might arise and had given William Morrow a warning that all plans might be off, and we had discussed a fall-back position of Gerry's doing interviews with the US media from Belfast. Now Gerry told me that he would not be applying for a visa since the trip would definitely have to be cancelled and I conveyed the bad news to Morrow. In mid-January *The Sunday Times* reported that "In a significant reversal for the IRA, the Clinton administration has denied a visa to Gerry Adams." He had not, of course, applied for a visa, still less been denied one.

By January 1997 the British government seemed indifferent to the fate of its Irish province, concerned only to spin out its survival in power, for which it was dependent to a degree on the unionist parties. With the prospect of murderous mayhem breaking out during the marching season, John Major placed to one side the North report on parades and marches. As the *Guardian* remarked, "Northern Ireland's safety is being sacrificed on the altar of the British general election."

At the beginning of February Gerry and I agreed on the contents of a new and expanded edition of his *Selected Writings*, which we would publish in early June, at the same time as Mandarin would publish the paperback edition of *Before the Dawn*.

In April the *Sunday World* came up with another of the invented stories which characterised much media coverage of Gerry. "Adams Now To Be Movie Star" read the headline, with the sub-head: "SF leader may end up playing title role in his own life story". The story alleged that "Hollywood film moguls are negotiating for the rights of his book *Before the Dawn*", and even purported to quote an unnamed "Hollywood source" as saying that Gerry would be "acting himself in the movie about himself". It was rubbish. Film rights were held by Brandon, and no one was negotiating with us at all, let alone discussing casting.

On 1 May, as the British New Labour Party swept into office, Gerry won back the Westminster seat for West Belfast, defeating the outgoing MP, Joe Hendron of the SDLP, by 8,000 votes. His Sinn Féin colleague and fellow would-be peace negotiator, Martin McGuinness, unseated Willie McCrea of the DUP to become MP for Mid-Ulster. On 20 July the IRA announced "the unequivocal restoration" of the cessation of 1994.

Gerry was writing a regular column for the *Irish Voice* in New York, and the US publisher to whom we had sold US rights in several of his books, Roberts Rinehart, now commissioned a collection of the articles he had written, to be edited by Niall O'Dowd. I acquired Irish rights, and in August went to talk to him about promotional plans and to attend, as I had for many years, the West Belfast Festival, Féile an Phobail, which was celebrating its tenth anniversary. On Monday Gerry and I met in the Falls Library, where Don Mullan was addressing a packed audience about the events on Bloody Sunday in Derry. Gerry's schedule was under pressure: on Wednesday he was due to meet with Britain's Northern Ireland secretary, Mo Mowlam, for important discussions in the lead-up to Sinn Féin's scheduled entry into all-party talks on 15 September. Meanwhile, he was closely involved in the festival and committed to turning up at many of the plethora of events, which would continue for a week.

Nursing a couple of vol-au-vents, we snack-lunched as we talked in a side room, running through a series of points about the text of *An Irish Voice*, later moving on to discuss my plans for marketing and promotion.

Business concluded, I joined Gerry and Eamonn in a tour of festival events. Driving past the site of the Adams family home in Divismore Park, we arrived at the location for the barrack-to-barrack "guider" race, where Gerry was due to present a prize. Unable at first to spot any festival organisers, we were led after a while to the front garden of a house on the Springfield Road, where a battered specimen of a wooden chariot rested, surrounded by a few children, including its two proud, crash-helmeted pilots. On the walk over from the car, children clustered around Gerry, and inside the front garden banter was exchanged before Gerry presented a shield to the winners. Just then an organiser arrived to say that the presentation was supposed to be taking place on a stage set up on open ground across the road. So off we went for a second presentation ceremony, en route to which we were presented with excellent sausage-meat hot dogs. Back into the car, we moved on to Whiterock Road and a meeting with Pam Brighton, director of *Binlids*, a play opening the next day. Upstairs we viewed the local artists' group exhibition, before heading back to the car and on to St Mary's Training College and the opening of an exhibition on the Famine. Here Caitriona Ruane, festival organiser, presided, while Robert Ballagh and Declan McGonigle spoke. I was particularly fascinated to see a quilt made on a co-operative basis by women's groups, on which the Soroptomists of Bangor featured cheek-by-jowl with the Women POWs of Maghaberry Prison.

The West Belfast Festival had for ten years made a substantial contribution to the quality of life in the area, especially for young people. It had been originated, under the leading influence of Gerry Adams, with a view to providing a more peaceful focus around the anniversary of the introduction of internment than the previously habitual confrontations between stone-throwing young people and the British army. Now, on its tenth anniversary, it was reflecting an enormous growth in confidence amongst nationalist people in Belfast and was seeking, perhaps rather awkwardly, to reach across boundaries.

I published *An Irish Voice: The Quest for Peace* in October 1997. We were to launch it in the Arts Shop on the Falls Road, and as I approached the shop I saw Gerry sitting on a chair on the pavement, taking advantage of the autumnal sunshine while being interviewed by a journalist from the *Irish News*. Breaking from the interview for a moment to greet me, he told me that the interview schedule organised for earlier in the morning had gone haywire, but that things had worked out satisfactorily in the end. He had a cold but was in good form. The previous week he had met Tony Blair, and the British prime minister had been suffering from a cold. Two days later Gerry had felt the effects.

"We've been blaming Perfidious Albion for everything for years," he joked, "and I'm definitely blaming Tony Blair for this."

Inside the shop Marguerite and the others had a table set up, laden with sandwiches, biscuits, tea, coffee and orange juice. The atmosphere was relaxed, even when a British army patrol passed on the street outside. But later, as we were about to leave, happy with another successful book launch, we learned that loyalist paramilitaries had been spotted on the road outside but had been chased away by republicans who had been providing discreet security.

Now Gerry was more tied up in political work than ever, as the momentum built towards the Good Friday Agreement of 1998. He was unable to engage in much promotion for *An Irish Voice: The Quest for Peace*, and there was no question of his embarking on writing another book. He yearned, I knew, to write more fiction, but that would have to wait.

The Good Friday Agreement represented a triumph of politics over conflict. It represented a substantial reformist compromise for the once-revolutionary republican movement. Yet for a year the implementation of the agreement was stalled. As the anniversary and a new deadline approached, Gerry rang me from Dublin airport. He was due to meet both Bertie Ahern and David Trimble in an attempt to get some movement towards the implementation of the agreement.

"Any chance of any development before Easter?" I asked him.

"I think perhaps it'll be either a crucifixion or a resurrection," he replied.

The political process has taken him away from writing, but if he finds himself able to turn to writing again, it seems certain that he will produce more books, and he would certainly wish to write more fiction. To date he has shown a considerable capability as a writer, but he has never yet been able to give his undivided attention to his writing, and so his full potential has probably not yet been realised.

Chapter Ten

FIGHTING THE *FATWA*

O N 14 FEBRUARY 1989 Ayatollah Khomeini of Iran pronounced a *fatwa* – a religious edict – on Salman Rushdie and his publishers:

I inform the proud Muslim people of the world that the author of *The Satanic Verses* book, which is against Islam, the Prophet and the Koran, and all involved in its publication who were aware of its content, are sentenced to death.

"Anyone who dies in the cause of ridding the world of Rushdie," he said, "will be regarded as a martyr and go directly to heaven." On the following day, an Iranian cleric of the 15 Khordad Foundation offered a US$3 million reward to any Iranian and $1 million to any foreigner who kills Salman Rushdie.

The *fatwa* followed a vigorous campaign against the novel by elements within the Islamic world, especially in India and Britain. Opinion was divided amongst Muslims. When the Indian government had banned the book four months earlier, almost every leading Indian newspaper and magazine had deplored the ban.

The controversy had become a prominent world news item even before the *fatwa*, and it had boiled over with tragic consequences on 12 February when 2,000 protesters tried to storm the US embassy in Islamabad in protest at the forthcoming publication of the book in the US, and police opened fire, killing at least five people and injuring more than 100.

I was chairing a meeting as president of CLÉ, the Irish Publishers' Association, in the Arts Club in Dublin when news came
through of the *fatwa*. I immediately drafted and proposed a resolution in opposition to the *fatwa*, and this resolution was passed
by the meeting and later issued as a press release. I circulated our
statement to other organisations and sought to stimulate others to
take up the issue.

However, as the year progressed I observed with some disappointment and concern that the issue of the *fatwa* was not really
being taken up in Ireland. My term as president of CLÉ ended in
March, so I was not really in a position to bring any organisational
weight to bear, but I did feel that the various writers' and arts
organisations were disappointingly inactive, though a joint statement by the Irish Writers' Union and the Irish Translators' Association appealed to all Irish writers and publishers to express
solidarity with the author. Booksellers and librarians should, I felt,
also have stood up to be counted, but their associations were conservative and I didn't expect them to become involved in free
expression campaigning unless given a strong lead, and Ireland
had no freedom of expression organisation or campaign in a position to give a lead.

Internationally the *fatwa* was very widely regarded as bringing
censorship to a grotesque apogee, and people who had long struggled within their own societies for freedom of expression saw it as
an issue on which it was essential that they take an energetic stand.
The International Committee for the Defence of Salman Rushdie
and His Publishers (ICDSR) was founded at a meeting in London
attended by organisations and individuals representing writers,
publishers, booksellers, journalists, trade unions and human
rights, and proved an effective campaigning group. In the US,
PEN American Center condemned "the extreme action the Ayatollah Khomeini has taken in calling for the death of a writer for
exercising his internationally recognised right to freedom of artistic expression". A hundred intellectuals from Arabic and Islamic
cultures demonstrated against the *fatwa* in the Human Rights

Square in Paris, and there were actions by writers and others in support of Salman Rushdie in many European countries.

At a political level the issue was also prominent. The foreign ministers of the EC countries simultaneously recalled their heads of mission in Teheran and issued a joint declaration condemning the threats against Salman Rushdie and his publishers. United Nations Secretary General Javier Perez de Cuellar appealed for the death threat to be lifted.

However, there were, of course, other approaches to this issue. Censorship begot more censorship, and Lebanon, Kenya, Thailand, Tanzania, Venezuela, Singapore, Indonesia and Brunei joined countries that had already banned *The Satanic Verses*. Bomb threats and actual bombings were amongst the weapons of those who enthusiastically supported the *fatwa*. Bookshops were fire-bombed from Norway to London and from Australia to California. In July 1991 the murderous fundamentalism of the *fatwa* struck home in Milan, where the Italian translator of *The Satanic Verses* was beaten and repeatedly stabbed by a man claiming to be Iranian, who demanded Salman Rushdie's address. In Tokyo the Japanese translator of *The Satanic Verses* was stabbed to death.

As the second anniversary of the *fatwa* passed, I was dismayed at the lack of protest in Ireland. Then I became aware of plans in Britain and the US to mark the thousandth day of the *fatwa*. I had no organisational resources to call upon, and CLÉ, the organisation I had most been associated with, was undergoing chaos and division. In February 1991, in an unprecedented move reflecting extreme dissatisfaction, the CLÉ President's Report was rejected and the outgoing committee was instructed to prepare for an immediate EGM, which they then failed to do. I could expect no action from that quarter, but on 11 November, the thousandth day of the *fatwa*, I wrote to Gerry Collins, the minister for foreign affairs:

> The author Salman Rushdie has now spent 1,000 days under sentence of death. This death sentence was declared by the government of Iran for the "crime" of writing a book.

There can be no doubt that *The Satanic Verses* is a controversial book and that certain passages in it have caused offence to some (but not all) Muslims. It is also a book which has been widely admired and which has won literary prizes in Britain, Germany and Italy.

During the thousand days Salman Rushdie has explicitly and publicly apologised for any offence he might have caused Muslims no less than five times. On each occasion the apology, together with the halting of the production of English-language paperback editions of *The Satanic Verses*, has been promptly rejected by the Iranian authorities.

As a writer and publisher I wish to express my unconditional solidarity with Salman Rushdie and his publishers, and to suggest that the Irish government has a positive duty to maintain strong diplomatic pressure on the Iranian government to remove the death threat against Salman Rushdie and against those associated with the publication of *The Satanic Verses* and to declare void the obscene bounty on the author's life.

I then sent a copy of this letter to a wide range of writers', artists' and arts' organisations, together with a covering letter, asking them to send a similar letter to the minister and to use any other appropriate means available to them to generate and contribute to pressure on the Iranian government to remove the death threat in relation to *The Satanic Verses*.

Unfortunately, the response was so muted, it was almost silent. Shortly afterwards I became aware that in many countries writers, publishers and people in the media and human rights organisations would be marking the third anniversary of the *fatwa* with events to draw attention and build opposition, but in Ireland it seemed there were no plans. So I wrote just as an individual to a number of writers and asked if they would agree to take part in a reading in solidarity with Salman Rushdie.

February 14, 1992, will mark the third anniversary of the sentence of death against Salman Rushdie. On February 16, 1989, as the then President of CLÉ, the Irish Book Publishers' Association, I issued a statement in support of Salman Rushdie and his publishers. Since then there seems to have been rather less solidarity with Salman Rushdie than one might have hoped. Now I wish to propose that if the death sentence is not rescinded in the meantime a day of action should be held in Ireland with the full support of a wide range of individual writers, publishers and artists, and of all relevant organisations, such as Aosdana, Irish PEN, the Irish Writers' Union, Poetry Ireland. . .

If you send a letter to the Minister, please send me a copy. If you support the holding of a day of action in February, please let me know.

In the meantime the German newspaper *die tageszeitung* launched a campaign of letters to Salman Rushdie to mark the approaching third anniversary of the pronouncement of the *fatwa* against the author. The campaign was taken up by newspapers in twenty-two other countries, including *The Irish Times.* A reasonable number of writers agreed readily enough to take part in the reading in Dublin in solidarity with Salman Rushdie, and the writers', translators' and journalists' unions expressed their support. I booked the Irish Writers' Centre in Dublin and sent out press releases. I approached RTÉ Radio with a proposal that they broadcast the reading, and when they declined I succeeded in convincing BBC Radio Ulster to record the proceedings for a special Easter Sunday programme. I travelled from Dingle to prepare and chair the event, and it went off well. Pleased that Ireland had not been one of the few European countries to allow the anniversary to pass without protest, I fed details of our reading to the International Committee in London.

The following month I met members of the International Committee in London, and they asked me to explore the possibility of Salman Rushdie's visiting Ireland. This was something which would have to be decided at cabinet level and which would involve both the Department of Foreign Affairs and the Department of

Justice, which would have to arrange and provide security. First I contacted Gerry Collins, minister for foreign affairs, who seemed well disposed in principle and who invited me to make a specific submission when we had dates and other details of a proposed visit. Shortly thereafter the International Committee and I discussed my proposal that Salman Rushdie visit Listowel Writers' Week. They thought it a good idea, so I approached the Writers' Week organisers, who were delighted at the prospect, and I approached the Department of Foreign Affairs again, where there was a new minister, David Andrews.

Meeting him in his office, I learned that he enjoyed a good and personally amiable relationship with the representative of the Iranian government in Dublin. However, he agreed that the *fatwa* was insupportable, and he would be happy to raise the matter at cabinet. I briefed him fully and he indicated that it would not be necessary for me to contact the minister for justice separately. He was able to come back to me later with the cabinet's agreement in principle that a visit could go ahead. However, meanwhile the International Committee had got back to me to tell me that the dates of Writers' Week conflicted with other plans of Salman Rushdie's. They still hoped to be able to arrange for him to come to Ireland, but at a later date.

My involvement with the International Committee led to their approaching me about the possibility of publishing a book of letters from writers in support of Rushdie. The idea arose from the initiative of *die tageszeitung*, which had commissioned writers to write public letters to Rushdie. Apparently the campaign had experienced some difficulty in placing the project with a British publisher, since much British liberal opinion was concerned that defence of freedom of expression in this instance might be regarded as anti-Islamic, anti-Muslim; this clearly included a certain security risk. My attitude was that I didn't care whether it was Muslims, Christians, Buddhists or Seventh Day Adventists who had placed a would-be sentence of death on the author; they should be opposed, whoever they were. To oppose the *fatwa* was nothing to do with opposing Islam; indeed, I was aware that there were many Muslims who were disgusted by the *fatwa*, regarding it as more blasphemous than anything Rushdie had written.

Of course, there was a security issue to be considered: clearly the net was being cast wider than Rushdie himself. Publishers and translators had been violently targetted. But I felt that in the south-west of Ireland we would not be at much risk. The greatest risk might come when I carried out publicity engagements, in London in particular; but such risk as might exist I was happy to run in the circumstances.

For myself there was another issue, of greater importance. I had little experience of the Muslim world and Muslim points of view. I wasn't sure how much honesty and integrity I would feel I possessed if I were to take a very public position in editing, publishing and promoting this book if I did so with my lack of personal experience of Islam. Muslims all over the world had demonstrated against *The Satanic Verses*, and demonstrators had been killed. Clearly the book had provoked outrage even amongst many Muslims who did not support the *fatwa*. Some Muslims had taken courageous stands against the *fatwa*. In Paris, for example, the Arab Association of Human Rights had issued a statement, signed by many writers, including Naguib Mahfouz, journalists, filmmakers, poets, actors and academics:

> No blasphemy does as much damage to Islam and to Muslims as the call for the murder of a writer. Disturbed by the latest developments in this affair and the ways they are being interpreted, we call on all those who, like us, are attached to Arab-Muslim civilization, to reject without qualification calls for murder which designate all Muslims as potential assassins; confront the hysteria in the media and elsewhere which is provoking racial confusion and prejudice against Arab and Muslim cultures and peoples; and reverse the escalation (of this situation) which is endangering understanding between peoples, and endangering the situation of immigrant communities in France and Europe.

I was relatively confident of my stance as regards the *fatwa* itself: it must be opposed, and so I had no doubt about proceeding with publication of *The Rushdie Letters*, but I resolved to visit a Muslim country and come to at least some understanding of how ordinary Muslims viewed the elements involved in the issue of the *fatwa*.

I deeply appreciate that Salman Rushdie and the *fatwa* were responsible for my learning a good deal about Islam and at least one Islamic country and forming warm relationships with a number of Muslim people. I found that *The Satanic Verses* were unequivocally condemned by everyone I met, and condemned sight unseen. No Muslim I have ever met with whom I have discussed the Rushdie affair has ever read even an extract from the book. (Nor, for that matter, had Ayatollah Khomeini, who had pronounced the *fatwa*.) As regards Salman Rushdie himself there was complete agreement that he was an exceptionally bad man who had done an evil thing. But there was no unanimity as regards the *fatwa*. Few of the people I met were sympathetic to fundamentalism; some felt that Rushdie deserved to die and it would be a good thing if he were killed; many saw the *fatwa* as an extreme response characteristic of Iran but not of most other Muslim countries.

In January 1993 Salman Rushdie visited Ireland to speak at a conference on freedom of expression entitled "Let in the Light" and organised by a group of that name. My earlier application to the minister for foreign affairs having been approved in principle, it remained for the conference organisers to tie up the details and, in particular, to liaise with the police. On his arrival he was brought to a party at a private house in Dublin attended by about thirty people, including Bono of U2 and former Taoiseach Garret FitzGerald. As Salman Rushdie and I spoke, we discovered that he remembered being taught by my father at Rugby School, and that the experience of his schooldays had not been a particularly pleasant one. That I as my father's son should be engaged in campaigning in his support was an irony I think he appreciated.

The following day he had a private meeting with the president, Mary Robinson, at Áras an Uachtaráin, and held meetings in Leinster House with political leaders, and in the evening he made a dramatic entry to the Let in the Light conference in Trinity College. The secret of Rushdie's scheduled arrival had been guarded for obvious security reasons, with the media being advised shortly before, but in Ireland such secrets can frequently circulate with exceptional speed, and there was an inescapable air of expectation. When he stepped out on to the stage an audible gasp was quickly overwhelmed by the sound of a standing ovation.

In an entertaining and quite inspiring speech, he emphasised some of the practical challenges of opposing censorship. "There is this point about freedom of speech," he said. "It has to be the thing you loathe that you tolerate, otherwise you don't believe in freedom of speech."

From the conference we brought him to *The Late Late Show*, where he received a very warm reception.

On Saturday we held a press conference to launch *The Rushdie Letters*, for security reasons revealing to the press the location – in the Abbey Theatre – only at the last moment.

Overall, his visit was a success in terms of the international campaign, while also succeeding in bringing wide popular attention to the issues of censorship placed on the agenda by the Let in the Light conference. It had dominated the front pages of the national newspapers and elicited leading articles which focussed not only on the issue of the *fatwa* but on questions of censorship in general.

Some fuss was made over the fact that the taoiseach, Albert Reynolds, did not meet Rushdie, but as far as I, and the international campaign, were concerned we were happy that in meeting the president he had been received at a higher level in Ireland than in any other country.

The Let in the Light conference was an enormous success. Originally planned for a small venue – even the back room of a pub had been mooted – it had been held in TCD's Edmund Burke Theatre, holding more than 500, and hundreds more had had to be accommodated in a nearby hall, where loudspeakers were rigged up to carry the proceedings.

The *Cork Examiner* editorial observed:

> The veils of secrecy which are thrown over the inner machinations of big companies and of the processes of government itself, are far more pervasive and penetration-proof than the average citizen realises.
>
> If it achieved nothing else, the weekend conference on "Censorship, Secrecy and Democracy" at Trinity College highlighted this reality.

In all media coverage particular attention was given to the need for a Freedom of Information Act. The editorial in *The Irish Times,* entitled "Right to Know", called attention to the timing:

> It is especially apposite that Dublin this weekend should host a successful and challenging conference on freedom of expression, secrecy and censorship just as a new Government comes to office, proclaiming openness, trust and accountability. . .
>
> Secrecy is bad and divisive; and the converse is also true. Openness is good and unifying, because it associates those in government with the people they rule. "Let in the Light" is a prescription for happier and more adult times.

To see discussion of censorship and freedom of expression take centre stage was a rare pleasure. Even more encouraging was the fact that there had been such enthusiastic attendances at the conference. As Mary Holland wrote in *The Irish Times*:

> It was clear, long before Salman Rushdie appeared from behind the curtain in the Edmund Burke lecture theatre, that something out of the ordinary was about to happen. . . The lecture theatre was packed with people sitting on the steps and standing at the back. The overflow hall was full and people had to be turned away. . . It reflected. . . a mood which has been growing since the

general election and the formation of of the new government. People are hungry for change, for accountability in public life, for a more honest way of conducting our politics.

I was delighted with the response, but I was concerned that there seemed to be no strategy for carrying forward the momentum evident at this event. Conference organiser Patrick Smyth promised that the conference was only a beginning, and that Let in the Light would become a campaigning organisation, but in truth it almost immediately reduced itself to a small group of Dublin-based journalists quietly lobbying on an occasional basis, for the most part behind the scenes. Brandon published the proceedings of the conference under the title of *Let in the Light: Censorship, Secrecy and Democracy*, but in the intervening time between the conference and the book, no direction and no leadership had been offered to those who had so enthusiastically packed the halls in Trinity. Some influence was undoubtedly exerted on the government, and a muted Freedom of Information Act was brought in, but the hunger for openness was largely dissipated in cynicism and depression at the performance of Labour in government.

In Britain the publication of *The Rushdie Letters* provided the main focus for marking the campaign of the third anniversary of the *fatwa*, and I joined Frances D'Souza, Carmel Bedford and others of Article 19 in holding a launch in the House of Commons. I had hoped that Salman Rushdie might be able to be present, but it was not possible; nevertheless we were provided with a Special Branch security detail and ushered through the members' entrance. The campaign had been finding it difficult to interest the British media in the long-running issue, and I was pleased to find that our publication of the book provided a new media angle and resulted in very substantial coverage in the features and review sections of the press.

The Sunday Times published some kind of profile of me in the context of the publication of *The Rushdie Letters*, and I received one of those curious letters that arrive with surprising frequency:

I have just read the piece about you in today's *Sunday Times*. I care little for Salman Rushdie and less for Gerry Adams. And I care nothing for the pretensions of the item above your name. One thing only caught my attention on that page – they call you a maverick. Send me ten photographs of your choice and I will write you a manuscript which will enhance both our reputations.

The word "maverick" seems to stimulate a strange response in many people. The same day I received letters from three other people, picking up on the same word in the article, each of them promising not that my reputation would be enhanced but that I would become a millionaire if I published their books!

On Friday 21 May in Dublin I attended the first day of the hearing of our high court challenge to the broadcasting ban on the advertising of Gerry Adams' *The Street and Other Stories*, and on the following day I was in Listowel to perform the launch of Michael D. Higgins' book of poetry, *A Season of Fire,* at Writers' Week. I was not present for the second day of the high court proceedings, or any of the succeeding days. On 26 May I flew out of Shannon airport to to Miami via New York. I was travelling to the American Booksellers' Association convention in Miami Beach, where I had been invited by the American Booksellers' Foundation for Free Expression to speak about the international campaign in solidarity with Salman Rushdie. I would also engage in company business at the convention.

I spent several hours in JFK waiting to make my connection to Miami, and I felt the strain of recent weeks bearing down on me. It wasn't so much the strain of taking on RTÉ and, by extension, the government on the issue of censorship, it was that I constantly found myself alone in such struggles. Sandy Denny's "Solo" was playing in my head. I resolved to see if there was anything I could do in the United States to lessen this sense of isolation and bring some support to bear on the fight for freedom of expression. The First Amendment tradition was so strong a part of American life, with a plethora of organisations devoted to upholding, defending and developing it, yet in Ireland we had no such tradition, and no organisations dedicated to working on the issues.

On arrival in Miami airport I was exhausted as I looked for a taxi to my hotel, and I sighed with resignation when one taxi driver cut in aggressively in front of the one I had been about to board. A brief row ensued in which I was the tidbit being fought over, and the aggressive newcomer won out, so I threw my gear in the back seat and followed it with my person.

"Governor Hotel," I said, "South Beach."

"Okay," my driver said. "We go."

A couple of minutes passed as I surveyed the surroundings of our route.

"You going to the booksellers' convention?"

"Yes," I replied, wearily unwilling to be drawn.

"Will Salman Rushdie be there?" came the immediate query.

I was a long way from home, the only person attending the ABA to represent and advance the cause of Salman Rushdie, and a taxi driver who had been particularly determined that he should pick me up rather than any other driver was asking me about Rushdie.

"Why do you ask?"

"I am from Iran. He is an enemy of my country."

Well at least, I thought, he is straightforward. But how had it happened that I had wound up with an Iranian taxi driver in Miami? In cutting in on the other taxi driver, had he known who I was and had he deliberately targeted me? The Iranian bounty on the life of Salman Rushdie stood at $2 million, and they had already shown that they were quite prepared to cast their net wide, having killed the Japanese translator of *The Satanic Verses* and attacked others.

I was seriously concerned as to whether I would be delivered to my hotel. I was dog-tired, but the bizarre situation had my nerves on edge, and I was well aware that I had no one to whom I could turn.

He delivered himself of a number of uncomplimentary remarks about Rushdie and about the kind of hordes of scum who could be expected to attend the book convention in support of him. I experienced no difficulty in biting my lip, and eventually we pulled up outside an art deco building. It was the Governor Hotel, and I breathed a deep sigh of relief.

I guess he never knew why he got such a large tip.

I was scheduled to speak at a meeting of the American Book-sellers' Fund for Free Expression meeting on the morning of the 29th. I spent my first day in Florida travelling with colleagues from our British distribution company, Turnaround, up the Gold Coast. In the evening I sat down to work on my speech, which I knew would have to be short and which would therefore have to be carefully crafted.

However, the United States is a country which finds it almost impossible to concentrate on matters outside its own country unless it perceives that a "vital national interest" is involved. Every US speaker at the meeting was permitted to continue speaking far beyond their allotted time, and so international matters went by the board. My presence was acknowledged and I received a sweet little round of applause, but I was left to convey the contents of my speech in a series of private meetings over the ensuing days.

At a breakfast on 1 June with Margaret Thatcher, Margaret Atwood and William Styron, I found myself seated at a press table with journalists from the USA, Canada, Australia and the UK. All were fascinated by Thatcher's performance, most concluding with some amazement that she seemed to have lost her marbles. She spoke in blatantly self-glorifying terms, offering up an image of herself as having stood alone in heroic confrontation with the evil empire of Soviet communism. Just as Churchill had stood against and defeated the Nazi threat in the Second World War, she had stood against communism and defeated it. She had, she said, at all times been decisive, active and determined. Clearly she would, in her own view, go down as one of the great world leaders.

"It was fascinating to me," she continued, "that as I did things that were very difficult, people stayed with me. I've learned so well what Winston Churchill said many, many times. 'Trust the instinct of the people.' Deep down, the instincts of a free people are still there." Explaining why she had written her forthcoming book, *The Downing Street Years,* herself, she spoke about "the feeling, the passion, the motivation, about what drove one on, what made one say yes to the impossible".

Leaving Miami Beach the next day for Key West, I noted an item in the *Miami Herald:*

> The mother of a third-grader plans to ask the Lake County School Board to ban *Little Abigail and the Beautiful Pony* from school libraries because she says the book teaches children to manipulate their parents.

Chapter Eleven

A POSITIVE PERSPECTIVE

ONE DAY EARLY in 1987 I received an unsolicited manuscript of about forty pages from a woman in the County
Cork village of Innishannon. Its untutored style could
not disguise the fact that here was a writer with a strikingly fresh
perspective. It was an account of a childhood spent growing up
happily in a secure rural setting in the 1950s and it reeked of
authenticity. I read it at a sitting, then read it again.

At just forty pages it was far short of book-length, but perhaps
the author would be able to write more in the same vein. I considered the publishing prospects of a book along these lines. They
were not ostensibly good: the subject matter, tone and perspective
were all extremely unfashionable. But it coincided with my interest in accounts of the everyday lives of "ordinary" people. While
it seemed dissimilar from Patrick McGill because its social background and source were not proletarian, it shared for me the
appeal of writing such as McGill's because, at the level of narrative rather than social history, his writing had a universal resonance. Fashion had never been my arbiter, and I felt that most
readers were unconcerned about it, but for the trade it was an
important consideration, for the media a guiding principle. When
it came to rural Ireland, the Big House seemed to be perennially
fashionable with literary editors, the rarefied lives of the elite offering an exotic appeal in many forms. Also relatively fashionable was

212

the portrayal of the brutal miseries of life in the country, especially the miseries associated with sexual repression. Here, however, was an entirely positive account of the country childhood of someone who had grown up on a farm that was neither large nor small, who knew nothing of the high society of the Big House and yet who did not seem to have suffered any suffocation under the blanket of rural Catholic conservatism. It was by definition a determinedly unfashionable account. As such it ran the risk, I knew, of attracting the scorn of literary editors and reviewers, or else of simply being ignored. Nevertheless, my instincts were screaming at me, and I was determined to act on them.

I wrote to Alice Taylor, but time passed and no reply came. I had to believe, regretfully, that she just felt unable to write more. But I rang her at her home, only to discover that the letter, although it had arrived, had been lost before she could read it. I explained my interest and we arranged to meet.

Entering the Metropole Hotel in Cork on a fine spring day, I was looking for an elderly, homely looking countrywoman, a kind of latter-day Peig Sayers. Instead I encountered a surprisingly young, bright-eyed and smartly but unfussily dressed woman who was fresh faced and without make-up. Vivacious and warm, with an infectious laugh, Alice, who was only about fifty, had her own expectations of me. She had sent her manuscript to Brandon because she assumed, given our location in Kerry, that we would be country people from a similar background to her own. I learned later that she was for a moment taken aback to find that I was "a toffee-nosed Protestant from Dublin". Later still I learned that by extraordinary coincidence it was her Taylor ancestor who had, in the early seventeenth century, conveyed to my Mac-Donogh ancestor the English Privy Council's ban on the completion of the castle in Kanturk.

Despite our mutual misapprehensions, and our ancestral conflict, we got on well. Soft-spoken, frequently smiling, and with an occasional frown of concentration, Alice told me that she had written her manuscript because she wanted to record the way of life she and others had known during her childhood in the 1940s. On reaching fifty, with her family largely reared, she was aware that her children had no notion of the life she had lived as a child, before the advent of electricity, running water and motors cars, and no great interest in knowing about it. She herself had only now become interested in her parents' generation and was beginning to regret the fact that she hadn't really paid attention to the stories of the older generation. She wanted to create for her children a record of how things had been, so that they would have it later in their lives when, like her, they might perhaps be more interested. But also she wanted to leave a record of an "ordinary" life which might be read in fifty or a hundred years. Originally she had had no intentions of seeking publication, but she had showed it to a close friend who had encouraged her to send it off. The book she had been reading at the time was *The Bodhrán Makers* by John B. Keane, which she had admired enormously, and so she sent it to Brandon. As far as she was concerned, if I hadn't liked it she would not have bothered sending it to another publisher but would simply have tucked it away under her bed.

I listened to her, charmed by her laughter and the irony and humour with which she described herself and her literary efforts. Responding to her, I focussed completely upon conveying to her a very positive message. Although I knew that any manuscript by her would need a good deal of editorial work, I had decided that my approach would be not even to refer to questions of revision and rewriting but simply to assure her that what she had written to date was valuable and fascinating, and that I wanted to see more.

"You wouldn't want to change it, would you?" she asked anxiously.

"No, no, I like it as it stands."

"Only I was talking to my friend Ursula in Innishannon – it was she encouraged me to send it to you – but I said that if you wanted to change it, I would just put it away in the attic or under the bed."

"Well, all I want is to see lots more along the same lines. I'm sure you can manage it."

We discussed the length of manuscript I wanted and she was unsure whether she could write that much. She didn't want to commit to an agreement or contract at this stage, but would see how she got on with the writing.

"If you don't hear from me again," she said as we parted, "you'll know that I just wasn't able to do it."

"You'll do it," I said. "You'll do it all right."

I had felt that what she had sent me initially possessed a resonance which had the potential to convey itself to a wide range of readers – a universal resonance, in fact. And after meeting her I could see her interviewing well on radio or television, for she had an excellent, lively and sparkling way of speaking.

Some months later her additional manuscript material arrived and I set to almost immediately to edit it, sending Alice a letter in November outlining the editorial work I was doing and enclosing a revised draft of much of the manuscript. Conscious of her concern about changes in the manuscript, I wrote: "I hope that you won't feel that I have done violence to your original – if you do, you should let me know immediately." I asked her to write some extra passages, to develop her descriptions of aspects of the life she had lived as a child.

Fortunately, she was satisfied that nothing I was proposing was a change in the sense of a departure from her intentions, and she set to with a will and rapidly provided me with the extra passages of text I had asked her for.

We found it difficult to decide upon a title, tossing back and forth various alternatives: "An Irish Country Childhood" seemed too bland and routine; Alice suggested "A Country Cradle". Eventually, although I was worried that it seemed long-winded, we settled upon *To School Through the Fields*.

In January I visited Alice for the first time at her home in Innishannon. The house was at first acquaintance quite a warren, with the kitchen at its heart, where people moved in and out and to and fro as in a railway station. Some were staff at the general store, or small supermarket, attached at one side of the house, some were neighbours calling in for a cup of tea, and one was Con, a cousin who came to visit and stayed. So casually comfortable was the atmosphere that anyone with sense would want to stay. Upstairs, numbers on the doors of rooms dated from the time when Alice had run a guesthouse here, and in one of these rooms was Mrs C, an elderly lady who had come to stay and never left. Alice's husband, Gabriel Ó Murchú, was a solid, calm presence; he ran the post office which was attached to the shop, while Micheál (24), their eldest son, was taking over the running of the shop from his mother. Alice and Gabriel's daughter Lena, aged eight, was the one real child of the family and was naturally the closest to her mother; she regarded me with curiosity but her great burgeoning interest was horses. The three other sons were Gearóid (21), Seán (18) and Diarmuid (16).

High in the house Alice had an attic room pleasantly cluttered with books, an easel and pictures, furnished with a desk, a chair and a couch, and here she worked at her writing and painting. Although she had enjoyed writing since childhood, it was at painting that she has thought she might make a mark. Her writing she did with a pencil in a copybook such as any schoolchild might use; then she passed on her copybooks to a typist. We talked over a long list of editorial questions and discussed the publishing contract, the title, and ideas for a cover design.

I was convinced of the exceptional quality of the manuscript, and I felt that it could benefit from the support of a larger publishing company, so I sent a copy to Penguin in London, proposing that we co-publish the book and promote its author together. However, they felt that it "could form *part* of a 'childhood reminiscences' book, but not a whole text in itself. It in any case does not feel strong enough."

I wanted to get a cover for the book that was just right and I engaged in long picture research without success. We had scheduled the book for publication in September, but the sudden unavailability of a book scheduled for spring meant that we decided suddenly to bring publication forward to late May. The deadline by which we needed to have a cover design was almost upon me, and by the time it had passed I still wasn't satisfied with anything we had come up with. One Sunday in early March I left the Booksellers' Association Conference in Killarney for Innishannon to visit Alice, to talk to her about our publicity plans and to show her possible illustrations for the cover. I warned her that if things went well she might find that the writing of the book was the easy part; I was going to try to get great publicity for her and the book, and I would need her to throw herself into it. There was no guarantee, of course, that I would be able to rouse any interest in the media, but I had a strong instinct that we would get some momentum going behind the book and she might suddenly find that she was taken up in a media whirl. She said she hadn't really thought about the media, but she would take it as it came, so long as I would steer her along the way. I took some publicity photographs of her seated at her desk and we chatted away, and the next day I spent in Cork visiting galleries. There I finally came across in a catalogue something that I thought was just right: a watercolour by Mildred Anne Butler. The period of the painting was decades earlier than the time Alice was writing about, but it nevertheless felt spot-on for the book. I sent a copy of the catalogue immediately out to Alice before returning to the office in Dingle, and she approved it right away.

In my role as president of CLÉ, I was shuttling back and forth in the early months of 1988 to Dublin for monthly meetings of the national committee, for a "heads of companies" meeting in January, for the AGM in February, meetings about Children's Book Week, with the Arts Council and Coras Tráchtála, the export board; and in March after the BA Conference I was in London for several days at the London Book Fair. In the meantime I was handling all our publicity, as well as being the publisher, editorial director, sales and marketing director.

I met with wholesalers to promote our forward list, and to each of the wholesale reps I presented a different extract from *To School Through the Fields*.

"This," I said, "is one to watch out for, even though there are more obviously saleable titles on the spring list. I know she's unknown, and I know there's no scandal or controversy attached to it. But just read your extract: there's something really special about this book, and if we get the publicity you may well end up selling a lot of copies."

However, I was having particular difficulty in persuading the media to take any interest in the book. Again I said that they should take a special look at it, but the response of many was to sneer, dismissing it as mere nostalgia and sentimentality, questioning why I would publish something so rural when all the interest was in urban experience. Ireland was leaving behind all traces of the kind of society *To School Through the Fields* was describing, and good riddance – it was the last thing the readers of their newspapers wanted to be reminded of.

"This," said someone from *The Irish Times* after a glance at the text, "is women's magazine stuff. Not for us." However, it was to *The Irish Times* I returned when at last I got a breakthrough on the media front.

I wrote to Brigid Ruane, a researcher on *The Late Late Show*, in March, sending her an extract from the book: "I've been boring friends silly for months now," I wrote, "with my delight at the freshness of the book; it has a very sunlit atmosphere and it makes people feel good just to read it . . . I think that she would be an absolute gem for the programme." I met Brigid in Dublin and persuaded her to read the book and go down to Innishannon to meet Alice, while I ran through with Alice the approach I wanted her to take. On 6 April Brigid audio-taped a long, long chat with Alice, was enchanted, and returned to Dublin where she played part of an edited version of their conversation to Gay. The veteran broadcaster instantly caught and appreciated the potential appeal of Alice's lively, lilting telling of stories from the book, and he said immediately that they must allocate a slot of at least half an hour to her. However, as both the time of publication and the end of the spring season of *The Late Late Show* approached, it became clear that plans for the appropriate show were too packed with items to allow for a long item with Alice. When pressed, he promised to take her in the autumn; it was very unusual for him to make such a commitment, but for our part we could not afford to wait until then, and so he passed it on to his radio programme, the *Gay Byrne Show*.

Now I was able to go back to *The Irish Times* with the suggestion that they run an extract from the book on the front page of their Saturday supplement, illustrated with Mildred Anne Butler's painting, "Threshing". Fortunately, they were stuck for a good idea for that Saturday, and frankly I think that it was the Mildred Anne Butler painting they liked best, but for whatever reasons they decided to run the extract on 28 May. Meanwhile, the *Sunday Press* decided to commission Isabel Healy to do a feature interview with Alice.

It had been difficult to decide how many copies of the book to print. As a first book by an unknown author with a story which many in the trade regarded as being merely of local Cork interest, it would struggle to generate orders and command shelf space in competition with thousands of other new books by established authors and household names. In general the print-run for a new paperback of this kind was 2,000 – 3,000 copies, but that would imply a selling price over the popular paperback £5 threshold. Since the first day when I had received the manuscript I had been saying that there was something special about it, and so I would stick with the feeling, price it down at £4.95 for the popular market and print relatively long, at 5,000 copies. The trade was unsure, but prepared to take some notice of my enthusiasm, and some of them upped their orders when I got back to them to tell them about the publicity scheduled. Pre-publication orders stood at 2,000.

The *Sunday Press* interview, "Alice's Wonderland", appeared a week earlier than anticipated.

People who are broken by the false values and sharp edges of the world should go to Alice, and she would heal them with her serenity, her stories of people, of animals and sunlight on fields. But because you can't all troop up the stairs to her Innishannon eyrie – read the book instead!

On 26 May Alice and Gabriel set out from Innishannon, arriving in Dublin at RTÉ's radio centre just in time for her interview with Gay Byrne. Despite the fact that she had never been on radio before, she took only a minute or two to warm up. Soon I was tingling all down my spine, for I knew that we were on to a winner. Gay displayed his skill as an interviewer, having the nerve and judgement to leave her talk away, giving her only the most minimal of prompting questions. But it was, of course, Alice who was the star of the show, talking with wit, humour, liveliness, in a performance that bore the stamp of pure innate ability, that was so natural that it seemed she was sitting beside the listener telling her tales. Story followed story for forty-two minutes, and all over the country people stopped what they were doing and just listened. As Tom Widger wrote in his *Sunday Tribune* radio column:

> You could tell at once that you were in for a piece of classic radio. Alice Taylor's interview with Gaybo about growing up in north Cork in the 1940s was an entirely convincing and unsentimental piece of nostalgia with a brilliant cast of eccentrics. . . It was an endearing piece of "as we were then" radio. And when the interview was over I rushed out and bought the book, *To School Through the Fields*, and you can't get a fairer comment than that.

I was in Dublin that day and the next and I called to a number of bookshops: in each one the punters were coming in a steady stream looking for just one book – *To School Through the Fields*. Within the day we had orders from the trade for the balance of 3,000 copies we held in stock. Next morning the *Cork Examiner* reported on her "overnight success". I was quoted as saying:

From the feedback we are getting it appears the book is just running out of the shops. Cork can be proud of her; she has delivered a fantastic winner.

On Saturday at a signing session in Easons of Cork the queues stretched out of the shop and along the street. Some people queued for as long as ninety minutes to get books signed. First-time authors do not usually command a following for signing sessions, but we had succeeded, on the strength of the promised publicity, in scheduling a signing session for Cork, and as the size of her success became swiftly apparent we were able through signings and further publicity to maintain and develop the momentum established by her remarkable performance on the *Gay Byrne Show*. I allocated new resources to the promotional budget; it was a principle of mine that where success arose, promotional expenditure should follow to increase the level of that success. However, in our poor financial situation it was difficult to find any funds to allocate, and I spent hours designing and manufacturing display material myself; in addition I drafted press releases with new media angles all the time, to keep the publicity coming. Working every night and weekend, I was able to up the tempo of our efforts to meet the demand. The national media, which had been reluctant at the outset, were now jaded, feeling that they did not want to touch a story which had already made an enormous impact, but I targeted intensively the regional media, who responded with immediate enthusiasm. I also organised signing sessions in bookshops nationwide, and Alice and Gabriel were soon on a regular treadmill of Saturday visits to different parts of the country. Soon she had done four signings in Cork city centre, two in Newmarket, four in Galway, two in Dublin, and one in Kilkenny; she had opened an art exhibition and a photographic exhibition in Galway, an art exhibition in Cork and an agricultural festival in Newmarket. And so, by expenditure more of time and energy than of scarce cash, we managed to keep the momentum going to a remarkable extent.

Alice played her leading role admirably and with great energy. However, my own momentum ground to a halt for a while as I fell ill.

In June I licensed the *Irish Independent* to run an extract from the book, and licensed the *Corkman* and *Ireland of the Welcomes* to run two other extracts; concluded an agreement for RTÉ to broadcast the book on "Booktime", arranging to link this with display cards in bookshop windows advertising the nightly readings and the book, and secured a double-page spread in the *RTÉ Guide* in association with the "Booktime" readings.

At the same time I was embroiled in conflict with wholesalers and retailers. Demand for the book was so intense that booksellers were issuing hourly demands, increasing their orders beyond our reprint figure of 15,000 copies. Our shipment from the printers to our distributor's warehouse had been screwed up; I spent a week yelling down the phone before the books finally arrived. As we made our deliveries, complaints came from Cork that they had received their books hours later than Dublin, complaints from Galway that their books had arrived hours later than Cork's. Abuse came from competing elements of the trade; booksellers who a few short weeks ago could not be persuaded to take more than ten copies were now screaming blue murder because we were only able to give them 100 copies. These were, of course, the problems of success. Our reprint was sold out instantly and we ordered a further print-run of 20,000 copies.

On a visit to Newmarket, the town near which she had grown up, Alice called into the small store where shopkeeper Terry Eddie had a small rack of books amongst his general stock. In two weeks he had sold 800 copies of her book.

"Alice," he said, "there's feckers coming in here buying your book who wouldn't even buy the newspaper!"

It was true: Alice had succeeded in striking a resonant chord with the "plain people" of the country, people who were not regular book buyers. Even at her first signing session, at Easons in Cork, it had been clear, looking along the lines of people in the queues, that this was not a regular book-buying audience. They were Alice's people, women and men of the land, and Alice was radiant with delight at the fact that her book was reaching them.

My mind had quickly turned to the enormous Christmas market for books. It was a long way from May to December, but if we could keep the momentum going, with the book prominently displayed right through the Christmas period, then I was convinced that we could register record-breaking sales. Once she had been interviewed on the *Gay Byrne Show* it was understood that she would not appear on *The Late Late Show*, but I now planned to get her on to the television show for a long interview in the autumn run. It would help if I had a new angle, and the best form of new angle was a new book. Two weeks after publication of *To School Through the Fields,* I originated my first draft of an idea which was to become *An Irish Country Diary* by Alice Taylor. There was no way that she could write a book-length manuscript, but what I conceived was a diary with plenty of space for people to write their own thoughts, a diary illustrated with paintings by Mildred Anne Butler, in which each month was introduced by a couple of pages of text by Alice. I talked to Alice about it, she agreed that it was a good idea, and she started writing the small pieces of text I had identified. In something of a frenzy I set about researching the pictorial content of the diary and designing the combination of text and illustrations. Once I had a dummy made up I consulted with key wholesalers, who were immediately enthusiastic, insisting that we would sell at least 50,000 copies.

In July *To School Through the Fields* was already a phenomenal best-seller, and I went back to Penguin again with a proposal, thinking that they could access a substantial potential British and Commonwealth market, but again they declined to become involved. I also had discussions about British and Commonwealth rights with Pan and other London houses, convinced that with the right approach a large publisher could achieve a sale in Britain and the Commonwealth which we would never be able to achieve. In August the fourth printing of *To School Through the Fields* arrived in the warehouse, and a few days later I handed the completed typeset text and artwork for *An Irish Country Diary* to the printer. We had scheduled it for publication in mid-October. The next Monday I discussed with Alice the idea of publishing a collection of her poetry. She had self-published a pamphlet of her poems entitled *The Way We Are*, and I proposed to combine poems from that pamphlet with poems she had written for *To School Through the Fields*, and some more she had written.

By late October, when we published *An Irish Country Diary*, we had already sold 50,000 copies of *To School Through the Fields* in just five months. All through the summer Alice had been doing signing sessions, travelling the length and breadth of the country with Gabriel, and now she started a new series with a signing of the *Diary* in Cork. Since the end of May her phone had been ringing, week-in, week-out, with people wanting to talk to her; others called in to the family shop in Innishannon, and others wrote to her. I took on the role of unofficial agent, encouraging her to pass requests for public appearances on to me in order to take some of the pressure off her.

On 21 October she appeared on *The Late Late Show* and she gave a wonderful performance, which again lasted a remarkable forty-two minutes.

In the Christmas period sales soared: by mid-November we had sold 142,000 copies. The previous best-selling Irish-published title, Noel Browne's *Against the Tide*, had sold 60,000 copies over two years. Ironically, despite the enormous success of *To School Through the Fields*, it was not reviewed. Two sentences in the books pages of the *Irish Press* constituted the entire national review coverage of the most phenomenal best-seller in the history of Irish publishing. Having been ignored by the literary editors in May, we sent out review copies again in October to 150 Irish and British literary editors. Not a line of a notice appeared. In November we published the sixth and seventh printings, totalling a further 60,000 copies, in December the eighth printing, of 15,000 copies. On six days in November Alice did signing sessions, mostly of two hours, in eleven bookshops in Cork, Galway, Sligo, Waterford, Dublin and Enniscorthy. On 11 December Alice, after coping with her fan mail and a couple of signing sessions the previous day, wrote to me: "I kept you till last just to have someone to complain to. . . Yesterday evening I felt as if the inside of my head had been picked away by crows."

My thoughts had already turned to a sequel. The *Diary* had not sold as well as people in the trade had predicted, but it had provided a valuable focus for further publicity, stimulating sales of *To School Through the Fields*. What her readers would really want was a continuation of the story told in *To School Through the Fields*. Alice, I knew, would not wish to be rushed. As she expressed it in a letter, "My slow meandering mind was never meant to be channelling into a fast flow." She wrote for the pleasure of it, and I felt that if the act of writing became a chore for her she would lose the pleasure and the writing itself would suffer. She had set out to record the ways of life of her childhood, and she had done it. I sat down to discuss with her how she might carry the story forward, not at all sure that she would want to write anything more.

I worked on editing the book of poems over Christmas, and at the start of January wrote to Alice with a proposed selection and some notes on how she might "tighten up" some of the poems. A week later I received a tart reply, a poem protesting at my editorial demands. "Sometimes, Steve MacDonogh," she wrote, "I do not like you, so I shall call this poem 'Ode to a Verbal Butcher'. You can rename it 'Protestations of a Lazy Cow'."

We considered a number of titles for the collection – "Walk the Fields", "Back to Simplicity", "My Own Place" and "Close to the Earth" – and opted for the last of these. "I think that it's the right one," she wrote to me, "because it has a broader interpretation than the others, and has a softer sound." I sent her drawings by Brian Lalor, whom I was thinking of commissioning to provide pen-and-ink drawings to complement her poems, and I visited her in February, and we went through the collection poem by poem.

I sent her a draft cover rough, using one of the photographs I had taken on my first visit to Innishannon which had been used in the promotion of *To School Through the Fields*, only to discover that she disliked these photos, particularly because of her hairstyle in them – "my loaf of bread look", she called it. I hastily commissioned a new designer and secured another photograph of her. *Close to the Earth*, her book of poems, was published in May and sold well for a book of poetry. By the following month the Department of Education was using a passage from *To School Through the Fields* in an English examination.

Having failed to interest any British publisher in becoming involved in publishing *To School Through the Fields*, I launched a concerted approach to the media in Britain to support the marketing of our own edition there, and a year after its first publication the *Mail on Sunday* published an excellent illustrated profile of Alice by Stan Gebler Davis. "In Ireland," he wrote, "where scribblers are ten a penny, she has become the most universally loved author in memory."

Quench the Lamp, her second book of memoirs, was coming along in manuscript, and I visited Alice to discuss it on my way back from promoting another book in London. Leaving Brixton at 8.30 on a Sunday morning, I arrived in Innishannon dressed for the city, my feet sore from London's streets, but Alice was not in a merciful mood, for this was the day of the annual charity walk in Innishannon, and Alice was its sergeant-major. As we set out along the village's main street, Alice told me the stories of houses as we passed them. I had the sudden sensation of having jumped into the book I had been reading all morning on the tube, in the airport and on the plane, except that Garrison Keillor had become Alice Taylor and Lake Woebegon was Innishannon. At a rendezvous point at the side of the road, we chatted with some of the neighbours and Alice collected money, totted it up, compared the figures with the previous year's, and finally set her troops on their way.

For several miles we walked through the woods, along country roads and beside the river populated with swans, returning eventually to the Murphy/Taylor residence. Here, with the assistance of numerous cups of tea, we resumed the editorial session we had started on the previous Wednesday night when I had been on my way to London and had made my rash promise to go on the walk.

Alice's room at the top of the house is a refuge from the bustle and business below; it also recalls the childhood circumstances in which she began to write. As we talked over editorial issues, I was reminded of a passage in this manuscript:

> I was denied the luxury of a bedroom of my own because demand exceeded availability. . . but nobody else bothered with the black loft and so it became my private domain. In the summer it was very hot and in the winter it was freezing, and because the window did not shut properly the weather outside sometimes found its way in. High winds sprayed raindrops in and blizzards whirled snowflakes through to fall like thistledown on the bare, dusty floor. The conditions, however, did not deter me, and it was here on a woodworm-eaten and wobbly table with one short leg that I wrote my first story.

Now as an adult she brought her memories of childhood alive with the unchanged medium of pencil and copybook. But, of course, between her pencil on paper and the printed page comes editorial intervention, in which a different sensibility with different demands invades the quiet world at the top of the house. Alice did not relish invasion any more than the rest of us, and so our editorial process was not without its occasional fireworks. Our work on this occasion passed peacefully enough, and we got through it in a couple of hours; I reached home in Dingle just before midnight. A few days later I polished up some further editorial notes and sent them to Alice, only to receive by return of post a letter enclosing what she described as "a few stray murderous thoughts" in a poem entitled "MacDonogh Massacre".

Quench the Lamp was actually, I felt, a better book than *To School Through the Fields*. Her writing had matured, and the thematic coherence of the book around the changes associated with the coming of electricity, piped water and mechanisation of farming gave it a satisfying shape and an interesting balance between affection for ways that were passing and the advantages of modernisation. We published on 27 April 1990, and by 1 May we had sold out two printings and had placed an order for a third printing. On Monday, 30 April, Alice did signing sessions in Mallow, Charleville and Newmarket, signing 900 copies of the book, and over the following four weeks she toured sixteen towns and cities up and down the country, from Belfast to Kinsale. A successful British promotion followed, including a live interview on "Woman's Hour". I accompanied her on her tour of signing sessions, media appointments and readings in London, Liverpool and Manchester.

In March St Martin's Press had published an American edition of *To School Through the Fields*. I had experienced a great deal of difficulty in selling rights initially. First, our New York agent had declined to take it on, saying that "it's just not something for the US market". Then, when I submitted it directly myself, ten publishers turned it down, including St Martin's Press. However, I was convinced that the book would work in the US, and that it would sell to much more than the Irish-American market. I had met the head of St Martin's Press, Tom McCormack, briefly some years previously, and now I wrote to him personally to express my conviction that this was something special that he should look at, despite his editor's decision to say no. Tom saw its potential, and a hardback edition was published in the US in March. Shortly afterwards I was able to send them the manuscript of *Quench the Lamp* and St Martin's Press editor Calvert D. Morgan Jr wrote in May, offering to buy the rights: "I must say I found it, if anything, even more delightful than *To School Through the Fields*."

Conscious of the lack of reviews in Ireland for *To School Through the Fields*, I adopted a special approach to promoting *Quench the Lamp*, sending literary editors and others in the media copies of the many glowing US reviews of *To School Through the Fields*. But I also placed great emphasis on the regional media, since it was

228

clear that they were more open than Dublin's "national" newspapers, which were for the most part national only in terms of their distribution; in consciousness they were provincially anti-rural and anti-Irish. For the first time a perceptive review appeared in a "national" newspaper, Ita Daly writing that Alice Taylor

> . . . has a writer's eye and instinct and the world of her girlhood, which is evoked in this book, is fully realised, palpable . . . The world that she is writing about has all but disappeared, and I think that we are all in Ms Taylor's debt for having chronicled it for us with such simplicity and grace. If she has not chosen to dwell on the dark side, this does not make her vision any less true than those who have.

She also went on to suggest that Alice Taylor would never be fashionable. With perfect timing, the next day's *Sunday Tribune* featured a review by its fashion editor. This, to my considerable amusement, complained that this book (set in the fifties) failed to reflect the harsh reality of rural life represented by Anne Lovett (whose tragic death occurred in a midlands town in the eighties). I was reminded of the Soviet critic who complained that Joyce's *Ulysses* failed to mention the 1916 Rising.

In early June we arranged an author tour for her in England, and in late June she represented Ireland at Glasgow's European Cultural City Year. The schedule of signings in Ireland, which had begun on publication, continued after a short break on her return from Glasgow, and in the autumn interest in Alice and the book was strong enough to warrant a further extensive series of signing sessions.

Sales were magnificent, and by the end of the year *Quench the Lamp* had sold about three times as many copies as any other book in Ireland during the year. Nevertheless, the determination of literary circles to be out of touch with her writing continued: in April of the following the year a sneering review announced in *Books Ireland* that it "*will* no doubt sell very well indeed".

In a training lecture for CLÉ in 1987 I had warned of the dangers to a small company of having a big best-seller. *To School*

Through the Fields had been the best-seller of all time in Ireland in 1988, and now in 1990 we had another massive best-seller. I had collapsed in the midst of the most frantic period in 1988 – fortunately for only a brief period – but here we were now having to respond to an enormous level of enquiries and correspondence, and I was again making the mistake of believing I could take most of the load on my own shoulders. Week after week requests were coming in for licenses to broadcast and quote extracts: teachers' audio tapes, "Reading Aloud" on BBC Radio, "Booktime" on RTÉ, "Morning Service" on Radio Ulster. . . We were also beginning to receive large numbers of manuscripts which sought to emulate Alice Taylor's achievements.

Publishing inevitably attracts cranks on occasion, and people who are just a little odd; our publishing of Alice gave rise to a particular kind of letter, in which people insisted that they had written manuscripts just like *To School Through the Fields*, "only much better"; they then proceeded to abuse Alice while proclaiming their own genius. These manuscripts almost invariably used the word "remember" and its synonyms at least three times in the first page. Polite rejection sometimes brought furious responses. "Seems you have a Mr MacDonogh," wrote one charming lady, "who can't recognise a futiristic [*sic*] classic." Her book, she insisted,

> is a brilliant work, extremely well written. It leaves Alice Taylor miles behind . . . My work is beautiful, unlike the soulless wonders that get into print these days. It's out of order for such an ignorant man, MacDonogh, to make such negative remarks, he doesn't know what he's talking about, as he hasn't even read or understood anything about such a great work, it's beyond him. It's most unfortunate for the publishing line to have someone so unsuitable like that in the business. . . Like the proverb says, 'Cast not pearl before swine.'

Hostility towards a publisher is entirely understandable, because so much of a person's heart, soul and/or ego may have been invested in the writing of a manuscript, no matter how bad, and the experience of rejection can cause a searing pain.

Hostility towards Alice was also to some extent understandable, the resentment of success, or begrudgery, being an acknowledged Irish characteristic, which I had also found to be enthusiastically embraced in many other countries. But I was surprised by how frequently and spontaneously it emerged in all kinds of people who, as far as I could see, had no reason to resent her or be jealous of her.

"You're Steve MacDonogh," someone would say as I was trying to have a quiet coffee or a convivial pint of Guinness. "God, how I hate that woman, Alice Taylor!"

It was uncanny. Someone would approach me, ostensibly to talk about Gabriel García Marquez or Philip Larkin, and within minutes it would become clear that what they really wanted to tell me was how much they hated Alice Taylor. The most frequent and ferocious expressions of this hostility came, unmistakably, from people who could generally be described as belonging to the liberal intelligentsia.

"Oh god!" they exclaimed, "how I hate that woman!"

But what was there to hate? What was the problem these people were suffering from? Had they nothing to do with their lives, nothing to occupy them more positively?

What soon became clear was that those who threw such strangely fierce resentments at me had one thing in common: they had never read a word she had written, and they had never met her. The hostility was directed not at any aspect of the real person of Alice Taylor but at a notion, an image of down-home, rural wholesomeness which had proved for so many people born in the forties and fifties to be not only illusory but far from healthy.

In the late summer after the publication of *To School Through the Fields,* I met a prominent Irish literary figure to discuss our autumn list. Without my even mentioning the book, he offered the remark: "*Of course* I haven't read *To School Through the Fields,* but I believe it's dreadfully badly written." It was not that his words were exceptional; on the contrary, many others in similar positions adopted similar postures.

Alice Taylor's sin was not that she had written about rural Ireland, but that she had written positively about it. She had also written in a way that was accessible to readers who could not at all be said to belong to a bookish elite. Her writing was far from bad, but there were those who perhaps assumed that bad writing was the hallmark of popular success. There were those, too, who wished books to be the preserve of a narrow intellectual class; the descent of the mountainy men and women from the hills to buy copies of Alice's book was for them not a cause of celebration: rather, it sent a frisson of horror through their sensibilities.

There was something more at play in the hostility towards Alice Taylor's memoirs, something that related perhaps to the prejudice in respect of Joanne Hayes, something that related certainly to the reluctance of literary editors to review or even to recognise the existence of Irish-published books. When in May 1988 we published *To School Through the Fields*, it very quickly became the biggest-selling book ever published in Ireland. Yet it was not reviewed by a single national newspaper in Ireland. Three years later it was published in hardback in London after I had done a deal with Century, designed to exploit the potential for a larger, London-based publisher to achieve greater British and Commonwealth sales than we could. Shortly after Century's publication of their edition, I received a phone call from the office of the *Irish Times*/Aer Lingus Literary Award, informing me that *To School Through the Fields* had been nominated for the award and asking me for a few details. But, of course, in order to have been eligible it would have had to have been first published less than a year previously. It was already the biggest-selling book ever published in Ireland, yet someone associated with the award had recognised its existence only on its publication in Britain. It was perhaps a case of the same mindset which saw Irish publishing almost completely ignored by so many literary editors in Dublin.

The Irish Times purports to be a national newspaper of record, yet if one looks at its book pages through the 1980s and 1990s one will look in vain for the record of Irish publishing in that period. Irish literature has been poorly served by all the national newspapers, particularly in their review coverage.

At the higher end of the scale of writing and book publishing stands original literature: new novels, collections of short stories, collections of poetry. And it is important for the development of literature that such material should be published in a context of critical response; that the work of the writer should evoke an intelligent response from people able to offer valuable assessments. This context is created by literary magazines, radio and television programmes and, in particular, by the book review sections of national newspapers. In the literary magazine *Cyphers* the editors wrote:

> The immediacy, the wide potential readership of book reviews makes them important to writers; being a variety of journalism they are elusive and yet highly revealing about the whole of our culture rather than just its officially literary aspects.

Some kind of response, some kind of atmosphere of discussion, appreciation, criticism and debate is important, too, as regards books which are not so elevated, books which reflect the way we live, the processes of change which society and the people in it are undergoing.

From the mid-seventies, and through the eighties, Irish book publishing developed at a phenomenal rate. Admittedly, it started from a very low base, but in no country was there as rapid a growth and development. This phenomenon involved not only high literature by any means; in fact, one of its most notable elements was its contribution to political debate and discussion, with books such as Tim Pat Coogan's *On the Blanket*, Noel Browne's *Against the Tide*, Gene Kerrigan and Derek Dunne's *Round Up the Usual Suspects*, Gerry Adams' *The Politics of Irish Freedom*. The range has been wide, from scholarly delvings into previously ignored corners of our history and folklore to popular celebrations of the lives of ordinary people; from literary criticism to children's books; from feminism to cookery books.

233

The public response as indicated by sales of these Irish-published books has been enthusiastic. When the Irish Writers' Co-operative started publishing in Dublin in 1976 the presence of an Irish-published book in the best-sellers lists was a rare event; now Irish publishers are fighting it out week-in week-out on almost equal terms with their much larger competitors from London.

But the response of the literary editors has been entirely different. In 1990 I conducted a survey of book reviews in Dublin's national newspapers. In 54 issues a total of 796 books were reviewed; of these books 702 were published in Britain and only 94 were published in Ireland, north or south. This represented 89 per cent British, 11 per cent Irish.

I also looked at the paperback best-seller lists for the same period, because I wanted to compare what the public was reading with what the literary editors were reviewing. The result showed a startling difference. British-published books accounted for 57 per cent of best-sellers, Irish-published books for 43 per cent.

So, Irish-published and British-published books were running neck-and-neck as far as the reading public were concerned, yet literary editors were choosing to under-represent to an enormous extent the books published in their own country.

I went public with my analysis of the prejudice of the literary editors, opening an article in *Books Ireland* with the straightforward statement that "Irish published books are getting a raw deal from key literary editors." I also used speeches at literary festivals and other functions to draw attention to the situation. I availed of the letters pages of newspapers and spoke in radio interviews about the issue. To my disappointment but not surprise my colleagues in other Irish publishing companies refrained from expressing their views publicly, though several of them were happy to bend my ear in private with their complaints. But it was understandable that they felt that if they raised their voices in criticism the literary editors might decide to ignore even more the books from their companies. Some felt that I was mistaken in my approach, in that encouragement rather than criticism might yield better results. Some felt that my analysis of the predilections of the literary editors was something of a hobby horse, but I was by no means alone in my analysis, or at least in parts of it.

The poet and critic Edna Longley identified in an article in the *Times Higher Education Supplement* a post-independence hang-up in the south of Ireland which she called "cultural cringe *vis-a-vis* London". And she suggested that Dublin's literary editors "remain cramped in that old cultural cringe", leading to them ignoring Irish-published books in favour of British-published books. And she pointed out that "the development of indigenous literary criticism requires that Irish books, wherever published, should be more widely and deeply discussed". Yet the neo-colonial factor ensured that it was not considered intellectually respectable to concern oneself seriously with the products of one's own society.

Author, critic and *Irish Times* columnist Fintan O'Toole, in *Cyphers*, pointed to "the failure of any of the literary pages to give priority to the reviewing of Irish books, though this is in general truer of Irish-published books than of books by Irish authors published in England". He remarked that "not being reviewed at all seems to be the most valid complaint that can be made against the literary pages and until the prejudice against Irish-published books is dropped and space is increased, that complaint is going to remain". Writer and academic Richard Kearney in the same magazine described the literary pages of the national newspapers as: "Disappointing, unless [the book] is published by UK or US publishing houses." Academic and editor Ailbhe Smith suggested that "the tendency everywhere is for non-Irish-published books to dominate".

I kept up my campaign about the newspapers' prejudice against Irish-published literature, and was gratified when the board of directors of *The Irish Times* had a discussion about the literary pages of their newspaper, to which I and another publisher contributed briefing documents. I was not privy to their conclusions, but in the months that followed there was a sudden efflorescence of reviews of Irish-published books in *The Irish Times*. It did not last.

Internationally there was a more positive response by literary editors and reviewers. Much of our fiction was now published in translation, and as we published more books by Alice we succeeded in selling more international rights: to Lamuv in Germany, Shinjuku Shobo in Japan, Pax in Poland; and large print and audio rights. Meanwhile St Martin's Press continued their successful publication of her works in the US. *Quench the Lamp* was followed by *The Village* (1992), *Country Days* (1993) and *The Night Before Christmas* (1994), which was especially successful in the US as *An Irish Country Christmas* (1995).

Initially Alice had set out to offer an account of her childhood which her children could read on reaching a time in their life when they might be curious to know. Now she had stretched her recollections over five principal books. I found *Country Days* somewhat below the standard of her previous books, and I raised with her the suggestion that she had perhaps exhausted the well she had drawn from so successfully and that she might think about writing a novel. She was a natural writer who wrote for her own enjoyment, but to make the transition to fiction she would need to transform her approach, to study and work at the craft of fiction. She agreed that she had achieved what she had intended when she started out, and then some, and she said that she would give serious thought to embarking on a novel during the winter. Meanwhile, however, I also indicated to her that I felt her greatest strength to date lay in her ability to bring childhood experience to life on the page, and I asked if she might be able to give me a book about the Christmas season as she had experienced it in her youth. The result was *The Night Before Christmas*, in which she returned to her best form in evoking, from the perspective of a young girl, the sights, sounds and smells of an Irish country Christmas in the fifties.

She struggled with the novel for two or three winters, but when it seemed that she was stalled and confused I persuaded her to let me look at the manuscript as it stood. She had written a few chapters, but what she had written was raw material, and in fact it was mostly the kind of raw material that novelists need to leave out. I was not dismayed, because I felt that she had performed a useful function in clearing her way through this quite dense material, which could, if she left it behind, form a useful unseen backdrop to a novel once she really got started on a narrative. I think she was teetering on the brink of saying to herself that she wasn't cut out to be a novelist, of admitting defeat. But she is a doughty person as well as being a more skilful writer, in my view, than most observers would credit, and I felt that she could, if she were prepared to engage in the deliberate and considerable effort necessary, learn the craft and provide a narrative which would work and would create for her a whole new writing career.

She worked intermittently at the novel, particularly over the next few winters. Then, in 1997, six years after she had first begun to address the question of novel-writing, she delivered the manuscript of *The Woman of the House*. Far longer than any of her previous books, and quite different in creating a real, imagined, fictional world, it was a considerable achievement, and I was delighted with it. I had had faith in her as a writer from the time in early 1987 I had received from her the first forty pages of *To School Through the Fields*. I had not been sure if she could make the transition to novel-writing, but I had been confident that it was well worth encouraging her in that direction. And now here was a triumphant achievement which I was sure would sell well.

Alice Taylor has succeeded in writing for a very wide audience whose interests are rarely if at all catered for by the metropolitan media. "Who," Daniel Corkery once asked, "is writing for the people who attend the GAA Munster Finals?" Who, in others words, was writing for the "plain people" of Ireland outside the Pale? Well, Alice Taylor has done so, and not only outside the Pale, for she has also written for readerships of many backgrounds from Dublin to London, from New York to Tokyo and from Göttingen to Gdansk.

Chapter Twelve

CIVIL WAR

AFTER WITHSTANDING MANY struggles with exterior forces, it was civil war that brought Brandon to its knees and almost to extinction. I had long felt that the company could not develop without major changes, and I was concerned about my long-term health prospects. Bernie Goggin, who had been my business partner since we set up the company in 1982, is in many ways a delightful person: an extremely enthusiastic environmentalist with an exhaustive knowledge of the flora and fauna of the Dingle Peninsula, he can talk endlessly with great passion about sand dune systems and the iniquities of developers whose schemes threaten special habitats. He is knowledgeable and enthusiastic, too, about geology and archaeology, and he put these enthusiasms to use by devoting time to An Taisce, attending conferences on various aspects of the environment and by guiding groups of visitors around the peninsula. However, our relationship had become very poor; we were not communicating, and I felt that we were missing too many opportunities to develop the company and make it more effective and more profitable through our shared problems of communication. He must also have been experiencing his own disappointments and reservations about how matters stood. He had capitalised the company in 1982, and it was his properties which provided the collateral for all our loans and overdraft facilities. And it was he who had lived with intense anxiety at the prospect of losing everything – his livelihood and his properties – if the company should fail.

In April 1996 I told him that I wanted to bring our partnership to an orderly end; I really didn't feel that we could carry on as we were. There were, I felt, insuperable problems in the partnership, which were adversely affecting the company, and I proposed we should discuss between ourselves the best way to arrange to go our own ways. It would, I said, surely be a relief to him to be free of the tensions that had for too long been bedevilling the partnership and the working of the company, and I hoped we could resolve matters between us to our mutual satisfaction. I was extremely reluctant to precipitate a situation in which our staff would lose their jobs, but I felt quite confident that a reasonable ending of the partnership need in no way mean the end of the company. I opened informal discussions with other publishers to explore the possibilities of their making an offer to take over the company.

The most seriously interested publishers, who were familiar with the company, suggested that the best outcome would be to retain its independence and to retain me at the helm. I was pleased with their interest, and I also had discussions about the possibility of running Brandon as an imprint within a larger company. A couple of publishers indicated that while they were not interested in acquiring Brandon, they would be willing to offer me interesting and challenging employment, if I were prepared to leave Dingle. Another company felt that I was essentially an independent, and that was what gave Brandon its character. What they proposed was that they would advance me a loan to enable me to buy my partner out and keep the company going under my sole direction. This was contingent, of course, upon the price for buying out being a reasonable one.

There were no developments over the next five months; we continued working and, although I was keen to see matters resolved, I was concerned that the company was in danger of going downhill due to the deterioration in relations with my partner. In September I received a letter from a firm of solicitors in Bandon, County Cork,

informing me that they represented Bernie Goggin and were prepared to discuss the ending of the partnership with me. I had hoped
that we could avoid the road of working through solicitors. Partly
this was because the logic of the law was adversarial, partly because
whatever value resided in the company could quite easily be eaten
up in legal expenses if the process brought us into the high court.
Clearly I had to accept that the matter would now be dealt with
through the solicitors. In another ironic twist, the solicitors were of
the same family that had bought my Sullivan grandfather's family
home in 1919.

Bernie gave me the company's books to study over Christmas:
they indicated that our trading position had deteriorated significantly since the previous April. Finally, in January, nine months
after I had first opened discussions, Bernie agreed to another
meeting between us about the dissolution of the partnership.
Clearly he had no wish to buy me out, yet the kind of figure he
wanted from me to buy him out was far in excess of what I felt
the company was worth.

I advised everyone working for Brandon that there was a serious financial crisis and announced some measures I proposed to
take to cut costs and some to secure extra income. At the end of
April Bernie provided me with management accounts, which I felt
I needed in order to speak to potential backers. They showed that
our financial position was now serious. In late May I received a
new proposal from Bernie's solicitor, but again it struck me as
being in excess of what I felt the company was worth, especially
in the light of the financial information I now had. At the same
time I received more bad news about the financial position. Over
the months the tension in the workplace had been inescapable.
My assistant editor, Peter Malone, decided to resign.

I made a new written offer to buy out my partner at the beginning of June, but we were still some distance apart, and the tension
rose towards the end of June. I had suggested that Bernie could buy
me out; I could buy him out; we could sell the company or we
could put it into liquidation. But he presented a different scenario:

that the company would cease trading without going into liquidation; all the staff would be laid off and its assets would be sold off gradually. Crucial to this proposal was that whereas in a liquidation rights would revert to authors, in the situation of simply ceasing to trade the rights would remain with the company. I opposed this proposal, feeling that if the company was no longer going to trade, then it should be put it into liquidation, allowing rights to revert to authors.

The board, consisting of the two of us as the two directors, was deadlocked. I advised everyone working for the company of the situation. I told them that I was trying to rescue the situation, but that I did not hold out a lot of hope. Although I had received and replied to many letters from Bernie's solicitors, I had declined to retain solicitors myself, but now I took legal advice. Various courses of action were, it seemed, open to me, but most options would take both time and money.

I wanted urgently to advise my authors of the situation. I was already extremely upset over the turn of events: everything that I had worked for fifteen years to build up was coming crashing down. I felt that the authors I had worked with had every right to know what was going on, but I was unable, in the legally fraught circumstances, to send a letter of explanation. However, I picked up the phone to a couple of our authors whom I regarded as particular friends.

One of these was Gerry Adams, and on the tense eve of the July 1997 confrontation at Drumcree he travelled to Tralee to speak at a Sinn Féin celebration of Martin Ferris' outstanding performance in the general election as the Sinn Féin candidate in North Kerry, and to sign copies of his books. As I brought the books to the hotel, I felt that this was probably the last occasion on which I would publicly represent the company. After sharing a meal with Martin Ferris, Richard McAuley and others, Gerry and I went off on our own for a chat in the grounds of the Earl of Desmond hotel. Gerry knew how traumatic the situation was for me, and I was extremely glad of his sympathy. He returned to the packed social occasion indoors, as I headed back home to Dingle. In the early hours of the morning he made the long journey from Tralee to Belfast, receiving by phone as he travelled the first reports of the attack on the people of the Garvaghy Road to clear the way for the Orange parade.

Unable to continue to publish at Brandon, and for the moment apparently powerless as one of the two directors, I had two principal options: to fight my corner, taking a high court action; or to withdraw, surrendering the field to my fellow director. I was distraught at the turn of events, and I realised that if I devoted my energies to a fight for possession of the company, not only might both our resources be consumed by legal fees, but my resources of energy and creativity would be consumed in a battle which was in some ways more about the past than the future. I resolved therefore to move immediately to set up a new publishing company. Although my name was synonymous with Brandon, and it was being said that Brandon was dead, I could walk away from the situation with my publishing creativity intact.

I sounded out Alice Taylor and spoke to Gerry Adams again. As far as they were concerned, they would be sorry to lose their association with the Brandon imprint, but they would be happy to continue to be published by me.

I worked at breakneck speed, consumed with the challenge of starting afresh with nothing but my own publishing instincts. At the same time, the strain of events and the sense of grief was destroying my appetite and ability to sleep. I found that the more I looked forward and the more I worked towards the future, the more I was able to approach some kind of equanimity, but then another letter would arrive from the solicitors and I would be thrust into a state of nervous agitation and exhaustion again. Nevertheless, I found that I was at my best when going forward, and I resolved that if I must lose Brandon, then so be it. What was most important was to imagine and build a viable future.

I seriously considered giving up publishing altogether. I was utterly dismayed at the situation I found myself in after devoting my energies for fifteen years to building up Brandon. I was also a writer: although my writing had been largely neglected in favour of publishing, I was nevertheless the author of six books, and editor of more; I had written newspaper and magazine articles; had made and presented a radio documentary. I had a number of writing projects at various stages of development, all of which had been placed on the back burner, owing to the constant demands of publishing, but which could all be brought forward. I reasoned that I could combine writing with some freelance editing and work as a publishing consultant, while organising my life in such a way as to keep my costs to a minimum. To a certain extent this was an enticing prospect of freedom and adventurous challenge. A number of my friends of long standing felt it was regrettable that I had let my writing play second fiddle to my publishing, and some of these now suggested that I should view the apparent collapse of Brandon not as a disaster but as an opportunity to realise the potential as a writer that I had largely suppressed.

I also found appealing the prospect of freeing myself of the role I had been playing throughout my publishing career: that of Mr Efficiency, allied with a touch of mother, father, social worker, financial adviser and psychiatrist. A large part of my function in Brandon had been to plan everyone else's work, to determine policy and to provide the working context. I had also had to be available on a more or less twenty-four hour basis to all our many authors, each of whom were naturally inclined to approach me as if they were the only author, their books the only books I was dealing with; some of them wrote frequently and at length, while others were frequently on the phone.

One of my better-known authors phoned me at 2.00am on a Sunday night to ask me would I give him the plane fare to go to the US, where he had acquired a job as guest writer in a university. On several occasions another author rang me whenever he was threatened with having his electricity cut off and whenever his wife was threatening to leave him, and in fact these two threats seemed often to coincide. It was obvious enough that he wanted me to pay his electricity bill, but I was never quite sure what he wanted me to do about his wife. I did on a few occasions meet him with his girlfriend, but for some reason I never met his wife. Another author had an uncanny ability to track me down wherever I might be. Even arriving somewhere at short notice, I might find a message from her awaiting me. Other authors have been inclined to ring me when major events occur in their lives, and on one occasion an author rang to say that it was her thirty-fifth birthday and she thought it was about time she got married; would I oblige and marry her? All of which left me feeling quite often that I had no life of my own. Indeed, looking back over the fifteen years I felt that I had allowed myself to live an underdeveloped personal life, an overcommitted working life. All the time I seemed to have a long agenda of things to do, top of which were the demands of authors and publishing, bottom of which were the demands of my own life. But it was not just a question of the amount of time and energy taken up, it was also that I had for years played a role which required that I misrepresent my own nature. Inherently I was not, I felt, the efficient, organised, dependable person I represented myself to be. I had been relatively successful in playing the role, but it was a long-held strain, and I experienced a sense of loss of the ability to be myself, and a sense almost of grief for that loss.

I thought about it deeply, and recognised that I had proved myself as a publisher of some character and ability; I had not proved myself to anything like the same extent as a writer. However much I might welcome the opportunity to explore my potential as a writer, this was a time to rely on the proven rather than to speculate on the unproven. I decided to put together a detailed set of financial projections for the establishment of a new publishing company. One aspect daunted me above others, and this was the question of financial management. I possessed neither experience nor natural aptitude in this area. I discussed my concerns with my accountant, my solicitor, with friends, and with the banks I approached. Out of all the discussions and consultations the principal conclusion was that my knowledge of all aspects of the publishing business should prove sufficient to make up for my shortcomings in terms of financial management skills. What I would have to do, I concluded, was devote a substantial proportion of my time to dealing with the financial aspects, my lack of natural aptitude meaning that I would have to make up with perspiration what I lacked in inspiration.

At first I planned to take a couple of months off to recharge depleted batteries and clear my mind and emotions. But I soon realised that – rearrange the projections as I might – I could not afford, if I were to set up a new company, with all its attendant costs, to miss out on the fast-approaching Christmas market.

It shouldn't have been possible, starting in July, but in a paradoxical and contradictory way the events around the break-up of Brandon had induced in me a feeling not only of despair but of a new appreciation of my own abilities, and a new consciousness of how other people in the business respected my judgement. I resolved to use my reputation as my principal capital. And it was on the strength of my reputation that I found that people were prepared both to pay me early and to advance me credit, and it was on my reputation that I relied crucially in approaching the banks. I decided to call the new company Mount Eagle Publications Limited, after the low mountain above Ventry in the southwest of the peninsula.

For six years I had been encouraging Alice Taylor to write a novel. She had made a false start but had showed the determination to go back and try again, and now, just as I was setting up Mount Eagle, she had completed a draft she was really happy with. I threw myself into editing what was a substantial novel. In normal circumstances I would not have dreamt of publishing it any earlier than the next spring, but the market potential for a first novel by Alice Taylor in the run-up to Christmas was considerable, and I needed to get the Eagle into the air. I had the advantage that I was receiving almost no mail, was working from home, had no employees, and thus had a less cluttered existence than I had known for many, many years.

The other project that was immediately available was *An Irish Voice* by Gerry Adams. It was being originated by Roberts Rinehart, the US publisher, and while I had some editorial input, it did not require nearly as much work from me as it would if, like his other books, I had been originating it.

There was no time to conclude Irish distribution and sales representation arrangements, such as Brandon had had with Gill & Macmillan, so I decided to market these first two books on a "wholesale exclusive" basis. I had to offer the wholesalers extra discount, in return for which their returns levels were capped, giving me a considerable degree of security, but at the same time I did not have to pay a sales representative or a distributor. I also decided to employ a different pricing policy to that we had applied in Brandon, and I priced both books relatively highly at £9.99 paperback. In the event both books performed well, Alice Taylor's *The Woman of the House* exceptionally so.

I could not afford to employ a publicist, so I did the publicity myself, and this worked well. However, as soon as news broke that I was publishing Alice Taylor and Gerry Adams, there was a strong reaction from Bernie Goggin's lawyers. A solicitor's letter demanded that I cancel publication of *The Woman of the House* immediately or face a high court action. It seemed to me, thinking of *One Girl's War*, that history was repeating itself as farce. From *One Girl's War* to *The Woman of the House*: would I have to come full circle back to the Four Courts?

Publishing contracts do not tie authors to publishing companies as commodities to be owned and exploited by the publisher. What they do is license the publisher to publish, promote and sell particular books. While some contracts include option clauses, which require the author to submit their next manuscript to the same publisher, it is not the case that publishers own authors. Both Gerry Adams and Alice Taylor were contractually free to offer their new books to any publisher they wished, and to conclude publishing agreements with no reference to Brandon. I had read reports in newspapers and journals that Bernie Goggin had announced that Brandon had ceased to trade, so clearly he was not in a position to publish any new books. I decided to ignore the solicitors' demands, and in response received a new demand – that I should convey income from sales of the books to their client.

In October and November *The Woman of the House* stood at number one in the paperback fiction best-sellers; *An Irish Voice* was also performing well. Mount Eagle was in buoyant flight. And at a board meeting of Brandon Book Publishers, attended by Bernie, me and our two solicitors, on 1 December the sad saga of our partnership was finally resolved. As a press statement I issued briefly put it:

> At a board meeting of Brandon Book Publishers Limited on 1 December 1997 the transfer of the ownership of the company to Mount Eagle Publications Limited was approved by the directors, and the retirement of Mr Bernard Goggin as a director of the company was accepted . . . The company intends to continue trading as a book publishing company.

The Brandon imprint became part of Mount Eagle Publications, and I moved back into the Brandon offices and resumed immediately the marketing and promotion of the books published by Brandon. Bernie Goggin was able to retire in his fifties in comfortable circumstances.

I set about consolidating Brandon/Mount Eagle, which a *Kerryman* journalist wittily dubbed "the Twins Peaks of Irish publishing".

I resolved to maintain a strong emphasis on fiction, and I was pleased to be able to sign up new novels by J.M. O'Neill, whose four previous novels had been published by large London-based publishers; by Lilian Roberts Finlay, previously published by Collins and Poolbeg; and by Liam Nolan, principally known as a broadcaster but also author of some five previous books. I also inherited titles which I had been working on in Brandon, such as a fine first novel by David M. Thomas and my own edited collection, *The Brandon Book of Irish Short Stories*.

On 25 March 1998, sixteen years to the day since I had arrived in Dingle from Dublin to set up Brandon, I made the return journey to relaunch the Brandon imprint at a press reception in Easons' O'Connell Street bookshop. Alice Taylor, Liam Nolan, Roddy Doyle, Dennis Cooke and Evelyn Conlon were amongst those present, and Gerry Adams, deeply immersed in political negotiations, sent me a message:

Lazarus a chara,

Well done on the relaunch of Brandon. Sorry I can't be with you. May all your publications be big ones.

In 1998, the first full year of the integrated Brandon/Mount Eagle, Brandon's backlist sales more than doubled. We were solidly back in business. Although I had been worried about my capacity and experience, or lack of it, in the financial area, I found I soon came to grips with the financial management of the company, and even quite relished the challenge.

I put new print-buying practices in place, and in general it proved possible both to extend the range of our publishing by buying print more widely and to increase profitability by working with printers to reduce costs while ensuring quality. I felt that in the past we had been inclined to under-price in pursuit of sales, with the consequence that when books did well they did not contribute enough to the bottom line. Now I priced up, as I already had with *The Woman of the House* and *An Irish Voice*, and the profitability of our publishing increased.

One problem was staffing. Of the previous staff of Brandon, two had moved on to other areas of activity, outside publishing, and Linda Kenny had set up in business as a freelance publicist. There were few experienced people available in Ireland, and fewer who would want to work in Dingle. For nine months from July 1997 I worked solo, using a mobile phone, two fax machines and two answering machines to impersonate an office and assigning some editorial and publicity work to freelancers. Then, in March 1998 I was joined by Máire Ní Dhálaigh as my secretary, a member of a well-known Blasket Islands family who had worked for many years in the Royal Irish Academy in Dublin. In the course of 1998 we published as many books as we had ever done in the past with a staff of five, but it was inevitably a strain. I had hoped to appoint a secretary earlier than March, and by March to have also appointed an experienced publishing executive with a background in print production as my administrator. After a number of interviews I had identified several people I wished to appoint as administrator; however, each proved in the final analysis unwilling to move to Dingle. Now grossly understaffed in relation to our level of production, we were hideously extended and at considerable risk of making serious and costly errors. I felt I was walking a tightrope while juggling grenades, but somehow we reached the year's end without disaster. Eventually I was at last able to appoint an administrator, and in mid-January 1999 we were joined by Siobhán Prendergast.

I looked back in wonder at the number of titles we had published in relation to our minuscule level of staffing. And I looked with relief, pride and satisfaction at the best year-end figures we had ever produced in all the years since 1982. Comparing the 1998 figures with those for 1996, I had succeeded in doubling sales while halving overheads. Beyond that, I had as vibrant and varied a forward list of projects as I had ever had in my publishing life. And I was happy in the confident belief that in the next few years I would be no stranger to controversy.

Publishing has changed a great deal since I started out as a nineteen-year-old in 1968; Irish publishing has been transformed since I took part in the Irish Writers' Co-operative; and international publishing now is barely recognisable compared to what it was when I set up Brandon in 1982. Back in 1971 the writer Jeff Nuttall wrote that I possessed "an abiding belief in the liberating power of literature". Despite all the changes in the world and in myself, I retain that belief as strongly now as ever.

EPILOGUE

A S A PUBLISHER I have rarely gone looking for trouble. It has been in the nature of certain establishments – British intelligence, Irish broadcasting, for instance – that they have visited trouble upon me (and, of course, many others) in pursuit of their denial of freedom of expression.

It is in the nature of authoritarian and paternalistic establishments, be they political, administrative or religious, to encourage and promote a context in which "Thou shalt not" is the first imperative. Both Britain and Ireland are societies in transition, and both retain authoritarian and paternalistic elements and reflexes. The censors' scissors have been blunted, and there have been advances in the acceptance of the public's right to information. Yet the Irish state retains an archaic Censorship of Publications Act, while the British state continues to insist upon extreme restrictions in the area of "Official Secrets". In Britain the people are still in many respects regarded as subjects, while in Ireland wartime emergency legislation from 1939 is kept in place. In neither Britain nor Ireland is there a deeply rooted tradition to compare with the First Amendment tradition in the United States of America.

Censorship is not a simple matter of being pro or con; it is a matter of balancing conflicting rights. Crucially it is a matter of starting point. I seek to start from a basis of the positive value of freedom of expression and information, and from the understanding that such freedom is a fundamental human right. To do so requires a reversal of the tradition inherited from the British and Irish authoritarian tradition as expressed both in government and in the two principal religious tendencies: Protestantism and Roman Catholicism.

Questions of freedom and diversity are not as simple as they are painted in the general media account. The collapse of the Soviet Union and specifically its Communist Party control is almost universally regarded in the west as simply a good thing for freedom, yet one might also consider some of the less welcome aspects of that freedom, some of the less favourable consequences. The conflicts in Azerbaijan, Chechnya, Dagestan, Bosnia and the former Yugoslavia are certainly associated with the consequences of the collapse of the Soviet Union, and the threatened wider Balkan war would possess the terrible added dynamic of intersecting explosively with the western capitalist nations' project of having the Islamic world take on the role of "Evil Empire" from the Soviets.

In considering the kind of freedom to which the citizens of the former Soviet Union and Warsaw Pact countries have been introduced, we have to include the new freedom now extended to millions who never experienced it before – the freedom to be unemployed; there is also the freedom to be a prostitute, which has been greatly increased; the freedom to build organised crime syndicates; and the freedom to have one's pension rendered worthless by inflation. The free market has meant the obliteration of social and cultural considerations; now, it may be a good thing that such considerations are no longer mediated by communist parties with all the repressive, authoritarian and bureaucratic problems associated with them, but is it entirely a good thing?

In the former Eastern Bloc we are seeing capitalism clawing its way into a new existence: it is bloody and brutal. In the western bloc free market ideology is taken for granted, and the march of privatisation proceeds.

Since the collapse of the Soviet Union, the Labour Parties in both Britain and Ireland have abandoned the elements of socialism they had inherited from the past, settling for roles as capitalist parties which act to promote an ameliorated form of capitalism rather than to oppose or overthrow capitalism.

Lord Gowrie, when chairman of the Arts Council in London, questioned whether even the tiny amount given to literature by the Arts Council – less than 1 per cent of its total grants – should be given at all. He is not alone in suggesting that matters should be left to the workings of the marketplace.

And at the level of the marketplace, what is happening? Conglomeration mania in the 1980s has seen the accountants in power in the 1990s, and has seen larger and larger multimedia companies controlling ever-increasing market share. Is it necessarily a bad thing, if a book one is reading is published by HarperCollins and they are part of News Corporation (Australia)?

Perhaps one might like to consider what are the priorities of a worldwide group in which publishing constitutes just 14 per cent of their turnover. What is the context in which editorial decisions are taken in HarperCollins? What are the priorities in Penguin, Viking and so on, where publishing accounts for less than half of the turnover of the Pearson Group?

Jill Paton Walsh, an author of over thirty books, was turned down by all the leading large UK fiction houses, including the publisher of her previous novels, when she submitted her novel *Knowledge of Angels*, which was subsequently shortlisted for the Booker Prize after she published it herself. She said:

> It is true that publishers seem to care very little for individual writers nowadays. They are simply interested in individual books, and what will sell. The idea of supporting and nurturing a writer has disappeared, and this is one of the consequences of conglomeration. They want instant sales and success. Fiction editors are feeling nervous, constantly looking over their shoulders and wondering what the accountants will say . . . There is this culture of anxiety which is unsettling everyone.

These conglomerates are now gearing up to determine the shape of the new electronic publishing; they combine newspaper, magazine and book publishing, broadcasting and cable tv; film; advertising; software development; theme parks and entertainment.

As for the present, in the greater part of the media generally politics is featured almost exclusively in terms of personalities and the parliamentary contests of Tweedledum and Tweedledee. The vital interventions of community groups, the struggles of rank-and-file trade unionists, are scarcely visible. Increasingly newspapers present material of no social or public significance; page after page is devoted to soap stars and other stars and a whole panoply of bland vicariousness. Economics are represented only in the narrowest "free market" terms. The many countries of Africa are lumped together as one indeterminate mass, featuring almost solely in terms of incomprehensible wars and natural disasters, mediated by the benign intervention of white people from the more developed capitalist countries.

There is a lack of diversity of views and experiences. It is claimed that more media means more choice, but the choice is amongst imitative, repetitive and limited options.

In book publishing much of the same syndrome has taken hold. Above all, the business of publishing, like that of newspapers, is seen as a process dedicated solely to the generation of money. More and more promotional budgets are devoted to a few ultra-hyped best-sellers, many of which are rubbish. There is an emphasis on "celebrities" and a concomitant ignoring of "ordinary" lives. It is symptomatic of the conglomerates that they have come up with the invented book by a celebrity of some sort. Thus we find acres of space in bookshops all over the world taken up with massive displays of essentially fake books. And newspapers from the *News of the World* to *The Irish Times* buy the hype, devoting acres of newsprint to covering the publication of the non-book.

I believe that this restructuring of the industry of publishing is antithetical to the art of publishing and thus to the long-term interests of the general public, the readers. It is associated with the kind of publishing which is based on computing the market in the

most exploitative and uncreative way. Market surveys show that
the principal reason a person buys a book is because he or she
knows the name of the author and feels in some sense interested
in that author. So, you get some hack to write a book related to
the sphere of activity of a widely known person, pretend that that
widely known person wrote the book, and Bob's your uncle. This
is the kind of publishing which seeks to devote ever greater
resources to a few hyper-best-sellers and to establish the lowest
common denominator that will allow you to sell the largest possible number of copies.

Its future lies in the ever-greater integration of the various
spheres of activity of the conglomerate. Right now we see the
entire future, structure and organisation of various sports being
determined by broadcasting companies. This tendency will be
extended by the conglomerates to cover ever greater areas of life.
The broadcasting company which will determine, for example,
when and in what circumstances a rugby international series will
be played and which countries will be involved will also control
newspapers which will report on the series; it will also be a sister
company within the conglomerate of the sports magazines which
will feature the series, and will be integrated, too, with the advertising company promoting the series. Key players will have personal business managers who will be part of the company owned
by the conglomerate and they will negotiate deals with other parts
of the conglomerate to arrange the exploitation of the key player
in endorsing products, opening supermarkets, and, as an inciden-
tal part of proceedings, publishing a book allegedly written by this
key player. Ninety per cent of book publishing thus becomes just
one aspect of a vast, self-contained entertainment industry.

But where is the room in this scenario for inventiveness in
publishing, for creativity, for a genuine contribution to social and
cultural life?

Where does a new Samuel Beckett, Grace Paley or James Joyce
fit into all this? Where is the creative publishing which requires
independence of mind allied with a willingness to take risks?

Fortunately, human beings are contradictory creatures, and the greatest successes in publishing are often unexpected successes. The openness and creativity of those independent of the conglomerates can nurture new voices which strike deep resonances in wide readerships. I believe now, as strongly as ever, that the achievement of any kind of real freedom requires not just vigilance but active opposition to political, economic, military, industrial and "security" establishments wherever they be. Freedom is indivisible and all around us; it is not some shining absolute principle on a pedestal, towards which we may afford to be passive. Freedom is something that we make and remake actively in a hundred small ways, or it atrophies. Occasionally big moments occur, big issues arise, and we stand at turning points, capable of pointing new directions. Mostly we live lives composed of small considerations, small struggles and crises. But it is out of these small conflicts that we can craft our collective, social sense of ourselves. I am a small player in the world of publishing, a minute player in the world of business and of public life. The large players seek to reduce us all to the level of atomised individual consumers, for the more effective operation of the market. This market they claim to possess the attributes of nature, yet it is an unnatural prison for the human spirit. It is for this reason that the role of independents – whether they be termed mavericks, "alternatives", rebels or revolutionaries – is important in asserting the primacy of the human title.